BIZARRE BATHROOM READER

DIEGO JOURDAN PEREIRA

BIZARRE BATHROOM READER

YOUR PLUNGING GUIDE INTO THE STRANGEST STORIES, ODDEST TRIVIA, INEXPLICABLE EVENTS, AND UNFATHOMABLE MYSTERIES THE WORLD HAS TO OFFER!

RACEHORSE
PUBLISHING

Racehorse Publishing books may be purchased in bulk at special discounts for sales promotion, corporate gifts, fund-raising, or educational purposes. Special editions can also be created to specifications. For details, contact the Special Sales Department, Skyhorse Publishing, 307 West 36th Street, 11th Floor, New York, NY 10018 or info@skyhorsepublishing.com.

Racehorse Publishing™ is a pending trademark of Skyhorse Publishing, Inc.®, a Delaware corporation.

Visit our website at www.skyhorsepublishing.com.

10 9 8 7 6 5 4 3

Library of Congress Cataloging-in-Publication Data is available on file.

Cover and interior art and design by Diego Jourdan Pereira

Mechanical design by Kai Texel

Scream Queen font designed by Nate Piekos at Blambot.com. Used under license.

Print ISBN: 978-1-63158-679-8

eISBN: 978-1-63158-680-4

Printed in China

To my wife, Icha,
who made a believer out of me.

BONUS CURSE

A medieval warning to book thieves
ancient and modern:

"The finished book before you lies;
This humble scribe don't criticize.
Whoever takes away this book
May he never on Christ look.
Whoever to steal this volume durst;
May he be killed as one accursed.
Whoever to steal this volume tries
Out with his eyes, out with his eyes! "

Mark Drogin (1936-2017), *Anathema! Medieval Scribes and the History of Book Curses* (Allanheld & Schram, 1983)

CONTENTS

BONUS QUOTES

"All the world is made of faith, and trust, and pixie dust."
—J. M. Barrie

"Analyzing humor is like dissecting a frog. They both die in the process."
—E. B. White

"A classic is a book that has never finished saying what it has to say."
—Italo Calvino

INTRODUCTION

"'We're all mad here. I'm mad. You're mad.'
'How do you know I'm mad?' said Alice.
'You must be,' said the Cat, 'or you wouldn't have
come here.'"
—Lewis Carroll

When Jesse McHugh at Skyhorse's Racehorse imprint requested a sequel of equal girth, yet different in tone from my *Astonishing Bathroom Reader*, I proposed an open-minded, in-depth follow-up of the fringe subjects I only managed to glaze over in that book, which had managed to capture my interest and fuel my investigative curiosity for months after the leaded black ink had been finally set in glorious, pulpy print.

The way I see it, a true skeptic's mind is drawn to the weirdest of things, if only to inoculate itself against the virus of certainty, which tends to clog intellectual growth more than any odd theory—however far-fetched it would seem to our well-meaning mind—because there is always room for healthy doses of doubt, no matter which side of the belief spectrum we are on. Case in point, see the photo below, taken years ago by my beloved Maritza "Icha" Mardones. I assure you it wasn't doctored in any way.

Maritza Mardones Castillo

What is that? A floating eye peeking through the steam, obviously, but whose? How? Where from? Well, I'll be damned if not knowing should prevent us from seeking the answers to this and other unfathomable mysteries! So, gulp down your Kool-Aid, and plunge into the rabbit hole of this *Bizarre Bathroom Reader* with me. I promise you won't regret it.

—Diego Jourdan Pereira

I

PUZZLING PLACES

"You unlock this door with the key of imagination. Beyond it is another dimension: a dimension of sound, a dimension of sight, a dimension of mind. You're moving into a land of both shadow and substance, of things and ideas. You've just crossed over into… *The Twilight Zone*."
— Rod Serling

A LAND OF SHADOW AND SUBSTANCE

I can think of no better way to open this volume than by interviewing fellow writer J. M. DeMatteis. A man known to many for his seminal work in comic books (including Justice League International, Spiderman, and Abdazad), the focus of this particular conversation nonetheless falls on his work for the 1985 The Twilight Zone TV series revival.

What made you want to become a writer?
I was always creative. Spent my childhood drawing. Started playing guitar in the fifth grade and began writing songs and playing in bands when I was a teenager. Writing was something that always came naturally to me, just another expression of that same creativity that came out through art and music. But it's the one that led to a career—first as a music journalist, then in comics, TV, novels, film . . .

What were your major writing influences as a young man, and what are your main ones now?
I think once you have your influences, they're the ones that stay with you for life; so, the same writers that inspired me when I was younger still inspire me today: Ray Bradbury, Rod Serling, Dickens, Dostoyevsky, Vonnegut, J. D. Salinger, Philip K. Dick . . . to name a few. In comics: Stan Lee, Jack Kirby, Steve Gerber, Len Wein, Will Eisner.

How did you break into comics? What was the state of the industry back then?

I broke in by sending submissions to DC. Paul Levitz was editing the anthologies, what used to be called the "mystery" books (*House of Secrets*, *House of Mystery*, *Weird War Tales*, etc.), and—long story short—I kept submitting till Paul bought one. The first story I sold was to *House of Mystery*, the first one that saw print was in *Weird War*.

How did you make the transition from comics to television?

I never saw myself as just a comic book writer, so I always wanted to expand out and write in as many forms and genres as possible. I'm a huge *Twilight Zone* fan and, back in the eighties, when I heard the show was being revived, I was very excited. I read in a magazine that Alan Brennert, who'd written some stories for DC, was working on the show so I tracked down an address, took a chance, and wrote him a letter. Alan, who is a brilliant writer and a truly nice human being, reached out, asked me to submit some ideas, and that eventually led to me selling my first script, *The Girl I Married*.

What was writing for television like in the eighties, and what was different from doing it for comics publishing?

The big difference in TV is that it's a group effort. In comics, we have a lot of independence to go off and tell our stories in exactly the way we want. Even when I'm writing the Marvel and DC icons, I have a tremendous amount of freedom.

You're generally dealing with an artist and an editor and that's it. So, you can really put a personal stamp on things. In TV, especially when you're a freelancer hired to write an episode, there are more people involved and it's much more collaborative. You're often hired to develop a story that the staff has developed with specific goals in mind. So your job is to execute their vision and, at the same time, bring as much of yourself, of your own ideas and personality, to the project. (TZ was different. It was an anthology, so the individual writers had to generate unique, stand-alone ideas for their episodes.)

As long as I take off my "personal vision" hat and put on my "collaboration" hat, working in television is tremendous fun. I get to work with extraordinarily talented people, bouncing around stories, creating things that will be seen by millions. Doesn't get better than that, does it?

What specific set of traits makes a superhero story good or interesting?
The same traits that make any story interesting. First and foremost, the stories have to be about deep, interesting characters. You have to root your tales in emotion and psychology. Without that, the cleverest plot in the world is just empty calories. You want your audience to think, to feel. To see themselves in the characters and, perhaps, learn something about themselves in the process. Some people write from the plot in. I generally write from the characters out. If you've got the characters right, the plot will form itself naturally.

What unique point of view, sensibility, and storytelling did you bring into the job?
Because TZ is an anthology, you can tell stories that are deeply personal. My episode came out of experiences in my own life, translated—via "the zone"—into fantasy. And that's the beauty of *Twilight Zone*—you can *literalize* the interior world. Our inner experiences are often fairly fantastic. TZ allows us to give them shape and form. I also think—and this is why I adore the show—that the outer world is far more fantastic and magical than most people realize (or admit). It's certainly been my experience that life is filled with magic and miracles. Which makes TZ a far more accurate reflection of what life really is than so-called "realistic" fiction.

What was the usual time frame when writing an episode for that show?
My memory is that a draft had to be turned around in two/three weeks. And then the rewrites would turn around a little faster. But it's been a very long time, so I can't swear to it.

Was there any reviewing and rewriting involved? How much input did you get from producers and directors? Any from CBS executives in general?
I was a freelancer, so I didn't have any dealings with the CBS execs. Alan was my contact, so he would pass the notes on to me. Rewriting? Absolutely. My episode was rewritten by another comic book writer, Marty Pasko, who, along with his writing partner Rebecca Parr, was on the staff of the show.

The staff often has to do the final pass because issues come up that have to be dealt with quickly and, as a freelancer living three thousand miles away in New York, it's not that easy for me to address everything. Also, this was my first TV script, and I still had a lot to learn. I'm sure Marty and Rebecca improved many elements of my original draft. I was very lucky, too, that the show's executive producer, Phil DeGuere, directed my episode. I went out to LA for the filming and had a wonderful time watching my story come to life. The first time I heard the actors speak my dialogue, I almost wept!

How do you think the 1986 revival holds up against the 1959 original?
Let's be honest: Nothing can compare with the original. It's a unique beast, guided by Rod Serling's vision—his heart, soul, and humanity—and featuring a small group of the finest fantasy writers of the era. That said, the eighties' TZ was incredibly well done and had some extraordinary episodes. (Alan Brennert's "Her Pilgrim Soul" remains one of the finest shows I've ever seen on television.) Taken on its own terms, that version of TZ was a pretty brilliant anthology series.

What did you learn from the whole experience? What did you bring back from it, into your comics and animation work?
The first time you work in a new form, it's a challenge. There are so many things to learn.

And it took me some time to get comfortable with the form. But in the end it's all about the story. And a great story is a great story, no matter the medium. You'll express it differently in a comic, a novel, a TV show, or a movie, but, at the core, you need a compelling story, told in a compelling way. I love writing TV and film, I love the collaboration, I love reaching audiences far larger than any comic could ever reach. There's something truly magical about it.

What would you say changed the most in television between the late 1980s and modern times?
Well, these days you see major movie stars, major directors, massive budgets. An hour of television can look as good as a feature film. But TV remains, as it always has, more intimate and, in many ways, more immediate than film. The ongoing television series allows you to connect with a group of characters in real time, week to week, and establish emotional connections that ripple through the storytelling, creating a relationship between audience and characters that movies often can't. In that way, TV is more like comics, where people get attached to certain characters and will follow them for years.

LOVE TRIANGLE

When "The Deadly Bermuda Triangle" was unleashed onto the unsuspecting readers of then-venerable sci-fi magazine Argosy back in February of 1964, little did Fortean writer Vincent H. Gaddis (1913–1997) suspect the moniker would ever cross over to the cultural mainstream, but it did.

1. Called the "Devil's Triangle" by more lurid journalists, it corresponds to a 500,000- to 1,510,000-square-mile patch of sea, roughly cut between Bermuda, Central Florida, and the islands of the Greater Antilles (Cuba, Hispaniola, Jamaica, and Puerto Rico), where mysteriously disappearing ships—and, as of the twentieth century, planes and submarines too—have been reported for centuries.

2. But not according to famous debunker Larry Kusche (b.1940), whose extensive research on the subject led to the publication of his 1975 *The Bermuda Triangle Mystery: Solved*, which threw a bucket of ice-cold water over Bermuda Triangle aficionados by clarifying most disappearances as either naturally caused accidents, human error, or plainly manufactured nonsense.

3. However, while traffic was and still is incredibly heavy in the region since the time Spanish vessels first sailed through the lane and were given a taste of its seasonally extreme weather conditions, not all disappearances can be chalked up to storms, hurricanes, or even the Gulf stream.

4. Unexplained magnetic anomalies have long been said to hit the area—which author Ivan T. Sanderson (1911–1973) claimed to be much broader, and "lozenge-shaped" (*Invisible Residents*, p.159, 1977)—in recurring waves. While this phenomenon could be a natural occurrence, some authors have suggested otherwise.

5. Charles Berlitz (1913–2003) notably attributed the phenomena to wrinkles in space-time, purportedly caused either by remnants of Atlantis technology, UFOs, or something in-between. Particularly, the 1968 discovery of the underwater "Bimini Road," a stretch of ancient stone "pavement" off the northwest coast of North Bimini Island, has lent some credence to the Atlantis hypothesis.

6. Within the Bermuda Triangle's bounds lies the Puerto Rico Trench, which reaches down to the infamous Milwaukee Depth, the deepest point in the Atlantic Ocean at -27,493 feet. Alas, the Triangle itself still hasn't been recognized by any nation, nor included in any official maps.

BONUS FACT

At the end of the 1980s, against a devalued ruble, PepsiCo opted to trade its popular soft drink in exchange for seventeen Soviet submarines, a destroyer, and other ships, briefly becoming the world's sixth-largest naval superpower, and its first fully privately owned one.

THE LIFE AQUATIC

While relatively smaller than claimed by many authors, the list of still-inexplicable incidents in the Bermuda Triangle area never ceases to amaze, beginning with none other than Christopher Columbus (1451–1506)!

1. Consigned by the great Admiral himself to the pages of his *diario* on the evening of October 11, 1492, a day before landfall, Columbus saw a shimmering light in the distance. " . . . and because the *Pinta* vessel was a better ship, she went ahead of the Admiral, found land and made the signals that the Admiral had ordered. A sailor called Rodrigo de Triana first saw this land, although at the tenth hour of the night the Admiral being on the stern castle saw a light, though it was a thing so dim, he didn't want to affirm that it might have been land." Despite this strange occurrence, it must be noted that neither Columbus nor his ships were swallowed by the Triangle itself.

2. In 1800, 1814, and 1824 three US Navy ships (USS *Pickering*, USS *Wasp*, and USS *Wild Cat*) all vanished at sea along with the totality of their crews (90, 140, and 14 people, respectively).

3. Dubbed "the single largest loss of life in the history of the US Navy not related to combat," the USS *Cyclops* and its crew of 306 men (and some civilian passengers) vanished without a trace on March 4, 1918, after departing Barbados.

She was carrying 11,000 tons of manganese ore, which is used to produce munitions. Her two sister ships, USS *Proteus* (fifty-eight men on board) and USS *Nereus* (sixty-one men on board), also disappeared at sea while carrying manganese ore, a month apart from each other in 1941!

4. On December 5, 1945, five TBM Avenger torpedo bombers collectively known as Flight 19 disappeared with their fourteen airmen during an exercise, as did the PBM Mariner flying boat and its crew of thirteen dispatched to search for them. While the loss of the flying boat was attributed to an explosion, nobody knows for sure what happened to the bombers, other than their compasses freezing suddenly as they flew into oblivion.

5. Two British South American Airways (BSAA) Tudor IV passenger planes, the Star Tiger and Star Ariel, vanished without trace in 1948 and 1949 respectively. The Star Tiger was flying from the Azores to Bermuda, while the Star Ariel was on the way to Kingston, Jamaica, from Bermuda.

6. In 1962, a USAF Boeing KB-50K Superfortress—huge!—and its crew of nine went missing en route to the Azores from Langley, Virginia. Three years later an Ercoupe F01—tiny!—also disappeared, seemingly into thin air.

7. Portrayed in Steven Spielberg's 1977 blockbuster film *Close Encounters of the Third Kind* as stranded by aliens in the middle of the Gobi Desert, the SS *Cotopaxi* carrier was originally christened after a still-active volcano in Ecuador by its builder, the Great Lakes Engineering Works, in Ecorse, Michigan, back in 1918. Seven years later, it went missing with its thirty-two men on board, while on the way to Havana, Cuba; a disappearance that was linked to the Bermuda Triangle until finally identified by diver Michael C. Barnette (b.1971) in January 2020 as the "Bear Wreck" found in the 1980s lying thirty-five miles off the coast of St. Augustine, Florida.

8. **While unexplained disappearances may have slowed down in the past couple of decades, people's fascination with the Bermuda Triangle continues to grow, as ships and aircraft keep on reporting strange occurrences in the area, such as the Turkish Airlines flight TK183 incident on February 23, 2017, which saw the Airbus take a detour from Havana to Washington Dulles Airport in Virginia on account of a strange electrical malfunction, or the unnamed twenty-nine-foot Mako Cuddy Cabin boat with twenty people on board, which vanished on its way to Florida from Bimini Island as recently as December 31, 2020. The mystery, it appears, continues to deepen.**

AXIS OF EVIL

"Vile Vortices" were first hypothesized by Scottish biologist and author Ivan T. Sanderson—him again?—after similar incidents from around the globe made him realize the Bermuda Triangle was far from an isolated phenomenon.

Bermuda Triangle: The first and best-known anomalous region, this infamous patch of salt water is already described at length in the preceding pages.

Formosa Triangle: Also known as the Dragon's Triangle. Like its Bermuda "cousin," this location had the same defenders (Berlitz, Sanderson) and detractors (Kusche) during the twentieth century. What stands out, however, is the Japanese government's recognition of the area as *ma no umi*, or "dangerous sea," due to the number of vessels that dared enter its waters never to return.

Hamakua Volcano: It is unclear which of the two volcanos in the Hamakua district of Hawaii Sanderson referred to, but the entire volcanic archipelago has certainly seen its share of marine tragedies, not all of them solved.

Easter Island: The nigh mythical island of the south Pacific, if only due to the hundreds of monolithic *moai* that litter its surface and even the bottom of the sea surrounding it, created by the island's original Polynesian settlers.

As with the hieroglyphic writing their descendants developed, the statues' true meaning has been largely lost to time.

New Hebrides Trench: On the edges of the southwestern Pacific Ocean's Coral Sea, between the islands of Vanuatu and New Caledonia lies a trench as deep as 25,000 feet, that according to recent exploration is teeming with marine life and may yield greater mysteries in years to come.

Wharton Basin: A marine depression at the northeastern quarter of the Indian Ocean, and connecting the India and Australia tectonic plates, which explains its seismic activity. Its floor remains uncharted territory and is yet to be thoroughly explored.

MohenjoDaro: The "Mound of the Dead Men" is all that remains of one of the largest cities of the ancient Indus Valley Civilization. Located in modern day Pakistan, it was built around 2500 BC, and to this day nobody knows why it was abandoned and forgotten six hundred years later.

Great Zimbabwe: Built with dry stone in the southeastern hills of Zimbabwe as the palace of a forgotten local monarch around 1000 AD, it was abandoned five hundred years later by the local Shona people under mysterious circumstances.

Algerian Megaliths: While often confused with the beautiful Madghacen, a royal mausoleum-temple of the Berber Numidian Kings which dates back to 150 BC, these refer to large paleolithic and neolithic semi-carved stones scattered across the Sahara Desert. Their original purpose, like Stonehenge's, is forever lost in the sands of time.

South Atlantic Anomaly: A scientifically sanctioned anomaly, the SAA is the region encompassing the south Atlantic and a large portion of South America where Earth's magnetic field is at its weakest, allowing the Van Allen radiation belt to get as close to Earth's surface as 120 miles, which means the whole region is supercharged solar energy particles!

North and South Pole: The two places on Earth where the planet's axis of rotation meets the surface, in the middle of the Arctic Ocean and Antarctica respectively. Norwegian explorer Roald Amundsen (1872–1928) was the first man to reach the South Pole in 1911 and led the first verified expedition to the North Pole aboard an airship in 1926. While the poles often shift, their rare reversal (the latest one taking place 42,000 years ago) can be catastrophic.

BONUS QUOTE

"Love is something that hangs up behind the bathroom door and smells of Lysol."
—Ernest Hemingway

DAVY JONES'S LOCKER

"Vile Vortices" are far from the most dangerous spots in the high seas, according to both a 2013 report from environmental NGO WWF (World Wide Fund for Nature), and a current one by private insurance corporation Allianz Global.

The Coral Triangle: The world's most dangerous part of the ocean on account of its dozens of yearly shipwrecks, the Coral Triangle encompasses the South China Sea and the East Indies (which include Indonesia, Malaysia, the Philippines, Papua New Guinea, Timor-Leste, and Solomon Islands), an area of well over two million square miles. Home to six hundred different species of coral, seven marine turtle species, and more than two thousand species of fish, the 120 million people living on its coasts threaten its fragile ecosystem with overfishing and pollution. According to the *Allianz Global Safety and Shipping Review 2020*, 228 ships have been lost there between 2010 and 2019.

Eastern Mediterranean and Black Sea: Holding the record for the second-largest number of shipwrecks in the world, this area reported a total of 137 shipwrecks between 2010 and 2019, but, in part due to the reduction in traffic caused by the global Coronavirus Pandemic, these numbers have shown a steady decline as of 2021.

The Sea of Japan: Surrounded by Japan, Korea, and North China, this body of water comes third with the 2010–2019 loss of 108 ships, according to the *Allianz Global Safety and Shipping Review 2020*. It is also the only area where real-world danger partly overlaps with Sanderson's Formosa Triangle "vortex."

North Sea and the British Isles: With steadily declining ship losses since 2013, this area (which includes the English Channel and the Bay of Biscay) still comes in at fourth place on the list. The *Allianz Global Safety and Shipping Review 2020* consigns the loss of seventy ships, but a staggering rise in accidents—605 in 2019 alone!

West African Coast: While the region registered a relatively small number of thirty-nine ship losses, the Gulf of Guinea, a piracy hotspot, concentrates 90 percent of all global kidnappings at sea!

BONUS FACTS

According to a 2002 AP report, two unnamed seventy-year-old Finnish twin brothers were killed hours apart from each other by different trucks while riding their bicycles on the same highway.

In 1832, after being refused the proper accommodations aboard a steamboat on account of the color of his skin, Brazilian immigrant Emiliano Mundrucu (1791–1863) filed the first court lawsuit against racial discrimination in US history.

INTERDIMENSIONAL BROTHERLY LOVE

Not all wrinkles in space-time occur due to natural factors or the undue meddling of suspected alien origin. Human beings, too, have a well-known track record for toying around with science they barely understand, which could potentially destroy us all.

1. A middling author of several UFO books which preceded the "ancient aliens" phenomenon by half a century, astronomer Morris K. Jessup (1900–1959) began to correspond with Carl M. Allen (1925–1994), writing as "Carlos Miguel Allende," in a way that mirrored the Raymond A. Palmer (1910–1977) and Richard S. Shaver (1907–1975) affair a decade earlier.

2. In his letters, Allen claimed to have witnessed a "cloaking" (invisibility to radar) experiment gone wrong. Conducted on October 28, 1943, aboard the USS *Eldridge* at the Philadelphia Naval Shipyard, the trial saw the destroyer allegedly vanish from sight in a blue haze, only to reappear in Norfolk, Virginia, 200 miles away, where it stood for some time until vanishing and reappearing back in Philadelphia ten minutes later. It had been plunged into a wormhole!

3. Supposedly based on Einstein's unified field theory about the interrelation of electromagnetism and gravity, the experiment allegedly left some

crewmen fused to the deck and others turned inside-out, while a few simply never reappeared. The very few who survived the ordeal were left raving-mad, according to Allen's account.

4. Needless to say, official Navy records completely contradict these claims, establishing the USS *Eldridge* to be on a performance tour in the Bahamas around the time the "experiment" allegedly took place, while later research sadly revealed Mr. Allen as a loner with a long history of mental illness. This, of course, didn't stop a flurry of writers from jumping aboard the *Eldridge* and taking us all for a ride. Case in point, *The Philadelphia Experiment: Project Invisibility: The Startling Account of a Ship that Vanished—and Returned to Damn Those Who Knew Why . . .* (1978) by William L. Moore (b.1943) and the aforementioned Charles Berlitz, a man who ostensibly never found a sea mystery he couldn't cash in on.

5. Beginning with a script written by none other than John Carpenter (b.1948), the Moore and Berlitz bestseller was faithfully adapted to the silver screen as *The Philadelphia Experiment* (1984), which was directed by Stewart Raffill (b.1942), with Michael Paré (b.1958) and Nancy Allen (b.1950) as the leading couple. Considered a minor cult classic, it did well enough at the box office to spawn an inferior sequel in 1993, and a somewhat decent 2012 TV-movie reboot, with the appropriate cameo by Michael Paré himself.

THE BLACK PEARL

Nothing jolly about them: ghost ships range from the truly spectral to the real-life derelict, drifting aimlessly with the crew either dead or missing, but let's focus on the former before jumping aboard the latter.

Flying Dutchman: Arguably the most famous ghost ship hailing from the 1790s, this glowing harbinger of doom—hurricanes!—is said to be a Dutch East India Company merchant ship that couldn't be steered into South Africa's Cape of Good Hope harbor, and forever remains lost at sea.

Caleuche: Sailing straight from the South Pacific folklore of the Chiloé Island, in Chile, this vessel is said to be manned by the enslaved souls of the dead, brought aboard by the Pincoy and the Pincoya, the "Donnie & Marie" of the mermaid world.

Ghost Ship of Northumberland Strait: Dramatically blazing, this spectral schooner has kept sailing the strait separating Prince Edward Island from Nova Scotia and New Brunswick, in Canada, for the last two hundred years. Burning ship apparitions are far from unusual; however, real-life 1813's *Young Teazer* and 1858's *Eliza Battle* are said to still be flaming their way through North American waterways.

Lady Lovibond: Appearing in fifty-year intervals since 1748, the *Lady Lovibond* is said to have been originally bound for Oporto, Portugal, on a honeymoon pleasure trip, when it was deliberately wrecked on the Goodwin Sands (Kent, England) by the jealous first mate.

Palatine Light: This particular apparition, based on the ill-fated voyage of the *Princess Augusta*, has been haunting Rhode Island since 1738. Its water supply became contaminated to the point of killing two hundred passengers and half the crew, the captain included, and severe storms subsequently damaged and forced the ship north, eventually wrecking it ashore at Block Island. Unsalvageable, it was finally pushed out to sea, only to sink forever into local folklore.

SS *Bannockburn*: Dubbed the "Flying Dutchman of the Great Lakes," this Canadian steel-hull freighter vanished from sight on a snowy November 21, 1902, with a cork life preserver being the only remnant found a month later. Reports of its ghostly sighting on the waters of Lake Superior continue to surface every now and then.

København: This five-masted barge vanished without trace en route from Buenos Aires to Sydney back in 1928, only to be seen sailing the Pacific with a broken mast, in spectral form, by passengers and crew of the *Mexico*, a Danish East Asiatic Company motorboat, a year later. Sightings continued over the following years, with reports from Argentinian, Chilean, and Peruvian fishermen finally dying out after a ship cadet's diary had been found in a bottle on Bouvet Island, telling of the *København*'s ultimate "death by iceberg," its survivors escaping aboard lifeboats, one of which was found, corpses still inside, in the southern coast of Africa.

HMS *Eurydice*: A victim of one of Britain's worst peacetime naval disasters, this corvette sank in 1878 during a heavy snowstorm just off the Isle of Wight, and over the years many reputable witnesses, including Prince Edward (b.1964), the Earl of Wessex, claim to have seen it.

RMS *Queen Mary*: Far from vanished, the venerable ocean liner permanently moored at the Port of Long Beach, California, houses restaurants, a museum, and a hotel. However, according to several accounts, it is also one of the most haunted places in America, with suite room B-340 being where the largest number of paranormal incidents have taken place. Scariest apparitions include a murdered cook, a mini-skirted woman who drowned in the pool, a woman in a white evening gown draping herself over the salon piano, and many, many more.

USS YMS-328: The 140-foot-long decommissioned US Navy Mine Sweeper was one of John Wayne's (1907–1979) most prized possessions. Renovating and re-christening her as the Wild Goose, the film star hosted many a party for the celebrities of his day on board, and apparently had such a good time he never really left, reportedly being seen and felt in the years immediately following his death, but no new reports have surfaced since, which explains why Hornblower Cruises still rents the ship for dinner cruises.

BONUS FACTS

While researching for a role in the film adaptation of *The Girl from Petrovka* (1974), Sir Anthony Hopkins (b.1937) scouted London's used bookshops in vain for a copy of the original novel only to find it on a subway station bench. Turns out it had been misplaced by the author himself, George Feifer (1934–2019), who was delighted when Hopkins returned it to him while shooting the film in Vienna months later.

With more than 6,000 confirmed fictional casualties, the largest body-count in any horror film goes to VHS ghost Sadako Yamamura (*Ringu*), a.k.a. Samara Morgan in the American remake, who has killed more Japanese people (and foreigners) than Godzilla!

A product of "hipster" subculture gone too far, "yarn-bombing" began in 2005, in Houston, Texas, when a local knitting club began wrapping city lamp posts, parking meters, telephone poles, etc. with spare knitted or crocheted material.

DEATH SHIP

While not as glamorous as the glowing, floating ghost ships of lore, real-life ocean drifters, their crew either mysteriously vanished or rotting on deck, still have many stories to tell.

Duc de Dantzig: An early nineteenth-century French private man-of-war, the *Dantzig* lived many high seas adventures, privateering throughout the Caribbean and the Atlantic from 1808 until 1811, when it was never seen or heard from again. Presumed lost at sea, the story goes that an unnamed French frigate found it drifting two years later, the rotting crew either hacked to pieces or crucified to the masts in what appeared to have been an epic bloodbath. It was set ablaze and left to scuttle.

SV *Mary Celeste*: Perhaps one of the most popular ghost ship mysteries ever, and rightfully so, the *Mary Celeste* was an American brigantine found abandoned midway between the Azores Islands and Portugal on December 4, 1872, by Canadian sailing ship *Dei Gratia*, under partial sail, with the cargo intact, and her lifeboat missing; her crew and passengers were never seen again. Impounded and salvaged while simultaneously immortalized in fiction by writers like Arthur Conan Doyle (1859–1930), it continued sailing under new owners until it was deliberately sunk off the coast of Haiti, in an attempted insurance fraud, back in 1885.

Marlborough: Disappeared at sea while on a voyage to London back in 1890, the fate of this merchant sailing ship and its crew remains a complete mystery after 131 years. One thing is certain though: the Bermuda Triangle had nothing to do with it, and the sea surrounding the British Isles remains as dangerous today as it did back then.

SS *Ourang Medan*: In an incident unreliably dated by various news sources as happening in 1940 or 1947–48, this Dutch sulfuric acid transport was found intact, floating aimlessly in the waters of the Strait of Malacca, somewhere between Malaysia and Singapore. The corpses of its crew, captain, and even a dog were discovered curiously frozen by the crew of passerby American vessel, the *Silver Star*, which barely managed to evacuate the *Ourang Medan* before a fiery explosion consigned it to the bottom of the ocean for good.

SV *Teignmouth Electron*: A forty-one-foot trimaran designed by Donald Crowhurst (1932–1969) for the *Sunday Times* Golden Globe Race of 1968–69, the unseaworthy yacht was found adrift and empty in the North Atlantic on July 10, 1969. The subsequent investigation yielded that Mr. Crowhurst had abandoned the race while falsifying his position reports, in an attempt to trick the world into believing he had completed the race, but the stress he was under led to his complete psychotic breakdown and eventual overboard suicide after seven months at sea. Crowhurst's story has caught the fascination of filmmakers for decades, its latest movie outing, *The Mercy* (2018) directed by James Marsh (b.1963), features Colin Firth (b.1960) in the titular role.

High Aim 6: Registered in Taiwan but sporting an Indonesian flag, this fishing boat was found adrift on January 8, 2003, at approximately eighty nautical miles east off the Rowley Shoals (a group of three coral reefs in Australian waters). The ensuing Taiwan police investigation located a single member of the crew who confessed that the other seamen (of course) had killed the captain and the engineer, then returned home, leaving the ship behind. A year prior, a similar crime had taken place aboard another Taiwanese fishing boat, the *Hairisheng 6*, in which ten crew members were arrested for the murder of both its captain and the engineer.

SS *Pyonyang:* For years, hundreds of rickety North Korean boats packed with bloated corpses kept washing ashore on Japan's north coast, over 600 miles away from their homeland, baffling Japanese authorities and international investigators alike. The numbers became so unprecedented back in 2017 and 2018 that it was speculated the vessels carried defectors away from the cruel regime of this secluded communist Asian nation. As it turns out, according to a 2020 Global Fishing Watch report, another communist nation is to blame: China, its massive "dark fishing fleets" pushing North Korean fishermen away into rough Russian and Japanese seas they were ill-prepared to face.

BURNT OFFERINGS

According to most accounts, hauntings may be classified into two different categories. There's the "movie on a loop," in which people who had once lived or frequented a property continue to replay their business, oblivious of their surroundings. Then there's the scary specter that's very much aware of us and tries to interact, which may lead to frustrating exchanges and even aggression.

Gakona Lodge: As stated at their website, "Alaska's oldest, continually operating roadhouse, Gakona Lodge has been sheltering, comforting, and thrilling Alaska travelers and adventurers since 1904." Unfortunately, Barbara and Jerry Strang, who bought the property in 1975 and kept it running for forty years also reported an unwanted, pipe-smoking apparition, with a proclivity to lock doors and stomp floors, with a serious dislike for the music of Joan Baez (b.1941).

Sturdivant Hall: A magnificent two-story columned southern house museum located at 713 Mabry Street, in Selma, Alabama, it used to be the mansion of the president of the First National Bank of Selma, John McGee Parkman (1838–1867), who speculated with cotton prices during the Civil War, was jailed for it, and died attempting an escape. Soon after, his ghost began to haunt the mansion, and continues to do so to this day, according to the 1969 book, 13 Alabama Ghosts and Jeffrey by folklorist Kathryn Tucker Windham (1918–2011).

Allen House: Located in Monticello, Arkansas, and promoted to tourists as "The Most Haunted House in America," this unusual Victorian-style manor built in 1900 by well-to-do planter Joe Lee Allen (1863–1917) is said to be haunted by the ghost of his dear middle daughter Ladell "Dell" Allen (1894–1948), who committed suicide by ingesting mercury cyanide, less than a year after her son, Allen Bonner, had passed from pneumonia at twenty-eight, and six months after her ex-husband, and Allen's father, Boyd R. Bonner also passed at fifty-six. Despite the house's fearsome reputation, "Dell" is said to be pretty harmless and less noisy than one would expect from someone dying in her circumstances.

Bodi: In a state defined as "arrested decay," this Sierra Nevada, California, ghost town of the Gold Rush era is apparently filled to the brim with very real ghosts. On record, it went from a population of 5,417 people in 1880 to zero inhabitants by 1950, but the non-living still walking its streets and roaming its houses count in the dozens. While most go about their business gently, there's at least a couple of credible stories of people who had the bad idea of staying the night, and more aggressive spirits attempted to crush and suffocate them.

Toys "R" Us: Back in the day, employees of the Sunnyvale, California, Toys "R" Us (built in 1970 over an old nineteenth-century ranch) reported numerous incidents involving unexplained voices, breezes, shoulder-tappings, shelf rearrangements, and all the usual creepy shenanigans you would expect from bored ghosts. In 1978 dubious psychic Sylvia Celeste Browne (1936–2013) claimed the ghost was a lanky Swedish preacher and ranch hand from the 1880s named "John, Yon, Jan, or Johan"—*make up your mind, Sylvia!*—Johnson, and a photographer she brought over supposedly even took a blurry infra-red photo of him which was widely circulated by the press. Not surprisingly, two years later, when *That's Incredible* (1980–1984) scheduled a new nationally televised *séance* and photo shoot with Ms. Browne at the store, "Johnny Johnson" didn't deign to show up. Ironically, while the haunted store closed for good in 2018 after Toys "R" Us went belly-up, the location was reopened a year later ... as a Spirit Halloween store!

Whaley House Museum: Like an awful lot of early nineteenth-century Greek Revival homes still standing in America today, this San Diego, California, landmark built by settler Thomas Whaley (1823–1890) is abound in apparitions, its ghostly residents including Mr. Whaley, his wife, a girl named Annabelle Washburn (who carelessly ran into a clothesline with tragic results), and "Yankee Jim," a drifter who tried to steal a boat, a crime which saw him promptly hanged by Whaley himself before the word "lynching" was even coined. Whaley was also a pioneer when it came to building his home atop native graveyards, well before it became a common trope of poltergeist lore.

Cherry Hills Country Club Clubhouse: Originally the lavish Cherry Hills (Denver, Colorado) home of George W. Gano (1871– 1930), president the Gano-Downs Clothing Company, and his wife Ethel Reed Gano Work (née Spooner; 1872–1960), "Bradmar Manor" was purchased by famed obstetrician Dr. Robert A. Bradley (1917–1998), creator of the Bradley Method of Natural Childbirth, two years after Ethel Gano's passing. According to a local legend, prior to her death Ethel requested that her coffin be brought before the main fireplace and claimed her spirit would then split one of the massive (four-foot-wide) cross ceiling beams, which is exactly what happened when her instructions were carried out! The Bradleys would soon find spirits definitely roamed the halls, with unexplainable blinking lights, footsteps, shouts, and music being heard while still renovating their new home. Undeterred and entrepreneurial, they decided to "make lemonade" by documenting all occurrences in the 1969 bestseller *Psychic Phenomena: Revelations and Experiences*, founding the Academy of Parapsychology and Medicine, and holding séances twice a month. While always describing their home's poltergeist incidents as benign, the Bradleys decided to sell the house ten years later anyway, via the following tongue-in-cheek advert: "Looking for a house with 23 rooms, five fireplaces, and possibly a resident ghost? Then your house is Bradmar. The fabled and gabled English Tudor house at 4100 S. University Blvd. that sits on four acres of ground and presently belongs to the Robert A. Bradleys is for sale." (*Rocky Mountain News*, February 17, 1972)

85 Woodland Street House: This red duplex set back from the street in Simsbury, Connecticut, holds a secret. According to *The Ghostly Register* (Arthur Myers, 1986), between 1977 and 1980, back when the Glowacki family (Richard, Virginia, their four children, and other relatives) was renting the then-yellow house, several apparitions—including a nondescript-but-inquisitive shadow, a talkative old Irish woman, and a playful, old, one-armed man with suspenders—engaged with them in various ways. They also witnessed dolls and other objects such as crucifixes and a picture of Jesus Christ being moved, turned, and dropped on various occasions, but neither psychics nor a Catholic priest managed to cleanse the residence, and the family ended up moving to another town.

Tuckaway House: Surrounded by century-old trees, this hospitable bungalow at 3128 Pennsylvania St. in Indianapolis, Indiana, is supposedly still inhabited by the congenial ghosts of former owners, fashion designer George Meier (1864–1932) and his wife, world-famous palmist Nellie Simmons Meier (1862–1944), and even their Dalmatian dog!

Liberty Hall Historic Site: Currently operated by the National Society of The Colonial Dames of America in The Commonwealth of Kentucky, this museum located at 202 Wilkinson Street, in

Frankfort, Kentucky, used to be the home of Senator John Brown's (1757–1837) family and descendants from 1796 to 1937, when an heir gifted it to the public. In hindsight, he probably was tired of sharing lodgings with "The Gray Lady," an old friend of the Browns named Margaret Varick, who made the house her permanent residence, and two other lesser apparitions said to occasionally show up on the grounds: a Spanish opera singer, and a lovelorn soldier in the War of 1812.

Myrtles Plantation: A fabulous bed and breakfast located in St. Francisville, Louisiana, the long history of the "One of America's Most Haunted Homes" began in 1796 with General David "Whiskey Dave" Bradford (1762–1808) and his family escaping persecution for Bradford's involvement in the Whiskey Rebellion, and later building the original cottage atop a Tunica nation burial ground. Home to an alleged dozen ghosts, the best known—and historically accurate—being attorney William Drew Winter (1820–1871), who was shot on the front porch by a stranger (to this day, visitors hear his dying footsteps). Other stories, like that of vengeful slave girl "Chloe," have long been proven to be complete and fairly recent fabrications.

Destrehan Manor House: Also in Louisiana, this neoclassical mansion in the French Colonial style used to oversee a major plantation of indigo and then sugarcane, switching owners over the centuries (the first construction was finished in

1790). By the late 1960s it had fallen into disrepair, until donated to the River Road Historical Society, a local nonprofit that restored it to the point it is currently a prized tourist attraction and filming location, with blockbusters like *Interview with the Vampire* (1994) and *12 Years a Slave* (2013) being filmed there. But not all its phantasms are the product of "movie magic." A white figure suspected to be the ghost of a former owner, Scotsman Stephen Henderson (1773–1838), has been seen and heard, still distraught by the death of his young wife. Another theory links it to pirate Jean Lafitte (c. 1780 – c. 1823), but for obvious reasons everybody hopes that isn't the case.

Stone's Public House: Originally called the Railroad House by founder John Stone (1779–1858) back in 1834, and John Stone's Inn in the last decades of the twentieth century, when reports of paranormal incidents began. These included doors that would not remain bolted, lights and water taps that would turn themselves on, ten dollar bills materializing in the tip jar, patrons feeling shoulder taps or hearing giggles, and a host of creepy stuff going on in the upstairs function room, and only intensified as the establishment was renovated into the current "gastropub" which sits on 179 Main Street, Ashland, Massachusetts.

The Mount: The museum, a National Historic Landmark since 1971, Edith Wharton's (1862–1937) Gilded Age mansion in Lenox, Massachusetts, has seen its share of supernatural incidents, ranging from "movie on a loop" occurrences (disembodied laughter and footsteps), to Edith Wharton, her husband (Edward "Teddy" Robbins Wharton; 1850–1928), her lover (William Morton Fullerton; 1865–1952), and what is thought to be none other than Henry James (1843–1916) himself trying to interact with visitors and employees in a friendly way. The spirits of the educated rich and famous, it would seem, remain well-mannered in the afterlife too.

Strand Cinema: If Stephen King's fiction is any indication, Maine is no stranger to the paranormal, and the still-standing Skowhegan movie theater, which opened in the 1920s when films were silent and now offers "Dolby Digital Sound," reported a mischievous ghost looking for a good time, if not popcorn, during the 1980s. While attempts were made to contact or record the entity, they yielded nothing conclusive.

Beckett's Castle: Facing Casco Bay, on the east side of Cape Elizabeth, Maine, the former summer home of writer Sylvester B. Beckett (1812–1882) is a two-story stone building with a three-story tower built in the early 1870s. Well preserved as a historic landmark, the Gothic "castle" is said to be haunted by Beckett himself, who walks around, rearranges paintings, keeps doors from shutting, and so on, but no actual apparition of the man has ever been spotted on the premises.

Crayhay Mansion: Still located at 15 Franklin Avenue, in Midland Park, New Jersey, this elegant, three-storied Civil War–era mansion set well away from the street is claimed to be alternatively haunted by the pushy ghost of former owner Max Crayhay (a wealthy lawyer who shot himself in 1911), a teenage girl named Rose who passed in tragic circumstances, a somewhat hostile floating old lady around which many theories abound, and . . . a yellow and white kitty, that has both manifested visually, or made its warmth felt around the house.

Sweetwater County Library: A modernist, red brick building built in 1980 atop a nineteenth- century graveyard, this library still serving the people of Green River, Wyoming, has seen lights turning on and off, doors opening and closing, names being whispered, and even typewriters and computers typing on their own, to the point the staff entertains itself by keeping a "ghost log" since the 1990s. It may be found online at: www.sweetwaterlibraries.com.

The Octagon House Museum: A National Historic Landmark built in Washington, DC, in 1799, the Octagon served as the temporary residence of President James Madison (1751–1836) for six months after the 1814 Burning of Washington. Purchased by the American Institute of Architects Foundation in 1898, which restored it as their headquarters, in 1970 it was turned into a public museum, and its employees as well as its visitors reported many a ghost sighting on the premises, including bell-ringing slaves, original Octagon owner Colonel

John Tayloe's (1721–1779) daughters climbing the curved stairway, a man in black nineteenth-century attire, and even First Lady Dolley Todd Madison (née Payne; 1768–1849), said to split her haunting time among various other DC buildings.

Old Stone House: The oldest unchanged building in Washington, DC, is a colonial era, L-shaped, three-story residence at 3051 M Street Northwest that's made of granite and fieldstone, still preserved on its original foundation. Several ghosts still live in the upper floors (currently closed for "renovations"), including a nasty misogynist named "George," an unnamed woman in a brown dress, a little boy who runs up and down the stairs, and a few others.

Edgar Allan Poe House & Museum: Echoing The Ghostly Register again, "Why on Earth Shouldn't Edgar Allan Poe's Old House Be Haunted?" Indeed, not a lot of good reasons the plain-looking, two-story brick-and-wood Baltimore home of America's horror granddad wouldn't be dealing with its own little poltergeist activity. Poe (1809–1849) himself has been rumored to turn the lights on at strange hours, open or close doors and windows, and even tap the shoulders of visitors, decades after his untimely passing. The stories kept away rioters in the 1960s and, according to the aforementioned Register, scared the daylights out of amateur psychics in the mid-1980s.

THE AMITYVILLE EXAGGERATION

On December 19, 1975, the Lutz family moved into their dream home in Amityville, Long Island. Twenty-eight days later they ran from it, never to return. Their story has been immortalized and magnified ever since, and it's time to separate fact from fiction.

1. At 3:00 a.m., on November 13, 1974, the five-bedroom, Dutch Colonial–style waterfront house with a heated swimming pool (and two quarter-round windows on the third floor, long since removed, which made the house look like a jack o' lantern) on 112 Ocean Avenue, became the scene of a gruesome crime.

2. Then twenty-three-year-old Ronald DeFeo Jr. (1951–2021) shot his sleeping parents (Ronald DeFeo Sr. and Louise DeFeo) and his four younger siblings (Dawn, Allison, Marc, and John Matthew) with a .35 caliber rifle, in a paranoid fit of drug-induced rage. For this heinous crime, DeFeo Jr. would remain behind bars for the rest of his life, finally passing on March 12, 2021.

3. Despite this, the property price dropping to a mere $80,000 (with the DeFeo family furniture thrown in for another $400) was hard to resist for George L. Lutz (1947–2006) and his wife Kathy Lutz (1946–2004), who knowingly bought the house, moving into it with Kathy's three children in tow.

4. According to the Lutzes, there were strange odors and sounds, such as the front door slamming in the middle of the night. They also felt chills around the place, and suffered from night terrors that woke them at 3:15 a.m. every night (around the same time the DeFeo murders took place) ... and that's basically it.

5. Granted, the above would be enough for *any* family to panic and flee such a place. The Lutzes certainly never deviated from this core version of the events, but it would seem the plague of flies, the green slime–oozing walls, the cloven hoof marks on the snow, the devil pig, the fire bats, and Kathy turning into an old levitating woman all came *after* the fact; embellishments first written by Jay Anson (1921–1980), to whom they originally sold their story rights (alongside a number of tape recordings they made at the house), and the many other authors who followed in the latter's footsteps.

6. Named as "Father Mancuso" in the Anson book, Reverend Ralph J. Pecoraro (1935–1987) in particular was adamant to declare that, other than the Lutzes calling him on the phone one time, he never even set foot on the property. Hence, it stands to reason that the story of the blessing, the hellish voice yelling at him to get out, and the hand blisters were all fabrications, but fabrications do sell books and movies.

7. Well-ingrained into America's folklore via pop-culture, Amityville would become a money-making machine through a series of novels and almost thirty movies. An "all-you-can-eat buffet of occult bullshit" according to horror writer Grady Hendrix (*Paperbacks from Hell*, p.108, 2017), fed and promoted by George Lutz himself. But the family that purchased, renovated, and lived in the property at 112 Ocean Avenue during the following decade stated they never experienced anything of the sort.

8. The Lutzes ended up reaching California, where the trauma resulting from a story they never backed down from, coupled with the pressures of newfound celebrity eventually split the marriage of George and Kathy up. The ensuing family feud over the franchise proceeds wasn't any kinder to them, and left Kathy's second son, Christopher Quaratino (b.1968) estranged from his stepfather whom, he later claimed, used to dabble in the occult and may have had a hand in what happened at the house.

BONUS QUOTES

"I would love to take you seriously, but to do so would be an affront to your intelligence."
—George Bernard Shaw

"The quickest way to a man's heart is through his chest."
—Roseanne Barr

GRAVE OLD WORLD

Across the pond, a relatively small town located twenty-seven miles northwest of central London appears to concentrate the most haunting reports in all of the United Kingdom: Amersham!

1. Originally known as *Agmodesham*, this market town has been sitting on the River Misbourne valley, deep within the Chiltern Hills in Buckinghamshire County, since pre-Anglo-Saxon times (in fact, archeological evidence of Roman presence has also been found), where it's thrived for millennia.

2. In the 1500s the Amersham Martyrs of the Lollard revolt, a Proto-Protestant movement, were imprisoned, tried, and brutally executed by both Church and state, in and around town landmarks now rife with paranormal activity.

3. Currently haunted public establishments include the Crown Hotel, a former Elizabethan inn populated by seven ghostly residents; the quaintly named Saracens Head Inn with two spectral patrons still in attendance; and The George and Dragon Hotel, where the disembodied footsteps of a local folk legend, "The White Lady," can still be heard.

4. The Hellfire Caves, a man-made network of tunnels excavated in the outskirts of town during the eighteenth century at the behest of Baron

Francis Dashwood (1708–1781), co-founder of the Hellfire Club, is said to be haunted by Hellfire Club Secretary Paul Whitehead (1710–1774), who supposedly asked for his heart to be put on display at the caves upon his passing. The theft of the urn containing it, however, caused his spirit to wander around ever since. A girl named "Sukie," supposedly stoned to death by an angry mob, has also been seen floating around.

5. Amersham's strangeness seems to radiate to nearby Chiltern towns and landmarks too, including the Standard Pub (Beaconsfield) parking lot, where the beating drum of a boy executed there during the English Civil War can still be heard; the graveyard of St. Bartholomew Church (Fingest) where an apparition dressed as a gamekeeper engages with visitors; and the understated Ickenham London Underground subway station, where a woman in a red scarf continues to replay her tragic fall onto the tracks, which happened back in the 1950s.

6. Perhaps the area's continued association to the supernatural stems from its own Spiritualist group that used to gather at Lyon's Tearoom on Church Street, in High Wycombe, which later coalesced into the Wycombe Spiritualist Church, and by 2017 had been reborn as the Wycombe Spiritualist Centre.

7. Sixty miles to the south from Amersham, in Sussex, another eerie British town garners not

ghosts but fringe cults (more on those later): East Grinstead. This real-life "Twin Peaks" is populated by Rosicrucians, Jehovah's Witnesses, Christian Scientists, and Mormons—all pretty innocuous compared to their neighboring branches of the Anthroposophical Society, Opus Dei (a Catholic sect with a BDSM fetish), and the Church of Scientology!

BONUS FACTS

Despite its dramatic name, the Exploding Head Syndrome (EHS) doesn't cause people's noggin to burst like a *piñata*, but rather endure unusual, and still-unexplained, loud noises and flashes of light which, while frightening, are basically painless.

Convicted Mormon forger and murderer Mark William Hofmann (b.1954) counterfeited documents related to the history of the Church of Jesus Christ of Latter-day Saints, and then car-bombed two people to cover his tracks in 1985.

As reported by *The Royal Gazette* in 1975: "Erskine Ebbin and his brother Neville were killed almost exactly a year apart after being involved in collision with the same taxi, driven by the same driver [a Willard Manders] and carrying the same passenger."

I DON'T WANNA BE BURIED IN A . . .

Ever since Siberian hunter-gatherers buried their newly domesticated companions—dogs!—with tokens of affection, mankind has found ways to memorialize the special bond we share with animals.

1. As the mummified remains of their pets attest, the ancient Egyptian culture believed they would keep their deceased company in the afterlife. Cats, of course, were the most popular (to the point of considering them deities), but dogs, mongooses, monkeys, gazelles, and birds also held the special affection of households, where the process of mourning them included wailing and the shaving of eyebrows.

2. Perhaps as a counterpoint to the cat-obsessed culture which enslaved them, ancient Israelis loved their dogs so much they created the very first dog cemetery around 500 BC. Overlooking the Mediterranean Sea, in what is now the Ashkelon National Park, the Ashkelon Pet Cemetery was the largest known cemetery of this kind in the ancient world, where thousands of carefully buried remains from what appear to be ancestors of the modern Canaan Dog breed have been found, including puppies.

3. Informally, beginning with the burial of pet dog Cherry at the park's gatekeeper's garden in 1881, the Hyde Park Pet Cemetery (also known as The Secret Pet Cemetery of Hyde Park) became the first, if informal, pet cemetery of the modern era. One thousand burials (mostly of dogs, but also cats, monkeys, and birds) later, in 1903, it was officially closed, but pets continued to be intermittently interred there until 1976. Maintained as a memorial, guided visits are occasionally allowed by the Royal Parks administration.

4. On the other hand, the first officially established modern pet cemetery is the Hartsdale Pet Cemetery of Westchester County, New York. Founded in 1896 by veterinarian Dr. Samuel Johnson (1854–1937) in his own apple orchard, it was soon filled with little headstones, flowers, and all the accoutrements usually applied to departed humans. "The Peaceable Kingdom" currently provides resting grounds for more than eighty thousand pets of many species (and hundreds of their owners too), including those belonging to Diana Ross (b.1944) and Mariah Carey (b.1969).

5. A historic monument since 1987, the Parisian *Cimetiére des Chiens et Autres Animaux Domestiques* (Cemetery of Dogs and Other Domestic Animals) in Asnières-sur-Seine, has been housing dog, cat, horse, lion, fish, and monkey remains since 1899, making it the world's second-oldest pet cemetery, and one of the best regarded. Notably, the tomb of Hollywood star, German shepherd Rin Tin Tin (rescued from a trench in French territory during World War I) can be found there.

6. The fifth-oldest pet cemetery still in operation in the United States, the Aspin Hill Memorial Park (Aspen Hill, Maryland) was originally founded in 1920 by Boston terrier breeders Richard C. Birney and his wife Bertha and is currently run by the Montgomery County Humane Society. It contains fifty thousand pet burials—and fifty human ones—including several dogs owned by legendary FBI Director J. Edgar Hoover (1895–1972).

7. The Los Angeles Pet Memorial Park in Calabasas, California, was founded by Hollywood veterinarian Dr. Eugene C. Jones in 1928 to supplement his thriving pet hospital business. True to its showbiz roots, it became the burial grounds of celebrity pets, including Kabar (Rudolph Valentino's dog), Jiggs ("Cheetah" in the *Tarzan* movies), Topper (Hopalong Cassidy's horse), Droopy (Humphrey Bogart's dog), Boots (Charlie Chaplin's cat), Scout (Tonto's horse from *The Lone Ranger*), Petey (the dog from *Our Gang*), Spot (the *Little Rascals'* dog), and Elmer (Steven Spielberg's dog, who appeared in *Close Encounters of the Third Kind*, 1941, and *Jaws*).

8. One of the most curious pet cemeteries in America, the Key Underwood Coon Dog Memorial Graveyard, has been serving as a coon hound–exclusive burial ground in rural Colbert County, Alabama, since 1937, when local huntsman Key Underwood informally buried his coon dog Troop in an old hunting camp. When other hunters followed his example, the cemetery as it is known today, with its mismatching gravestones and concrete pillar (representing two coonhounds treeing a raccoon) guarding the gate, slowly came to be.

9. In modern times, the lack of a common religious belief concerning the afterdeath fate of animals has seen some owners embrace the "New Agey" concept of a "Rainbow Bridge," where they will be reunited with their pets. For those not wanting to wait nor circumvent the various American and international legalities of human-pet burial, in 2010 the English hamlet of Stainton by Langworth (Lincolnshire) became the first, and so far, the only place in the United Kingdom where owners may be legally buried alongside their pets, in a sanctioned "green burial" plot.

10. Harmless and wholesome, especially when compared to their human counterparts, pet cemeteries got a more sinister rep in the last forty years, in large part due to a work of fiction, the 1983 novel *Pet Sematary* by Stephen King (b.1947). In it, an ancient Native American burial ground brings the dead back to life, only now possessed by murderous evil spirits! Adapted for the silver screen twice, its very author has claimed that, out of all his other horror books, this particular story scared him the most. It certainly continues to spook us.

HELLHOLE

At some point in history mankind started opting out of executing and burying its worst of the worst, instead choosing to lock it away from society. Having long since abandoned any rehabilitation pretense, these prisons have come the closest to hell on Earth.

Tacumbú Prison: Incorrectly labeled "The Most Dangerous Prison on Earth" by the Netflix show *Inside the World's Toughest Prisons*, this facility in Asunción, Paraguay, was built for eight hundred prisoners back in 1956, but currently holds 4,231, watched over by just forty untrained guards. About seven thousand uninspected visitors are also legally allowed in four times a week, which means prisoners are regularly fed, especially in the Adventist and Catholic wings, but drugs and weapons circulate unhindered elsewhere, fueling bloody gang wars every other month. Though hardly the most dangerous prison on this list, it still makes places like Rikers and Attica look like frozen yogurt shops.

Kamiti Maximum Security Prison: One of the worst prisons in all of Africa, this facility located in Nairobi, Kenya, is infamous for its abundance of brutality, and its lack of a reliable water supply (no showers, nor any sewage system), food (only two rations a day: porridge for breakfast, and a bowl of soup for lunch), and no health care, which means Cholera regularly claims the lives of dozens of inmates packed in one-hundred-square-foot cells.

Kamiti is best-known, however, as a prison where rape is aggressively practiced among prisoners.

Miguel Castro Castro Prison: This infamous penitentiary located in San Juan de Lurigancho, a district of Lima, Peru, keeps 11,500 criminals within its rotting walls (originally erected to hold only 2,500). Manned by a skeleton crew of 150 corrupt guards, with no segregation possible (which means hardened criminals "mingle" with younger offenders) the only way of keeping it from exploding is letting drugs, prostitution, and rape run rampant. Cockfights too! Ironically, guards also need to be bribed to let in the raw materials needed by the pottery workshop run on the premises by a Catholic nonprofit. In fact, a particular inmate got so crafty with clay, he managed to bury his girlfriend's corpse under the floor of his own cell, where it stayed undetected for weeks.

San Francisco de Yare Prison: The worst Venezuelan prison among several other horribly overcrowded prisons (including former Maracaibo National Prison, *"La Sabaneta,"* which closed in 2013) in that dystopia of a country everybody wants to escape from, the *Prisión de Yare* holds 44,500 criminals, hundreds of which die regularly on account of starvation, STDs, and violent clashes between armed drug gangs.

Bang Kwang Central Prison: Nicknamed "Big Tiger" on account of the many who lose their lives within its walls, or the more jocular "Bangkok Hilton," this prison at Thailand's Nonthaburi Province keeps over eight thousand death row and long-sentence inmates (in a space made for three thousand) behind bars. The difference between the two being that the latter only have to wear welded leg iron chains for the first three months of their sentence, while the former will keep them on until execution day. It offers only one meal per day—a bowl of maggot-infested rice and soup—per prisoner, which means those who cannot afford to buy from the prison canteen have to "work" for other prisoners in order to eat, a horrifying prospect not uncommon to most prisons around the world.

Camp 22: *Kwan-li-so* ("penal labor colony") No. 22, better known as the Hoeryong concentration camp, is a maximum-security camp located in North Korea. While supposedly closed in 2012, satellite imagery taken in 2017 revealed it remains operational and has even been partly refurbished. A Nazi wet dream, its estimated fifty thousand emaciated prisoners (including their entire family and close friends, all deemed "guilty by association" according to the State) never leave its grounds alive. Meanwhile, they will be made to long for death as they are subjected to various forms of torture and forced labor. Fed only 6.3 ounces of corn per meal twice a day, inmates will need to hunt for insects, rats, and snakes, or even resort to cannibalism (the reason many lack a limb or two) if they intend to survive.

Children, of course, don't last very long, and neither do the elderly.

Penal de Ciudad Barrios: A maximum security joint originally built by the Salvadorean government to keep arrested members of the powerful MS13 gang (*La Mara Salvatrucha*) apart from other gangs, its 2,500 prisoners now run the prison as their very own "members-only" headquarters, from which they direct various criminal operations and impart their own brand of justice. No guards are allowed inside, and it is so dangerous the military ended up guarding the prison perimeter, only to prevent these nefarious criminals from physically escaping to the outside world, while their power and influence rot the beautiful country from the inside out.

Gitarama Central Prison: Fairly labeled as the world's deadliest prison, this Rwandan facility, found thirty-seven miles southeast of the capital Kigali, was built for four hundred prisoners but currently keeps almost seven thousand incarcerated. Stacked together like cattle all day long, inmates stand shoeless on floors so deplorably filthy (there is no sanitation) dozens die every day while attempting to cut off their gangrene-infected limbs. Others are simply killed and eaten by other prisoners (there's no food either).

The observant reader will find "supermax" prisons like ADX Florence (Florence, Colorado), and the infamous "Black Dolphin"(Penal Colony

No. 6, in Orenburg, Russia) absent from this list, but the truth of the matter is that, while the very dangerous criminals (including terrorists and serial killers) they hold have to endure harsh isolation, these facilities at the very least provide sanitation, running water, health care, dental care, and regular meals. They also are neither overcrowded, nor under-guarded, and present no institutionalized cases of predatory sodomy that we know of.

BONUS QUOTES

"There's a phrase we live by in America: 'In God We Trust.' It's right there where Jesus would want it: on our money."
—Stephen Colbert

"Never interrupt your enemy when he is making a mistake."
—Napoleon Bonaparte

"Being in the Army is like being in the Boy Scouts. Except the Boy Scouts have adult supervision."
—Adam Sandler

"Time and tide and hookers wait for no man."
—Rodney Dangerfield

DARK WATER

Imagine a prison where inmates are not adults, but children kidnapped from their families at a young age. Kept packed together with aggressive strangers in cold water cells under total darkness at night, and then forced to learn and perform a grueling circus routine by day, or else be deprived of food as a form of punishment. Well, that's only part of the living hell orcas go through in captivity, where most die, and a few simply snap, with tragic consequences.

1. Commonly referred to as "killer whales," in reality, orcas are the largest species of marine dolphins. These far-ranging apex predators have a diverse diet which includes fish and other sea mammals, but no instances of orcas eating humans has ever been recorded—which may well prove they have some standards.

2. One hundred and sixty-six orca calves have been abducted from their families at sea since 1961; 129 of which are now dead, including the seven infamously captured at Penn Cove, Washington, in 1970, a haphazard operation that killed five other members of their pod in the process.

3. Wild male and female orcas have a maximum life expectancy of sixty and ninety years respectively, but captive ones rarely pass their thirties. So far, a total of 168 imprisoned orcas have died, not counting thirty miscarried and stillborn calves.

4. As of March 2021, officially fifty-eight orcas are held in parks and aquariums around the world, twenty-seven of which were captured at sea, the rest being born into bondage. There's one in Canada, six in Spain, four in France, three in Russia, one in Buenos Aires, seven in Japan, fifteen in China, and twenty-one in the United States.

5. Twenty of the American orcas currently struggle with life at the infamous SeaWorld Parks, including Corky, the oldest surviving orca in captivity (captured in 1969). None of her seven children, however, managed to survive, adding to the forty-nine other orcas who have perished at those dreadful parks.

6. Just as it happens with jailed humans, imprisoned orcas are also traumatized by being constantly abused by their fellow inmates. The case of Morgan, a SeaWorld loan to the *Loro Parque* (Tenerife, Spain) stands out, as she tried to save herself from bullying cage mates, first by bashing her head against the metal grate, and then "beaching" herself over the concrete slab above the pool. It must be noted that the shallowness of pools, combined with very transparent chlorinated water allows for the sun to cause them severe burns. These are not happy "sea pandas" by a long shot!

7. If anything, orcas are intelligent, willful creatures, and those who refuse to seek the sweet release of death fight back, which explains the dozens of attempted trainer pin-down drownings and rammings reported since the late sixties, including:

- Invited to ride the original Shamu in 1971, SeaWorld secretary Anne E. Eckis (b.1949) was thrown off, grabbed by the leg, and dragged through the pool by the animal, until trainers managed to corner and pry her mouth open with a metal pole to release poor Ms. Eckis, who received twenty-five stitches as a result.
- During the 1970s, beloved Hugo and Lolita of the Miami Seaquarium repeatedly lunged and snapped at trainers, sometimes refusing to let them out of the water, and once playing tug-of-war with a trainer named Bob Pulaski as the rope.
- Orky II was an orca that tried to kill and maim several of its trainers during the seventies and eighties, and was moved from one sea park to another as a result, finally passing at the San Diego SeaWorld in 1988. Particularly, back in 1987 it dropped its five-tonne mass on a trainer named John Sillick (twenty-six) while he was riding another whale, breaking his back, hips, pelvis, ribs, and legs.
- Another 1987 incident involved SeaWorld trainer Jonathan Smith (twenty), who was tossed around by two six-tonne female orcas, Kenau and Kandy, during a show. Smith continued to pretend everything was fine so as not to panic the cheering crowd while the

whales continued to pass him around like a rag doll. Fortunately, he managed to escape the ordeal with a ruptured kidney and a six-inch laceration through his liver.

8. Then along came Tilikum (c.1981–2017). As shown in the ground-breaking documentary *Blackfish* (2013), "Tilly" became unnaturally aggressive after repeated mistreatment in the hands of trainers *and* other orcas, earning the "killer whale" moniker by killing three humans:

- His first victim, trainer Keltie Byrne (twenty-one), was a group affair, as Tilly and two of his abusive cage mates, Haida and Nootka, drowned the poor girl on purpose in 1991.
- His second victim, interloper Daniel P. Dukes (twenty-seven), got naked and plunged into Tilly's tank at night, his badly bruised corpse found draped over the orca's back the next morning in 1999.
- In 2010, after a "Dinner with Shamu" routine—I'd be pissed too!—Tilly grabbed his most notorious third victim, trainer Dawn Brancheau (forty), by her ponytail, and dragged her to the depths of the pool, fracturing her spine and tearing her scalp off, resulting in her death.

9. As is the case with most corporations, for decades SeaWorld Entertainment Inc. denied any wrongdoing on their part, moving violent orcas around its parks, and burying legal suits by any

means necessary—even going to the extreme of spying on activists—but the outcry resulting from the *Blackfish* documentary sent its share values into a pronounced decline, leading to its CEO's resignation, and a change of focus from animal attractions to mechanical rides, with orca breeding gradually being phased-out. While the strategy proved effective in reversing the company's fortune, it would be a tiny microbe—the Covid 19 virus—rather than an orca, that finally managed to bite a significant chunk off company revenue, but the cruel circus still continues . . .

10. In light of all the attacks and killing perpetrated by orcas with the sole purpose of striking back at their captors, Arthur Herzog's (1927–2010) wild claim about orcas being "the only animal other than man who kills for revenge" now rings true. An author of both thrillers and true-crime books, Herzog's 1977 novel *Orca*, as well as the De Laurentis film adaptation based on it, deals with a male orca tracking down a boat captain for killing the whale's pregnant mate and their unborn calf. Prolific British novelist Peter Tonkin (b.1950) kicked things up a notch a few years later with his bombastic thriller *Killer* (1980), the cautionary tale of five men stranded on an ice floe at the mercy of an entire orca pod, led by a mutated, oversized alpha male—let us hope the latter stays within the realm of fiction!

SIERRA MADRE

Nothing dispels the dark like the golden glow of real buried treasure. Technically, a treasure trove (called a "hoard" or a "cache" when of archeological significance) is any amount of money, coin, or refined metal found hidden or buried. Let's have a look at the most famous—and valuable—found so far.

Cuerdale Hoard (1840): A lead box filled with 8,600 items unearthed by workers repairing an embankment on the southern bank of the River Ribble, in an area called Cuerdale near Preston, England, this is one of the largest Viking-era silver caches ever found, which also includes items imported from as far as Northern Italy, and even Byzantium (modern day Istanbul), and is valued at $3.2 million.

Hoxne Hoard (1992): Consisting of 14,865 Roman gold, silver, and bronze coins and approximately 200 items of silver tableware and gold jewelry from 400 AD, this treasure valued at $3.8 million was buried in an oak box (its items carefully sorted in smaller wooden boxes, bags, or wrapped in fabric), and accidentally uncovered by retired gardener and metal detectorist Eric Lawes (1923–2015), while helping a friend find a lost hammer.

Staffordshire Hoard (2009): Found by metal detectorist Terry Herbert (b.1945) and valued at $4.1 million, it is the largest trove of seventh-century Anglo-Saxon gold and silver metalwork discovered, and includes almost 4,600 objects, all but three of which are military (uncommon, since most Anglo-Saxon finds contain domestic objects as well).

Saddle Ridge Hoard (2013): Deep in California Gold Country, "John and Mary" (their true identities kept a secret) were walking their dog around their property when they stumbled upon a half-buried rusted can containing 1,427 nineteenth-century mint-condition gold coins worth 27,980 dollars in their day, which have been assessed to be worth $10 million.

Le Catillon II Hoard (2012): Following a story told by a farmer's daughter, after thirty years of methodically searching a field on the British island of Jersey, in the English Channel, detectorists Reg Mead (b.1942) and Richard Miles (b.1963) found the biggest-ever hoard of Iron Age silver and gold coins in the UK—69,347 of them, entombed in a mound of clay—valued at $15 million.

SS *Central America* (1988): Sunk in 1857 by a category 2 hurricane while off the coast of the Carolinas, the *Central America* lost 425 lives (out of the 578 originally aboard the ship), including its captain, along with a precious cargo of gold valued at $8 million in its day ($550 million by modern standards), which was partially recovered by a Columbus-America Discovery Group team lead by Tommy Gregory Thompson (b.1952) in 1988, which was awarded an estimated $100 million for the find.

Spillings Hoard (1998): One day while plowing his field in Gotland, Sweden, a farmer named Bjorn Engstrom came across a Viking coin. Calling a friend from the local museum, together they soon uncovered another 150 coins. The following year they resumed their search, and on July 16, 1999, came across the biggest 800 AD treasure hoard ever discovered—14,295 Islamic, Persian, Byzantine, and Danish silver coins, 486 Viking armlets, and many other silver and bronze artifacts, weighing a total of 187.4 pounds. Deemed invaluable by the Swedish government, which paid Engstrom a hefty $242,400 fee for it, over the next twenty years more than seven hundred caches containing over 2,200 pounds of silver, including 168,000 coins, have been found buried all around the island.

Sroda Treasure (1985–1988): In 1985, a vase filled with approximately three thousand Prague *groschen* (fourteenth-century Bohemian silver coins) was found during the demolition of the local telephone building in the town of Środa, Poland, but no further archeological research was conducted in the area, until three years later when another demolition nearby revealed an even bigger cache, which included silver and gold florin coins, but most of them were taken away by individual looters before the government secured the site. As the "gold fever" took hold of the entire town, people started to rummage through other demolition sites, uncovering more caches, including a woman's gold crown, various pairs of gold pendants, jewel-encrusted gold rings, and a bejeweled gold clasp.

While the entire treasure's value hasn't been fully appraised, it's estimated worth has been set at $120 million.

Whydah Gally (1984): Commanded by the wealthiest pirate in history, Captain Samuel "Black Sam" Bellamy (c.1689–1717), the *Whydah Gally* disappeared off the coast of Cape Cod, Massachusetts, until found again by archeological explorer Barry Clifford (b.1945) in 1984, buried under 50 feet of sand. Its original 4.5 tons worth of gold and silver coins, coupled with the historical value of the two hundred thousand recovered artifacts (after all, it's the only fully authenticated eighteenth-century pirate shipwreck ever discovered), set the value of the find at an astounding $350 million, all of which belong to Mr. Clifford.

Nuestra Señora de las Mercedes (2007): The wreck of this Spanish Navy frigate, which sank in 1804 carrying a precious cargo of Latin American gold and silver coins, ingots, and jewels, was originally found by American company Odyssey Marine Exploration. However, after a protracted five-year legal dispute, it was declared Spanish heritage, and the fourteen tons of recovered treasure worth almost $500 million was promptly shipped to Spain.

Panagyurishte Treasure (1949): This Thracian thirteen-pound cache of 24-karat gold religious artifacts (a vial, an amphora, and seven animal-shaped drinking horns) was accidentally found by brothers Pavel, Petko, and Michail Deikov while searching for clay at a tile factory near Panagyurishte, Bulgaria. Quickly seized by the state, its value has been deemed to be incalculable. Further Thracian hoards found in Bulgaria include the Valchitran Treasure (1924), the Lukovit Treasure (1953), the Borovo Treasure (1974), and the Rogozen Treasure (1985).

Caesarea Sunken Treasure (2015): Diving off the coast of the ancient port town of Caesarea, Israel, after it had been battered by a storm, a man named Zvika Fayer spotted a golden coin. Then he found another, and another, and another, all littering the seabed. Immediately reporting the find to the Israel Antiquities Authority (IAA), before another storm hit the area Fayer, his friends, and a group of IAA officers managed to salvage two lumps made of thousands of tightly-packed 24-karat gold coins (which used to be transported in pottery jars), as well as various other artifacts, including a bronze lamp depicting the image of the Roman sun god Sol, another lamp in the shape of a Nubian slave, and a figurine of the moon goddess Luna, among other assorted fragments. A priceless discovery, while initially misreported to be of Arabian origin, all items turned out to be part of a 1,600-year-old shipwreck from the time of Constantine (312–337 AD).

Edgar Church's Collection: Strangely enough, one of the world's greatest treasures ever found was not made of silver or gold, but cheap, yellowing paper. Edgar Church (1888-1978), a commercial artist working for the Colorado Telephone Company, kept thousands of periodicals and art clippings for reference; among them were over twenty thousand well-preserved comic books from the 1940s. Without knowing these comics were already fetching exorbitant prices in auctions, the real estate agent tasked with selling Church's old home ended up contacting budding comics retailer Charles Rozanski (b.1955), who purchased the whole priceless lot at a bargain, including Action Comics #1 (Superman's first appearance from 1938), currently valued in the range of $10 million, and Marvel Comics #1 (1939) currently valued at $1,260,000. Needless to say, the collection made Rozanski the fortune on which he cemented his Mile High Comics business.

Bactrian Gold (1978): A collection of about 20,600 jewelry ornaments, coins and other 100 BC artifacts, all made of gold, silver, bronze, ivory, and lapis lazuli, this hoard was dug from six burial mounds, collectively known as *Tillya tepe* ("Golden Mound") by a Soviet-Afghan team led by the Greek-Russian archaeologist Viktor Sarianidi (1929–2013). Presumed lost during the 1990s, the entire treasure was found in 2003, secretly stashed under the central bank building in Kabul, Afghanistan, where it was placed for safekeeping due to its incalculable worth.

English Gold (2019): With a record 1,311 treasure troves found during 2019 in England, Wales, and Northern Ireland, we could say metal detecting has become a national hobby in the United Kingdom, where it engages 1.8 percent of the population. Particularly, the small, and sparsely populated five-town county of Shropshire on the Welsh border has seen an unprecedented 123 treasure trove findings between 2012 and 2020. No wonder *detectoring* is the preferred leisure activity of 3.6 percent of adults there! Recent Shropshire finds include the notorious 2017 "Piano Hoard," a cache of gold found hidden inside an old piano, and the 2018 "Wem Hoard," a bullion of fifth-century hacked-up Roman coins discovered—or should we say, detected?—by three *detectorists* named Steve Lord, Steve King, and Andy Bijsterbosch.

BONUS FACT

Englishman Joshua Abraham Norton (1818–1880) proclaimed himself "Norton I., Emperor of the United States" in 1859, becoming a folk hero of sorts in San Francisco.

A year later, Frenchman Orélie-Antoine de Tounens (1825–1878) proclaimed himself king of the Araucanía and Patagonia regions of South America, but was quickly imprisoned and deported back to France, where he would die a destitute two years later.

THE DESOLATION OF SMAUG

Lost to the sands of time, the following treasures continue to capture the imagination of the public at large, inspiring literature, movies, and more than the occasional wild goose chase around the world.

Tucker's Cross: In September 1955 diver and marine explorer Teddy Tucker (1925–2014) was surveying the shipwreck of the *San Pedro*, a Spanish galleon sunk off the coast of Bermuda in 1594, when he chanced upon a number of gold ingots and buttons. Among them, a somewhat crudely made gold cross lying face down in the sand caught his eye. Turning it around, it revealed seven encrusted emeralds as big as musket balls! Valued at $250,000 by the Smithsonian, at the time it was considered to be the most valuable single object ever found in a shipwreck. Sold by Tucker to the Bermuda Government for $100,000, it was kept at a local museum, until stolen and deviously replaced with a replica in 1975—right before a visit from Queen Elizabeth II—never to be seen again.

Mosby's Treasure: A burlap sack containing over $350,000 worth of gold, silver, and jewelry looted from the homes of wealthy Virginia planters was allegedly taken by Confederate Colonel John Singleton Mosby (1833–1916), a.k.a. "The Gray Ghost," from the Fairfax Courthouse, and buried between two large pine trees in the woods of

Fairfax County, Virginia, where it supposedly remains to this day. After his official pardon, Mosby enjoyed a long life of service to the United States government (including a post as Consul in Hong Kong) apparently never managing to return for it.

The Patiala Necklace: Created by the Parisian firm Cartier for Maharaja Bhupinder Singh (1891–1938) in 1928, this lavish necklace contained 2,930 diamonds, including the 428 carat "De Beers" yellow diamond, as well as a number of Burmese rubies. After vanishing from the Royal Treasury of Patiala in 1948, its "De Beers" diamond reappeared in 1982 at a Sotheby's auction in Geneva, where it fetched $3.16 million. Sixteen years later, part of the necklace was found by chance at a secondhand London jewelry shop, but the rest of its original diamonds and rubies remain missing.

The Royal Casket: Assembled by Princess Izabela Czartoryska (1746–1835) of Poland in 1800, this large chest contained seventy-three valuable relics, including gold and silver jewelry, watches, and other priceless mementos that had once belonged to Polish royalty. A casualty of World War II, it was sadly looted by the *Wehrmacht* at Czartoryski Museum in 1939 and lost to history ever since.

Yamashita's Gold: Named after General Tomoyuki Yamashita (1885–1946), the man who conquered British Malaya (Malay Peninsula and Singapore) in seventy days, *Kin no yuri* ("Golden Lily") was the alleged code name for the transport operation of this vast treasure (an estimated 6,000 tons of gold looted from Southeast Asian countries) rumored to have been orchestrated by Prince Yasuhito (1902–1953) himself, and stashed underground in secret vaults scattered across the Philippines by General Yamashita, who took the secret of their location to the grave when executed in 1946.

Lost Dutchman's Gold Mine: Believed to be in Arizona's befittingly named Superstition Mountains, this is America's most famous "lost mine." Searched for since the late nineteenth century, its existence is enmeshed in legend and lore to the point where fact and fiction cannot be told apart, but trust-worthy sources relate the story of a German (referred to as "Dutch" back in the day) prospector named Jacob Waltz who supposedly discovered a vein of almost pure gold in the vicinity of the Superstition Mountains. Some say he didn't find any; others claim that he did. Whatever the case, he owned a 160-acre farm by 1870, which he apparently lost along with his life after the Phoenix flood of 1891. Before passing, however, he managed to draw a map to the vein for his caretaker, Julia Thomas, who unsuccessfully spent several years trying to locate it. To this day, nine thousand people a year still follow in Thomas's footsteps, and a few have lost their lives in the process, but for the time being the mine remains out of reach.

Blackbeard's Treasure: The original pirate of the Caribbean, Edward Teach (c. 1680–1718) had a preference for theatrics (he used to tie lit fuses to his bushy beard strands), and he often raided the American Carolinas with his own private fleet, even settling in Bath, North Carolina, for a short while before going back to his criminal ways, which would eventually see him beheaded off the shores of Ocracoke Island (also in North Carolina). "What about his treasure?" you might ask. Well, in his own diary Blackbeard claimed the vast wealth he accumulated "lay in a location known only to him and the devil," but with no X-marked map to go by, all archaeologists have found while searching the sunken shipwreck of the pirate's main ship, the Queen Anne's Revenge, are faint traces of gold dust.

Montezuma's Treasure: Emperor during the heyday of the Aztec Triple Alliance, an empire of three city-states in modern-day Mexico, Moctezuma II (c.1466–1520) ruled over the biggest and richest of them all, Tenochtitlan (modern-day Mexico City). Initially receiving Hernán Cortés (1485–1547) into his own palace, when Cortés returned to the city after facing off against rival Pánfilo de Narváez (c.1473–1528), he found his men had taken Moctezuma II under house arrest as leverage against the Aztecs, who were growing restless about their presence. This caused a revolt that ended with the emperor stoned to death by his own enraged people, and the Spanish dumping all their looted treasure in the waters of Lake Texcoco while fleeing town. Never recovered, this hoard is said to still rest under Mexico City, which was built atop that very lake.

Treasure of Lima: Gathered by the well-to-do of Lima, Peru, in 1821, at the behest of the Spanish Viceroy, this hoard is supposedly hidden in the mountains of Cocos Island, Costa Rica, by the man commissioned to transport it, a Newfoundland trader named William Thompson, to the still-loyal Spanish Mexico. Promising to reveal where the treasure had been hidden upon capture, Thompson and his first mate instead bolted into the jungles of Cocos, never to be seen again. The list of valuables contained in the treasure is nothing short of amazing:

- One chest containing altar trimmings of gold cloth with canopies, monstrances, chalices all coated with gemstones of up to 1,244 pieces.
- One chest with two gold relic containers weighing 120 pounds with 624 topaz, carnelians, and emeralds, and twelve diamonds.
- One chest containing three relic containers of cast metal weighing 160 pounds with 860 rubies, nineteen diamonds, and other gemstones.
- One chest containing 4,000 Spanish gold doubloons, 124 swords, 5,000 Mexican gold crowns, sixty-four daggers, 120 shoulder belts, and twenty-eight round shields.
- One chest containing eight caskets of cedar wood and silver with 3,840 cut stones, rings, offering plates, and 4,265 uncut stones.
- Seven chests with twenty-two gold and silver candelabra weighing 250 pounds, and 164 rubies.
- One seven-foot, 780-pound solid gold statue of Virgin Mary with baby Jesus adorned with 1,684 jewels, and seven crosses made of diamonds.

The Ark of the Covenant: Arguably the most famous treasure of all time, according to the Bible the Ark was a gold-plated acacia chest with two cherubim on its lid. Commissioned to Moses by God Himself in order to carry the two stone blocks—rather than tablets—of the Ten Commandments (the New Testament's Hebrews epistle mentions it contained Aaron's flowering rod, and a pot of manna too) 2,600 feet before the marching Israelites. It remained concealed at all times (even from the priests and the Levites carrying it) until it was finally placed in a special room within Solomon's Temple.

Generally considered lost after the Babylonian destruction of Jerusalem in 587 BC, 2 *Maccabees* (a book regarded as canonical by Catholic and Orthodox Christians, but apocryphal by Evangelicals) describes with great detail how prophet Jeremiah hid it inside a cave within Mount Nebo, in modern-day Jordan.

BONUS QUOTES

"The dumber people think you are, the more surprised they are going to be when you kill them."
—William Clayton

"When people ask me if I see too much sex in the movies, I tell them, how should I know? I watch the film, not the audience."
—Mel Helitzer

NATIONAL TREASURE

A treasure means nothing without a place to keep it, and the more valuable an item gets, the best-guarded and hidden from prying eyes it must become. Welcome to some of the safest, most inaccessible places on Earth!

Oak Island Money Pit: Discovered in the late eighteenth century, this deep network of timbered tunnels and chambers in Oak Island (a forested 140-acre island in Nova Scotia, Canada) became the focus of a treasure-hunting frenzy in the mid-1800s when a slab of stone was found, a coded message engraved on its flat surface: "Forty Feet Below, Two Million Pounds Are Buried." However, the frenzied excavation activity led to most of it being ultimately flooded by sea water, its rumored treasures—ranging from Captain Kidd's hoard, Marie Antoinette's jewels, William Shakespeare's true identity, and even the Ark of the Covenant—forever irretrievable.

Vatican Apostolic Archive: Located within the massive walls of the Vatican enclave, and formerly known as the Vatican Secret Archives, the *Archivum Apostolicum Vaticanum* holds some of the most valuable historical information in the world since 1612, including all acts promulgated by the Holy See itself, diplomatic letters from several eras, and significant exorcism transcripts. It is also rumored to keep valuable religious relics ranging from Saint Peter's bones to the Holy Grail itself, remnants of an alleged "chronovisor" (a contraption that would let us see events from the past), an original copy of the Grand Grimoire (a legendary black magic book containing instructions for summoning Lucifer), and even indisputable proof of extraterrestrial life.

Fort Knox: Built in 1937 in Fort Knox, Kentucky, away from coastal cities to make it less vulnerable to foreign military attack, the United States Bullion Depository is a fortified vault building operated by the Department of the Treasury. Within it's razor-wired, mine-fielded perimeter, its granite walls encase a steel-plated, concrete encased vault (with an impenetrable time-locked twenty-one-inch-thick door) holding not only 147 million troy ounces of gold bullion (over half of the Treasury's stored gold), but also ten 1933 Double Eagle gold coins, a 1974-D aluminum penny prototype, and twelve gold (22-karat) Sacagawea dollar coins that flew on the Space Shuttle Columbia. During World War II, the signed original Constitution of the United States, the Declaration of Independence, Articles of Confederation, Lincoln's Second Inaugural Address, drafts of Lincoln's Gettysburg Address, a Gutenberg Bible, a copy of the *Magna Carta*, and even the Holy Crown of Hungary were also entrusted to Fort Knox for safekeeping.

Bank of England: This bank , which has never been robbed since opening in 1694, is the second-largest custodian of gold in the world. It holds around four hundred thousand bars belonging to several nations and worth a roughly estimated $280 billion, within its eight-foot-thick walls, and equally impenetrable layers of electronic security. If all else fails, physical security also includes a three-foot-long key to the vault door itself.

Federal Reserve Bank of New York: The world's main guardian of gold keeps an estimated 497,000 gold bars belonging to different nations and official organizations (private companies and individuals not allowed) securely stacked in its fifty-feet-below-sea level, bedrock-built, compartmentalized vault, right under its Manhattan headquarters at 33 Liberty Street, New York.

Iron Mountain: An American enterprise information management, destruction, and backup services company founded in 1951 in Boston, Massachusetts, Iron Mountain Inc. has 1,500 storage locations around the world. While most of these are run-of-the-mill, above-ground facilities, the company is famous for converting old mines into high-security underground bunkers (such as the ones in Boyers, Pennsylvania, and Greenfield, Rhode Island) which safekeep the most beloved possessions of Earth's greatest and mightiest—a clients' list which includes the Smithsonian, Universal Music, Time Warner, Sony, and Bill Gates (b.1955) himself.

Granite Mountain: The Granite Mountain Records Vault, a.k.a. "The Vault," is a large Church of Jesus

Christ of Latter-day Saints long-term storage facility and state-of-the-art archive excavated 600 feet into the north side of Little Cottonwood Canyon. It holds all of Utah's genealogical history, or about three billion pages of family records which the Mormon Church has been digitizing since the late 1990s.

Greenbrier Bunker: Commissioned by Dwight D. Eisenhower (1890–1969) in 1955 as a means to ensure the continuity of government should Washington DC ever be atomized, this formerly top-secret facility was built 720 feet under The Greenbrier, a luxury resort in White Sulphur Springs, West Virginia. Completed on October 16, 1962 (right on time for the Cuban Missile Crisis!), the 112,544-square-foot, two-level nuclear shelter was designed to keep the entire United States Congress safe from fallout. Maintained by around twelve permanent undercover government employees for three decades, it was quickly decommissioned in 1992 upon exposure in the pages of the *Washington Post*. Since 2006, guided ninety-minute tours are offered to guests and the general public from 9:30 a.m. to 3:30 p.m.

Hitler's Secret Archives: Holocaust deniers should take a trip to the quaint German town of Bad Arolson, where 50 million files recovered from concentration camps—as well as jewelry items belonging to those killed in them—are kept in sixteen miles' worth of shelves. The Nazis were famous for their record-keeping obsession, so their

Totenbuchs detail how one prisoner was shot every two minutes ... as well as the number and size of lice in their heads! The archive also contains the famed Schindler's List, and Anne Frank's (1929–1945) camp registry card.

Switzerland: The only thing safer than a given bank vault is a landlocked tax-heaven enclave of a country filled with banks sworn to the utmost secrecy, and that's just what the Swiss Confederation is. Famed for its chocolate, cheese, and neutrality, which allowed them to bypass two World Wars, they even subverted detailed German plans for a World War II invasion by granting Nazis laundering opportunities for their $400 million worth of looted gold, extracted both from occupied nations and concentration camp victims.

BONUS FACT

Reunited after thirty-nine years, separated-at-birth twins Jim Lewis (b.1940) and Jim Springer (b.1940) found they had both become policemen, had taken up carpentry as their hobby, had married and divorced women named Linda, named their sons James Alan and James Allan respectively, remarried to two women named Betty, and owned dogs they named Toy. They also drove Chevys, and vacationed at the same Florida beach.

BESTSELLER

From Edgar Allan Poe (1809–1849) to Hergé (Georges Remi; 1907–1983), treasure hunt stories deliver clue-solving thrills only paralleled by "whodunit" literature, but with a far more rewarding ending payoff.

"The Gold-Bug" (Edgar Allan Poe, 1843): Originally submitted to a Philadelphia Dollar Newspaper literary contest and nabbing its grand prize, this short story follows William Legrand's mad pursuit of Captain Kidd's treasure, via a cryptogram found written with invisible ink on a piece of parchment. Quickly becoming one of Poe's most popular tales during his lifetime (only surpassed by *The Raven*), it also inspired another writer's masterpiece: Robert Louis Stevenson's (1850–1894) *Treasure Island*.

Treasure Island **(Robert Louis Stevenson, 1883):** The granddaddy of all pirate novels, this one has it all, from one-legged seamen bearing parrots on their shoulders, to X-marked treasure maps. Originally serialized in *Young Folks* children's magazine from 1881 through 1882, it features the sea-faring adventures of young Jim Hawkins, who survives a mutiny (orchestrated by his friend, pirate Long John Silver, while posing as a cook aboard the fictional ship *Hispaniola*) and finds the long-lost treasure of Captain Flint.

King Solomon's Mines **(H. Rider Haggard, 1885):** An immediate bestseller, this first African adventure of character Allan Quatermain, a Victorian

75

"Indiana Jones" precursor, sees the white hunter's expedition follow a map written in blood into the lost African kingdom of Kukuana. Styled as gods by the locals, Quatermain and his men stage a coup and civil war in true Hernán Cortés (1485–1547) fashion before finally managing to escape to England with their pockets full of diamonds taken from the fabled mines.

The Hobbit (J. R. R. Tolkien, 1937): Entertaining Catholic children and American hippies since the 1930s, the quest of Bilbo Baggins (member of an imaginary race of hole-dwelling creatures) and a merry band of twelve dwarves led by wizard Gandalf to reclaim the treasure of Lonely Mountain from the evil dragon Smaug has been adapted into and ripped off by other media *ad infinitum*, and with good reason. After all, Bilbo's chance finding of the One Ring which rendered him invisible would lead to the great fantasy saga of the twentieth century, *The Lord of the Rings*.

***Red Rackham's Treasure* (Hergé, 1944):** The basis of Steven Spielberg's 2011 CGI film *The Adventures of Tintin*, this graphic novel revolves around the exploits of Belgian cub reporter Tintin and his raging alcoholic of a friend, Captain Haddock, as they follow a series of clues left by a Haddock ancestor to an unknown island 120 miles north of the Dominican Republic, where they find the wreck of a seventeenth-century ship, *The Unicorn*, but no trace of any treasure. Back in Belgium, however, a search through Haddock's ancestral country estate,

Marlinspike Hall, reveals the *Unicorn*'s treasure hidden in a secret room.

The Da Vinci Code **(Dan Brown, 2003):** The second in a fairly repetitive, but highly entertaining bestselling series of thrillers by Brown (b.1964) enmeshing cryptography, semiotics, and conspiracy theories. It stars fictional Professor Robert Langdon, who becomes involved in a high stakes chase to find the Holy Grail which, as Langdon discovers, turns out to be Mary Magdalene's sarcophagus, hidden below the Louvre.

Treasure Chest of Fun & Fact **(1942–1972):** Catholics' well-documented obsession with treasure (Hernán Cortés, J. R. R. Tolkien, and Hergé come to mind) came to a head with this American educational comic-book series published in Dayton, Ohio, and distributed in parochial schools all over the country for thirty years. It featured a veritable treasury of stories both fictional, Biblical, and biographical, written and illustrated by a who's who of comic creators of the day, ranging from Reed Crandall (1917–1982) to Jim Mooney (1919–2008).

BONUS QUOTE

"One picture is worth a thousand denials."
—Ronald Reagan

SCAVENGER HUNT

Bleeding from the printed page into the real world, real-life "armchair treasure hunts" require solving puzzle or riddle clues embedded within a book's writing or art to find very real, and often substantial, hidden prizes. Some of these contests have taken months and even years to complete, while others remain either partially or completely unsolved.

The Copper Scroll: Currently on display at the Jordan Museum in Amman, the last and most mysterious of all the Qumran Dead Sea Scrolls, "3Q15" is a copper-engraved inventory sheet written in Biblical Hebrew, which lists sixty-four burial spots for an assortment of gold and silver artifacts, presumably rescued from the Second Temple before the Romans looted it in 70 AD. Intensive searches of the locations pinpointed on the list conducted since the early 1960s have yet to yield any treasure at all.

The Beale Papers (1885): One of these three cryptographic pamphlets allegedly pinpoints the location of a buried three-ton treasure of gold, silver, and jewels (worth an estimated 43 million modern-day dollars) supposedly buried by a man named Thomas J. Beale in Bedford County, Virginia, sixty years prior to their publication. It is regarded by most as a hoax concocted by the man who printed the ciphers (a James B. Ward), only the second of which has been decoded so far.

Masquerade (1979): The book that inspired every armchair treasure hunt since, Kit Williams's (b.1946) lavishly illustrated Masquerade sent its British readers scrambling after a jewel-encrusted, eighteen-karat gold hare, which had been buried in a clay box to throw off metal detectorists. In 1982, a "Ken Thomas" (real name, Dugald Thompson) found the box in the dirt piles left by two other *Masqueraders*, after cheating his way to the foot of the Catherine of Aragon statue in Ampthill Park, Bedfordshire, where the hare was buried—he got the approximate location via Williams's ex-girlfriend. Years later, the jeweled hare sold at Sotheby's for 31,900 Sterling pounds to an anonymous East Asian buyer.

The Secret: A Treasure Hunt (1982): The product of many creative hands under the guidance of editor Byron Preiss (1953–2005), its twelve illustrated verse pages leading to twelve ceramic *casques* (figurine "keys" that could be traded for a predetermined gem, all twelve amounting to $10,000 of the day) encased in clear plastic boxes scattered across different American cities, in a still-ongoing quest which has uncovered only three *casques* since—in Chicago (1983), Cleveland (2003), and Boston (2019).

The Bee on the Comb (1984): Yet another Kit Williams brainchild, this book was published without its title on the cover, as the competition was based on figuring it out, and then finding a way to express it to Williams himself in a creative yet non-verbal way, which winner Steve Pearce did by producing a decorated cabinet. The prize was a queen bee-shaped award, plus a one-of-a-kind titled edition of the book, awarded on British national television in 1985.

MAZE: *Solve the World's Most Challenging Puzzle* (1985): Defined as a maze in the shape of a book, it was created by reputed illustrator Christopher Manson (birth date unknown), and published by Henry Holt and Company, offering a $10,000 award to the reader that cracked it. Since nobody did, in 1987 the contest was declared void, and the prize was split among the twelve people who came closest to solving it. Still in publication, it has since inspired a video game, clue websites, and many podcasts.

Fenn's Treasure (1988): Hidden by art dealer Forrest Fenn (1930–2020) in the Rocky Mountains, the location of this twelfth-century engraved silver chest filled with gold and jewels (valued at $2 million) was clued in a self-published poem which led an estimated 350,000 people to frantically search for it—five of whom died as a result of the pursuit. It was finally found in an undisclosed Wyoming location by thirty-two-year- old medical student Jack Stuef in 2020, just a few months before Mr. Fenn's passing at ninety.

On The Trail Of The Golden Owl (1993): *Sur la trace de la chouette d'or* is a French armchair treasure hunt book created by puzzle maker and author

Régis Hauser (1947–2009) under the pen name Max Valentin, in association with an artist named Michel Becker, who illustrated the book and sculpted the valuable buried prize: a gold owl (worth 1,000,000 francs of the day). While the author estimated the book's riddles could be solved within a year, as of 2021 the chouette remains as elusive as the Maltese Falcon.

BONUS FACTS

In 2021, a fifty-year-old male Japanese biker named Soya used a face-editing app to make himself look like a striking young woman, attracting many followers to his social media accounts.

According to official government statistics, two thousand Indians on average are killed by lightning strikes each year.

Likely used for electroplating objects, a set of three ancient artifacts—a ceramic pot, a tube of copper, and a rod of iron—was discovered in modern Iraq, and named the "Baghdad Battery."

The Everglades National Park in Florida is the only place in the world where crocodiles coexist with alligators.

FINDING NEVERLAND

An often-overlooked sight of how America got made are the continental territories that, unlike real-life scavenger hunts, never made it out of their paper existence after the final slicing of the map was set.

Transylvania: No connection to the fabled land of Count Dracula—though who's to say he wouldn't find the scenery lovely—but this unofficial fourteenth colony was set on land illegally purchased from the Cherokee nation. Located between modern-day Kentucky and Tennessee, Transylvania was absorbed by Virginia after the War of Independence.

Westsylvania: Yet another failed fourteenth colony/state idea, this stretch of land located between the British colonies of Virginia and Pennsylvania, lay beyond the reach of the pre-Revolutionary War Mason-Dixon line, so settlers of the region eventually petitioned the newly formed United States Congress for statehood. Congress basically ignored them, in order to give Pennsylvania and Virginia time to settle their dispute in 1780.

Delmarva: Developing a cultural identity of its own through partial geographical isolation, this large East Coast peninsula of the United States, currently divided between the states of Delaware, Maryland, and Virginia, unsuccessfully strived for its territories to split from their respective states and come together as one as early as 1776, and then again in 1833, and 1851.

Franklin: Located in modern-day eastern Tennessee, Franklin was created as an eventual fourteenth state of the new United States in 1784, to repay debts incurred by North Carolina during the War for Independence. A local government was even set in Greeneville, running in parallel to North Carolina's own for four years, when it became apparent the cession proposal wouldn't fly with Congress, and Franklin was assimilated back into North Carolina.

Deseret: Its name means "honeybee" in the Book of Mormon, and this provisional state, proposed in 1849 by the Latter-day Saints Church, encompassed nearly all of present-day Utah and Nevada, large portions of California and Arizona, and parts of Colorado, New Mexico, Wyoming, Idaho, and Oregon, which, in all truth, were barely inhabited and "up for grabs." In 1850, the Utah Territory was created by Congress, and a year later its government officially dissolved Deseret. While some Mormons never quite gave up on the idea of a much larger state, the arrival of the train made Deseret impractical by changing not only the landscape, but the population composition and density of the territories surrounding modern-day Utah.

Sylvania / Superior / Ontogagon: A fifty-first state combining Michigan's Upper Peninsula, northern

Wisconsin, and northeast Minnesota into a new state was first proposed in 1858, then resurrected in 1897, to no avail. Secession proposals for Michigan's Upper Peninsula on its own also surfaced during the 1960s and well into the mid-seventies but were never met with wide popular support.

Jefferson: Three American territories were proposed to bear the name Jefferson between 1859 and 1949, but if allowed to exist, social media "activists" today would probably be arguing for a name change.

The first was a democratically ruled territory created by a confluence of mining towns, which existed from October 24, 1859, to February 28, 1861, when it was superseded by what is now Colorado.

The second stemmed from the idea that Texas needed to be split into smaller states to be properly governed ("Texas divisionism"), with several proposals being drafted between 1870 and 1921, when the idea finally lost all traction.

A third State of Jefferson would be a proposed buffer state between California and Oregon, originally stemming from a Thomas Jefferson (1743–1826) vision for an autonomous "Republic of the Pacific" in the area. Rumors of secession have been flaring up in under-represented counties of the area since the early 1940s, but the idea never made it past leaflets and the occasional newspaper headline.

Scott: In 1862, when Tennessee left the Union to join the Confederate States of America, the people of Scott County, who held plantation owners in contempt, declared Scott a "Free and Independent State," effectively becoming a self-governing, though legally unrecognized, enclave by successfully foiling any invasion attempt (largely through the honored American tradition of guerilla warfare), and staying free for 125 years until readmitted into Tennessee back in 1986.

Nickajack / Winston: Rightly believing the Civil War would be a war for the rich, fought by the poor, this fuzzily defined region of North Alabama and East Tennessee aligned with the Union, though they never formally seceded from the respective Confederate States the area belonged to.

The now-legendary "Free State of Winston," encompassing Alabama's Winston, Cullman, and Blount counties also strongly opposed the Confederacy, refusing its army draft, sheltering thousands of deserters, and by 1862, actively joining the Union Army. However, much like Nickajack, Winston never formally split from its parent state.

Lincoln: Three states named after this president were proposed in 1865, 1868, and 1869, on different sides of the country.

The first, located within the northwestern "Inland Empire," was originally proposed by Idaho, with similar ill-fated proposals coming from Washington as recently as 1996, 1999, and 2005.

A second was attempted in 1868 when Lincoln was proposed as the name for the Wyoming Territory.

The third was actually pitched to Congress during the Reconstruction and meant to be a carved-out chunk of southwestern Texas, but it was finally buried under a ton of red tape.

Sequoyah: Proposed in 1905 by the Cherokee, Choctaw, Chickasaw, Creek, and Seminole nations, this could have been an all-native state in modern-day eastern Oklahoma, named after the great Sequoyah (1770–1843), who created the Cherokee syllabary in 1821. As usual, Congress dragged its feet at this formal proposal, and the decision fell on President Theodore Roosevelt (1858–1919), who opted to merge Sequoyah's and Oklahoma's own statehood proposal into a single state.

Absaroka: Its name means "children of the large-beaked bird," and this Crow and Sioux territory encompassed segments of Montana, South Dakota, and Wyoming, and made a bid for secession and statehood in 1939, but the coming of World War II saw the idea bite the dust.

CHAZ: Not quite a state, the Capitol Hill Autonomous Zone (alternatively known as Capitol Hill Occupied Protest, or CHOP) was established over six Seattle, Washington, blocks, and the Cal Anderson Park, on June 8, 2020, after that city's own George Floyd protests escalated beyond control the week before, forcing the Seattle Police Department to board up and abandon its East Precinct. Self-organized, and conveniently "without leadership," its size quickly decreased as rioters' rage cooled down, roadblocks started to be removed, and murders occurring within the protesting community made everyone realize police presence was indeed necessary. On July 1, the SPD finally cleared the area and reclaimed its Precinct.

BONUS QUOTES

"Accept that some days you are the pigeon, and some days you are the statue."
—Scott Adams

"Why do I care about the law? Ain't I got the power?"
—Cornelius Venderbilt

"Nothing is more dangerous than a friend without discretion; even a prudent enemy is preferable."
—Jean de la Fontaine

"The reason there are two senators for each state is so that one can be the designated driver."
—Jay Leno

"If you've never held a box of rat poison in your hand and stared at it for a good long while, you've never been in love."
—Chris Rock

BLACK COUNTRIES MATTER

While slavery indeed forced millions of Africans into lives of dejected poverty and suffering, a sad inheritance modern society still grapples with, many of those slaves with the power to break free, as well as those who were later emancipated, found themselves building settlements and nations of their own.

Yanga: Founded by Gaspar Yanga, a Gabonese warrior who escaped slavery and united other slave runaways (*cimarrones*) into an army that defeated the colonial Spanish Mexican army so badly, they basically agreed to legally free every escaped slave until then, and give their own Veracruz township, *San Lorenzo de los Negros* (which may be loosely translated into "San Lorenzo Now Owned by Blacks") in 1609. Segregated "in reverse" (whites were not allowed to stay the night—yes, the Americas' first "sunset town!"), the town prospered to such a degree Mexicans ended up moving in anyway, and by 1932 the town had been renamed after Yanga himself, who's now held as a national hero.

Angola Janga: *Quilombos* or *mocambos* (hilltop communities of escaped slaves) were a common sight in seventeenth-century Brazil, but most were swiftly squashed by colonial armies, and their people re-enslaved in the hellish sugarcane plantations. However, things were about to change.

Arriving a slave to Recife, Brazil, in the second half of the seventeenth century, Angolan warrior princess Aqualtune Ezgondidu (her exact birth and death dates are unknown), led thousands of slaves to escape to and then expand the Palmares *quilombo* into an independent nation, Angola Janga, a federation of city-states ruled from capital Macaco, first by Aqualtune, and then by her political heirs, Nganga Nzumbi (1630–1678), and Zumbi (1655–1695), for almost a century. In their day and age, Angola Janga's reputedly fearsome warriors were rumored to have developed a strange fighting technique that lives on to this day: *capoeira*, the Brazilian martial art.

Miskito Kingdom: At some point in the mid-1600s, both escaped and shipwrecked slaves entered the jungles of Nicaragua and were accepted into the Miskito tribe, resulting in a new Miskito ethnicity that still exists today. Seeing Spain as the bigger threat, these Miskito of African descent allied with the British during the following centuries; a mutually beneficial relationship which saw the Crown staging coronation ceremonies for Miskito kings, arming Miskito soldiers, and paying taxes to the Miskito when trading in their kingdom, a network of four coastal cities in modern day Nicaragua, until 1894 when the kingdom was finally absorbed into the latter.

Seminole Alliance: At some point during the eighteenth and nineteenth centuries, escaped slaves (called *maroons*) made their home in the swamps of Spanish Florida, running into the Seminole nation, itself also composed of escaped Muscogee (Creek) natives from Georgia and Alabama, their very name derived from the native word *simanó-li*, after the Spanish term for runaway, *cimarrón*, also the root of maroon. Living mostly separate lives in their own settlements, Black Seminoles did form a military alliance with Native American Seminoles that was strong enough to defeat the Federal government, forcing it to free Black Seminoles, well before emancipation was even in the cards for the vast majority of African Americans in the country.

Haiti: Despite their nation's troubled history, modern Haitians may stand tall knowing their ancestors fought a successful war of independence (1791–1804) against none other than Napoleon Bonaparte (1769–1821). Led by a former slave, and the first black general of the French Army, Toussaint Louverture (1743–1803), and his successor, Jean-Jacques Dessalines (1758–1806), they established the first maroon nation ever in 1804—and the first in the world to abolish slavery in 1805!

Republic of Maryland and Liberia: Decades before slavery was abolished in the United States, the repatriation of African American slaves had been in the mind of those whites (abolitionists and slavers alike) who feared freed slaves might try to take over the nation, as it happened in Haiti, or else never fully integrate into white society.

Pioneering this idea, the American Colonization Society, also known as the Society for the Colonization of Free People of Color of America, through its Maryland branch, proceeded to ship African Americans to a stretch of land they had purchased in the coast of West Africa: Cape Palmas. Soon others would follow, into separate settlements founded by ACS branches in Mississippi, Kentucky, and more, but the Maryland settlement was by far the most successful, even gaining full independence, but that wasn't meant to last. Under attack from neighboring African tribes, in 1857 it would join in with the Commonwealth of Liberia, formed by the other colonies a decade earlier.

Thus, the Republic of Liberia became Africa's first modern republic, but unfortunately its people, known as Americo-Liberians, failed to learn the lessons of history, and came to subjugate the indigenous African population for over a century, the ensuing civil wars sinking the young country into a spiral of violence and poverty it never quite emerged from.

Sierra Leone: Initially founded and supported as a British colony (Freetown) and Protectorate (Sierra Leone) in Africa by Jamaican Maroons, freed slaves (after the 1807 abolition of the slave trade), and African American Loyalists (who sided with the British during the War of Independence), by 1961 Sierra Leone had become an independent nation, evolving into a constitutional republic by 1971, but as many other Third World nations plagued by internal strife, disease, and poverty, to this day it struggles to find its own footing.

Linconia: An early American Colonization Society supporter, in 1862 President Abraham Lincoln (1809–1865) chose the Central American province of Chiriquí, in modern-day Panama, as the ideal location to start a colony where Blacks could be resettled after the planned emancipation. Lincoln even invited a group of important African Americans (including Frederick Douglass; 1817–1895) to the White House to discuss it, but the idea was met with derision not only from these men, but also in Central America, forcing the president to drop the idea altogether.

BONUS FACTS

In 2021, Argentinian police officer Rebeca Soloaga (b.1985) was sentenced to life imprisonment for the double murder of an elderly couple she perpetrated in order to pay for a trip to Disney World.

Buruli is a rare tropical bacterial infection which, if not properly treated, will cause gruesome open-yet-painless wounds (ulcers), which may leave a person permanently disabled.

The unnerving shrieking of fans was chiefly responsible for the Beatles ending all touring by August 29, 1966.

II

BEFUDDLING BELIEFS

"If one did not believe in demons, if one supposed that Man were good after all (as a postulate, of course), how would the evil get into him? What would be the source of these insane rages? What would be the source of his slips of the tongue? How would he come to know irrational fear?"
—L. Ron Hubbard

FOLLOW THE LEADER

Tersely defined as "systems of worship," cults as we understand them today are groups, movements, or factions (literally, "sects") exhibiting excessive devotion and dedication to a person, idea, or thing, and may be classified as follows.

1. Religious: The most common type of cult, it combines specific supernatural beliefs, a clear ethical system, and hero-worship into a single-minded attempt at permeating the culture and remaking the world in its image. If it achieves this goal, becoming the predominant world view in a given area, it will naturally find a balance (partly by merging or adopting elements of the surrounding culture, or by spotting and eliminating threats, either by reason or by force), and file off any extremist excess. While both Christianity and Islam are prime examples of this, a modern case study may be found in The Church of Jesus Christ of Latter-day Saints.

2. Political: These are groups, parties, or movements primarily concerned with direct political action to bring about abrupt change in the relation of power within a given society. They are extremely involved in a particular ideology (usually presented as a system of thought, a philosophy, or even plain economics) embodied in the leader of the day. Behaving much like religious groups, once domination is achieved (usually via revolt) these groups also bounce back into formerly despised traditional values—popularly known as a "Thermidorian Reaction." This is especially true with secular left-wing political partisanship.

3. Ethno-centric: When a group of people believe it possesses better behavioral traits due to its ancestry, nationality, or physical appearance, their misguided superiority complex (a.k.a. the Dunning-Kruger effect) will eventually lead to antagonism, prejudice, discrimination, segregation, racism, nativism, jingoism, and xenophobia. These groups normally align themselves with larger religious movements or political parties (both frequently conservative). Starting at the fringes, if the opportunity arises, they will strive to corrupt the very core of the infiltrated organization (i.e., recent GOP history).

4. Consumerist: Technically speaking, the least dangerous type of cult concerns groups of people inextricably linked to a particular product of their culture, though they regularly engage in similar dominion tactics in order to gain either a bigger chunk of the cultural fabric, or the vanquishing of a competing product. Beyond run-of-the-mill fetishism, this type of behavior is typically encouraged by the industry as a means to increase sales. Apple and Marvel fans come to mind in this category.

5. Destructive: Groups which have caused or are liable to cause harm among their membership, or the general public; with "harm" including refusal

of medical care, sexual abuse, violence, ostracism, and murder. Not every cult—be it religious, political, ethnic, or consumerist—is intrinsically dangerous, but they all include a seed of totalitarian thought worth keeping an eye on. Textbook religious examples include the Peoples Temple, the Branch Davidians, and Heaven's Gate. On the political end of the spectrum, we find the Weather Underground, the Black Panthers, and Antifa. The Ku Klux Klan, of course, is the prime example of destructive ethno-centric cultism, while sports hooliganism remains an obvious form of violent consumerism.

BONUS QUOTES

"Men should be like Kleenex: soft, strong, and disposable."
—Cher

"There is no greater sign of a general decay of virtue in a nation, than a want of zeal in its inhabitants for the good of their country."
—Joseph Addison

"My wife has a slight impediment in her speech—every now and then she stops to breathe."
—Jimmy Durante

"One may smile, and smile, and be a villain."
—William Shakespeare

FOUR REASONS WHY

Contrary to popular belief, joining a cult is not reserved exclusively for the brainwashed, the neurotic, the uneducated, or the poor, but seems to be an enduring trait of human culture as a whole, which is itself filled with movements, groups, parties, or clubs catering to every kind of person imaginable. True individuality established as the exception rather than the norm. The question is why are most people drawn to cults?

1. Ignorance: The old GI Joe motto, "knowing is half the battle," rings true here. Most cults do not present themselves as such. Herbalife Nutrition, Lululemon Athletica, and Tupperware parties are "marketing" schemes. The Freemasons, the Elks, and Rotary International alternate between "fraternal orders" and "social clubs." The Church of Scientology is, of course, a "church," or is it?

2. Idealism: There's a reason most cults—as well as the entire advertising industry—cater mainly to the sixteen- to thirty-five-year-old crowd: teens and young adults are the most prone to wanting to "change the world"; but having achieved little on their own, with no money, nor any real power, they seek to effect change via a fashionable group effort. Greenpeace is an "NGO," #MeToo, a "movement," and The Ayn Rand Institute purports itself a "think tank."

3. Inclusiveness: An awful lot of lonely people just need to be hugged. Seriously. Wherever family, spouse, or societal support is lacking, cults offer not only the safety blanket of communal experience, but self-esteem-boosting peer accolades, and a contacts network for career advancement. In the broadest sense, any group offers this, be it the Boy Scouts or Twitter—*none of them "cults," of course* . . .

4. Inspiration: Great leaders help people see the best in themselves and the world around them, but what transpires is often plain old cult of personality. As is usually the case, these leaders will seem selfless and self-effacing, devoted to the ideal alone. Forget now-obvious monsters from the past like Josef Stalin (1878–1953) or Jim Jones (1931–1978); how about we give a long, hard look at current idols in the making? The answer may surprise us.

BONUS FACTS

Unlike fully domesticated dogs, who will protect their master fiercely, cats will not get in harm's way for the sake of their owner.

Spotted sticking out of the mud after a downpour, a 2,500-year-old bronze figurine of a bull was unearthed near the ancient site of Olympia, Greece, in 2021.

CULT-URE CLUB

Oprah's Book Club notwithstanding, let's have a look at some of the other deranged cults operating in America today.

Congregation for the Light: This highly secretive Manhattan-based cult supposedly originated during the 1960s (though it claims to be much older) and believes its two hundred well-to-do members descend from the master Aryan race, and believes that after the Apocalypse takes place (a reason they receive regular weapons training), they will reincarnate on a planet called Nay as genderless, stomach-less aliens. Taught to avoid contact with "know-nots" (the rest of us) as much as possible, they may be spotted as avoiding any home decor unless owl-shaped or marked with an "X," but the Aryan race bit should be warning enough.

Eckankar: Out of Las Vegas, Nevada, but headquartered in Chanhassen, Minnesota, since 1986, this cult, er, "new religious movement," was founded in 1965 by Paul Twitchell (1908–1971) and presents a relatively harmless mishmash of Hinduism and Sikhism beliefs, only sprinkled with a few vaguely Christian concepts (e.g., Holy Spirit, soul, etc.). Admittedly not as dangerous as other "movements" on this list, nevertheless they don't hesitate to cajole their followers and batter their critics with defamation lawsuits.

The Family International: An international child sex abuse ring posing as the prototypical "summer of love" beach cult, it was originally founded by notorious anti-Semitic pedophile David "King David" Berg (1919–1994) in 1968 as Teens for Christ, and later renamed as The Children of God, which was nominally dissolved in 1978 in light of its sex abuse scandals, only to be renamed The Family (of Love) and expanding overseas. While seemingly abandoning paraphilia, both in writing and in practice, or so we hope, The Family International continues its spiritual warfare, purportedly with the help of "Loving Jesus," angels, Aphrodite, the Snowman, Merlin, Elvis, and possibly even Santa Claus. And if you think "Loving Jesus" is a sexual fetish, you're absolutely right.

The Brethren: A nameless (it's been alternatively known as the Brothers and Sisters, the Church, the Assembly, and The Body of Christ) and secretive nomadic Doomsday Christian cult founded by Jimmie T. Roberts (1939–2015) in 1971, like Cathars and Waldensians before them, the Brethren renounces material possessions and family, deliberately staying away from the limelight, and hiding in plain sight among the masses of homeless drifters. Harmless, right? Not according to the many families who lose their children to this cult every year, never to see them again.

OSHO International Foundation: First established in 1974 as a "movement" by Indian bioterrorist Bhagwan Shree Rajneesh (1931–1990), a.k.a. Osho, it combined standard Hinduism theatrics (chants, colorful clothes, and communal lifestyle) with a brash hedonistic philosophy, which surely fit Osho's own unquenchable lust for gold Rolex watches, Rolls Royce cars, and nubile devotees. After relocating to Oregon in the early 1980s, in 1985 he masterminded a plan to influence local elections by infecting salad products in local restaurants and shops with Salmonella, poisoning several hundred people. Letting his movement's higher-ups take the blame and be imprisoned, he was deported back to India, where he passed five years later, but his writings and followers continue to swindle the unsuspecting public to this day.

Kashi Ashram: Founded in Sebastian, Florida, in 1976 by enterprising Jewish housewife Ma Jaya Sati Bhagavati (born Joyce Green; 1940–2012), it is one of the many bogus commune cults influenced by Hinduism, attracting college students and misguided celebrities alike to its retreat center, yoga school, and sustainable farm (not to mention other schemes usually shut down after government funding runs out). With branches in New York, Los Angeles, Chicago, Colorado, Santa Fe, and Atlanta, this cult has been accused of emotional, physical, sexual (including forced marriages), and—unsurprisingly—substance abuse. To be fair though, all of these have been considered standard "ashram" practices for decades.

Aggressive Christianity Missions Training Corps: A "Salvation Army" from hell, this fringe cult was originally established in 1982 Sacramento, California, as the "Free Love Ministries" by "General" James Green (b.1945) and his wife, "General" Deborah Green (b.1947). Fleeing from the law in 1988, in the face of an abuse and kidnapping lawsuit, they established a new ministry in Oregon, the quaintly named "Death Force Team," only to run again to New Mexico, where they set up a new compound, but in 2017 justice finally caught up with the Greens, as Deborah, James, son-in-law Peter, and other members of their group were arrested and sentenced to prison for countless charges of child rape.

Order of the Solar Temple: Claiming to be rooted in Knights Templar lore, the Swiss l'*Ordre International Chevaleresque de Tradition Solaire* (later renamed *Ordre du Temple Solaire*) was founded in Geneva in 1984 by Luc Jouret (1947–1994) and Joseph di Mambro (1924–1994). If you think it coincidental that both founders died in the same year, well, they were among forty-eight members who took part in the first of the order's carefully staged Québec mass-suicides, on October 5, 1994, after a "rehearsal" had already taken the lives of five members the month before. Sixteen more acolytes would kill themselves in 1995, and another five two years after that. You'd think the cult would have run out of members by now, but they remain active, and several attempts at even more group suicides have since been thwarted by the police.

Buddhafield: Still active in Hawaii, where it hurriedly relocated to from Texas after the 1993 Waco massacre, this cult preaches the usual motley assortment of New Age beliefs to yoga practitioners, under the hypnotic leadership of speedo-wearing, cosmetic surgery junkie Jaime "The Teacher" Gomez (b.1965). A former gay porn actor, Mr. Gomez, now calling himself "Andreas" or "Michel," still rules his little commune with an iron-fist, while charging fifty to a hundred dollars per "cleansing" session, as revealed in the 2016 documentary *Holy Hell*.

Church of Euthanasia: Self-styled as a "non-profit educational foundation devoted to restoring balance between Humans and the remaining species on Earth," this anti-humanity cult was founded in 1992 by Chris Korda (b.1962), a transgender, vegan techno musician, software developer, and all-around environmental nutcase, who claims she was contacted by an alien intelligence known as The Being—guess Thanos was taken—who confirmed that our planet's ecosystem is failing, and this may only be reversed by a massive voluntary population reduction, or as this church succinctly puts it: "Save the Planet, Kill Yourself." Well, at least one person followed their advice and took her own life in 2003, but Korda herself keeps finding excuses not to follow The Being's main command.

Falling into the cult trap, or being born into one, may happen to anyone, as attested by many well-known celebrities. Leaving out Scientologists (already mentioned in the pages of the *Astonishing Bathroom Reader*; Racehorse, 2020), the list includes former Breatharian Michelle Pfeiffer (b.1958), Kabbalist Madonna (b.1958), Christian Scientist Val Kilmer (b.1959), former Children of God Joaquin Phoenix (b.1974), Jehovah's Witness Serena Williams (b.1981), NXIVM's Allison Mack (b.1982), and Orgonite Jaden Smith (b.1998). Rapper R. Kelly (b.1967), on the other hand, took things a step further by running his own sex cult, and is currently incarcerated for his crimes.

BONUS QUOTES

"Beware the fury of a patient man."
—John Dryden

"Forgive your enemies, but never forget their names."
—John F. Kennedy

"Bargain: Something you can't use at a price you can't resist ."
—Franklin P. Jones

"If you think your boss is stupid, remember: You wouldn't have a job if he was any smarter."
—John Gotti

"The less men think, the more they talk."
—Montesquieu

SPEAK OF THE . . .

If most cults try, or pretend to align themselves with positive—"godly," even—values, where does that leave those cults straightforwardly seeking evil? In order to ground the search, first we have to look at the personification of evil itself.

What is it?
The Greek root of the word "devil" (similar in every Western language, and a number of religions) is *diábolos*, meaning slanderer. This isn't gratuitous, but an accurate description of an entity whose main job is to pervert speech, thus turning people against God and each other.

What is it called?
The creature is basically nameless. Satan means "adversary" rather than a name in itself, as the Bible describes it in moral, rather than visual terms: *tempter* (Matt. 4:3; 1 Thess. 3:5), *enemy* (Matt. 13:39), *evil one* (Matt. 13:19, 38; 1 John 2:13; 3:12; 5:18), *adversary* (1 Peter 5:8), *father of lies* (John 8:44), *murderer* (John 8:44), *sinner* (1 John 3:8), and *deceiver* (Rev. 12:9). All still easily summed up by "slanderer."

   Lucifer, the Latin word for the morning star (the planet Venus), has long been established to be a misnomer for the King of Babylon used by prophet Isaiah, rather than a name for the devil itself. Another misnomer, "Beelzebub" colorfully refers to an ancient Canaanite god of fertility and agriculture named Hadad (Baal) as a "lord of flies," or a rotten idol. Later depictions of the devil in Medieval art showing a beast with horns, tail, and cloven hoofs (and bat wings imported from Eastern art much later) are simply a mockery of various pagan agricultural gods not very different from Baal.

What does it actually look like?

In the Bible's book of *Genesis*, the devil is described as a crafty serpent which came into the garden of Eden intending to corrupt men, but apparently it had legs, since God cursed it to lose them and forever "eat dust." Later, the book of Revelation would use similar imagery often comparing it with a dragon or a big, old snake. It is also from Revelation that we get the full picture of its defeat in battle against archangel Michael, and being cast out of heaven (that is, God's presence) alongside other rebellious angels.

The picture currently most associated with the devil, that of fictional character Baphomet, a goat deity supposedly worshiped by the Knights Templar, was concocted 165 years ago by a French renegade priest turned poet and "occultist" named Éliphas Lévi (born Alphonse Louis Constant; 1810–1875). We owe the inverted pentagram image with Baphomet's inscribed head to yet another mad Frenchman, Stanislas De Guaita (1861–1897).

What about the inverted cross?

Well, in the Catholic tradition that would be Saint Peter's Cross, named for the apostle who felt unworthy of being executed in the same manner as Jesus.

A papal symbol of humility (not to be confused with the Papal Cross), it was nonetheless appropriated by misinformed late twentieth-century pop culture (including films and heavy metal music) to represent some laughable form of "satanism."

Where does it live?
Another inverted cross–level frequent misconception puts Satan and its angels living in a fiery version of Hades. According to the Bible, however, they live here on Earth, right among us humans. They hold on to power destroyed by Jesus's crucifixion and resurrection, and will eventually be defeated when the Son of Man comes around and throws them into a lake of fire to be destroyed. Their effigies, however, are an entirely different matter: the Žmuidzinavičius Museum in Kaunas, Lithuania, collects and exhibits devil imagery from all over the world, including paintings, sculptures, masks, pipes, and other objects, which range from the humorous and folkloric, to the academically realistic.

What does it want?
According to the Bible, the ultimate reason it engages in all sorts of deceitful tactics to bring about the downfall of man is manifested in Matthew 4: 1-11: **it wants to be worshipped! The following chapter will attempt to describe how far it has gotten in that respect.**

DON'T PANIC

While the very word "Satanism" conjures images of robed men gathering at a cemetery crypt at night to sacrifice babies or goats—or baby goats!—to the sound of either Latin chants or heavy metal music, in reality satanic cults have more to do with provocative mid-1960s "performance art" than anything else. Oh, and technically there's only two of them.

1. A product of baby-boomer ennui, early 1960s college kids reclaimed stale European devil imagery (just as hippies would incorporate nineteenth-century Art Nouveau into psychedelia later on) and made it a symbol of their rebellion against the square culture of the preceding decade.

2. Equal parts Aleister Crowley (1875–1947) and Svengali, showman Anton Szandor LaVey (born Howard Stanton Levey; 1930–1997), in particular, took the act the furthest, capitalizing that decade's fascination with Satan into his own "Church of Satan," founded in 1966, and a series of books, including the laughable, pseudo-philosophical The Satanic Bible (1969).

3. The time was ripe then for "devil worship," and bestselling novels like Ira Levin's 1967 Rosemary's Baby, or the Rolling Stone's hit 1968 single "Sympathy for the Devil" were eager to capitalize on the trend. Quite ironically, the inspiration for the Stones' song was none other than anti-Marxist satire The Master and Margarita from Mikhail

Bulgakov (1891–1940). This novel, as you may have guessed, only found a posthumous publisher in 1967.

4. Unlike its "Summer of Love" counterpart, the leather-clad, devil-fueled pop-culture machine didn't halt when the sixties drew to a close. Terrifying crimes, like the Tate-LaBianca murders and the Zodiac killings, reminded the public of the dreadful reality of true evil, while stimulating the emergence of a new generation of rebellious "Satanists"(remember when KISS was controversial?), inventive horror novelists, *and* equally over-the-top evangelists preaching against it all.

5. In fact, it would be up to overbearing televangelism to solidify Satanism's popularity, by promoting lurid "memoirs" of alleged satanic child abuse, starting with *The Satan Seller* in 1972, by discredited pastor—and equally fake Satanist—Mike Warnke (b.1946). Warnke would become quite the mainstream media celebrity during the following decade, after the publication in Canada of yet another fake memoir, *Michelle Remembers* (1980), which took the world by storm. Before the decade ended, another bogus "memoir," *Satan's Underground* (1988) by professional con artist Lauren Stratford (born Laurel Rose Willson; 1941–2002) also fanned the flame of the Evangelical backlash against perceived forms of Satanism, which even caught board game *Dungeons & Dragons*, and cartoon show *The Smurfs* in its wake.

6. A form on collective hysteria which endures to this day, "Satanic Panic" also managed to coalesce the media, psychotherapists, self-help groups, evangelicals, and law enforcement into a single-minded witch hunt—devil hunt?—which spread internationally, and destroyed the lives of dozens of innocent people who were sent to prison after being falsely charged with belonging to a secret cabal of Satan-worshipping pedophiles. Case in point, the Oak Hill Satanic Ritual Abuse Trial of 1991, which saw the owners of a day care center, Fran and Dan Keller, falsely accused and convicted to forty-eight years of prison on counts of sadistic sexual abuse of children, all of which were finally overturned by 2017.

7. Regardless, Satan's grasp on the imagination of fans and detractors alike has been carried well into our twenty-first century by The Satanic Temple. Established in Salem, Massachusetts, in 2016, by Lucien Greaves and Malcolm Jarry (both pseudonyms), this tax-exempt religious organization claims to advocate for freedom of speech, among other redundant pursuits—the usual litany of well-meaning clichés repeated since LaVey's time— but what it lacks in originality, it more than makes up for in membership; its chapters are present in every state, plus Canada, England, and Australia.

8. Behaving more like a political grassroots movement than a religion, The Satanic Temple quickly seized the opportunity to leverage its clout

against streaming giant Netflix in 2018, with an alleged copyright infringement lawsuit over the use of a Baphomet sculpture in the teen horror show *The Chilling Adventures of Sabrina*. Considering all images of this fantasy character are based on the same, public domain, nineteenth-century engraving, everybody was surprised when Netflix buckled, settling the case "amicably" out of court (i.e., burying Lucien Greaves and Malcolm Jarry in piles of money). Pathetic as the whole affair was, it served its purpose: putting The Satanic Temple under the media spotlight. It doesn't get any more satanic than that.

BONUS FACTS

More than six hundred attempts to kill Cuban dictator Fidel Castro (1926–2016) were made during his lifetime, including exploding cigars, poisoned diving suits, and psychedelic drugs to drive him mad—*in their defense, it was the 1960s.*

The world's greatest Star Wars collector, Steve Sansweet (b.1945), a former Lucasfilm employee, keeps an estimated 500 thousand unique items at his Rancho Obi-Wan museum in Petaluma, California.

In early 2021, Pakistani police deployed its first armed rollerblading unit in the busy streets of Karachi.

IN THE DETAILS

If Georges Méliès's (1861–1938) turn-of-the-century films devoted to the story of Faust are any indication, Satanic movies (those films involving the devil as a concept or a character) are as old as the art form itself. Let's forget the fundamental "trilogy" of Rosemary's Baby (1968), The Exorcist (1971), and The Omen (1976) though, and focus on thirteen—hell, yeah!—of the genre's modern jewels instead.

Bedazzled (1967): In the year Satanism began, the film industry's first reaction to the trend was to make a swinging sixties parody—as it had done with characters like Batman or Matt Helm—of the story of Dr. Faust. Written and starring British comedy legend Peter Cook (1937–1995) as the devil, and Cook's equally legendary comedic partner Dudley Moore (1935–2002) as a cook (pun most definitely intended) in love with a smashing waitress (played by Eleanor Bron; b.1938). In exchange for his soul, the devil grants the cook seven poisoned, but extremely comedic, wishes. This classic worth revisiting was directed by none other than Stanley Donen (1924–2019), better known for *Singin' in the Rain* (1952).

Phantom of the Paradise (1974): Rock musicians have been making Faustian deals ever since blues legend Robert Johnson (1911–1938) had his guitar tuned by the devil at a rural crossroads, and this rollicking Brian De Palma (b.1940) film that's equal parts

Faust (1832), *The Phantom of the Opera* (1910), and *The Picture of Dorian Gray* (1890), most definitely sold its own soul in exchange for one of the greatest scores ever (by none other than Paul Williams; b.1940), and a black light poster that still looks good today.

The Devil and Max Devlin (1981): This atypically well-written Disney romp starred Elliott Gould (b.1938) as the shady Max Devlin, who gets a parole offer from hell in exchange for damning three young souls, and Bill Cosby (b.1937) as the suave Barney Satin—the devil itself!—which in retrospect was as true-to-life a performance as it gets.

Legend (1985): A 1985 Ridley Scott (b.1937) masterpiece of the epic fantasy genre, which sees green man Jack O' the Green (played by Tom Cruise; b.1962) and beautiful Princess Lili (Mia Sara; b.1967) try to save the world and a couple of unicorns from the Lord of Darkness (Tim Curry; b.1949). Beyond the environmental, "unicorns as pandas or whales" motif, this is an excellent, practical effects film that stands up well today against "Rings" and "Potters" alike.

Angel Heart (1987): Adapted by Alan Parker (1944–2020) from the 1978 novel *Falling Angel*, by *Legend's* own screen writer, William Hjortsberg (1941–2017), this Carolco-produced neo-noir horror film is as brilliant as it is unnerving. Its twisting mystery involves private detective Harry Angel

(Mickey Rourke; b.1952), who gets hired by a man named Louis Cyphre—*wink, wink!*—played by Robert De Niro (b.1943), to track down crooner Johnny Favorite, who owes him his soul. Get ready for tons of machine fog, Persian blinds, rough sex, and a surprise ending that will blow your socks off.

The Witches of Eastwick (1987): Another mid-eighties gem (from George *Mad Max* Miller, no less!), this is a dark comedy with feminist undertones about three Rhode Island women who inadvertently develop witch powers after losing their husbands (through abandonment, divorce, and death), and band together to cope with the pain. Their unwitting coven summons Daryl Van Horne, who seduces them into a polyamorous relationship. Needless to say, things soon go south, and the witches end up using their powers to cast this devil out of their lives. The movie is based on the far-darker 1984 novel by John Updike (1932–2009), which featured a more demonic—and bisexual—Van Horne; a role that, as attested by the original film poster, was supposed to be interpreted by Bill Murray (b.1950), only to be devilishly replaced by Jack Nicholson (b.1937) after the former abandoned the production without notice.

The Day of the Beast (1995): As diabolical a comedy as they come, this over-the-top Spanish film by Álex de la Iglesia (b.1965) follows a ragtag group of demon-hunters (a defrocked Jesuit priest, an overweight headbanger, and a TV show host) as they search for ways to sell their souls to the devil in order to infiltrate a cabal of Satanists and kill the newborn Antichrist. Will they succeed? You'll have to see it to believe it!

The Devil's Advocate (1997): It was only natural for a decade thrust in the middle of an angel fad to produce a few fallen angel films along the way. This is one of the best or worst, depending on who you talk to. Based on the 1990 novel by Andrew Neiderman (b.1940), it starred Keanu Reeves (b.1964) as successful Florida lawyer Kevin Lomax, who gets his big break at a New York firm run by, you guessed it, the devil incarnate, John Milton, played by Al Pacino (b.1940). A cautionary tale about greed and vanity, its biggest flaw comes from revealing its supernatural elements brashly during its third act. Suffice it to say it's a fun flick, and well worth a look if only to see Pacino's zesty rendition of Faust's Mephistopheles, and not much else.

The Ninth Gate (1999): A horror thriller by none other than *Rosemary's Baby* director Roman Polanski (b.1933), it is based on a segment of Arturo Pérez-Reverte's 1993 novel *El Club Dumas*, involving an antique books salesman named Lucas Corso (Dean Corso in the movie, as played by Johnny Depp; b.1963) who sees himself entangled in a conspiracy involving an Alexandre Dumas Sr. (1802–1870) manuscript, and a non-related fictional book, *De Umbrarum Regni Novem Portis* ("Of the Nine Doors of the Kingdom of Shadows"), its engravings supposedly containing a puzzle which would unlock an entrance to hell. True to his horror roots, Polanski did away with the novel's literary plot to focus on the supernatural alone, which results in a stylish film well worth its runtime.

Bedazzled (2000): In this well-meaning Harold Ramis (1944–2014) remake of the 1967 original of the same name, nerdy computer programmer Elliot Richards (Brendan Fraser; b.1968) is offered the same Faustian bargain by a sexy devil played by Elizabeth Hurley (b.1965). The man's wishes are twisted to similar comedic effect, but with a far more asinine movie ending than its British inspiration.

Constantine (2005): Yet another slick Keanu Reeves shoot-em-up vehicle based on the main character of DC Comics' *Hellblazer* comic series (particularly the "Dangerous Habits" miniseries) created by Alan Moore (b.1953). Constantine offers a somber-yet-fashionable take on the titular anti-hero and his universe, with plenty of action, and Swedish actor Peter Stormare (b.1953) playing antagonist Lucifer Morningstar (sigh) with *gusto* to boot!

Drag Me to Hell (2009): Any film buff worth its salt knows he's in for a treat whenever a movie has Sam Raimi (b.1959) in its directing credits, and this one is no exception. Based on a plot by Ivan Raimi (b.1956) about a curse put on bank loan officer Christine Brown (played by Alison Lohman; b.1979), which has her tormented and pursued by the relentless demon Lamia, this movie delivers on its promises big time!

The Witch (2015): Stark and unflinching, yet beautifully shot, this diabolical period film by director Robert Eggers (b.1983) deals with an exiled New England Puritan family being torn apart by seemingly supernatural occurrences straight out of Medieval lore, which escalate out of all control. After it ends, the audience will never look at billy goats the same way.

BONUS QUOTES

"If you love something, set it free. Just don't be surprised if it comes back with herpes."
—Chuck Palahniuk

"A common mistake that people make when trying to design something completely foolproof is to underestimate the ingenuity of complete fools."
—Douglas Adams

"What are the thoughts of the canvas on which a masterpiece is being painted? 'I am being soiled, brutally treated and concealed from view.' Thus men grumble at their destiny, however fair."
—Jean Cocteau

"Alimony is like buying oats for a dead horse."
—Arthur Baer

TRUTH DECAY

Why do people believe the most outlandish things? Unfortunately, a well-known 2013 Public Policy Polling survey only confirms what many have long suspected: that "rationality" is nothing but the thin lemon glaze over the varying chocolate cake layers of mankind's inherent insanity.

1. Seven percent of American voters believe the Apollo 11 moon landing was faked.

2. Thirteen percent of voters believe Obama is the Antichrist.

3. Fourteen percent of voters believe the CIA distributed crack cocaine into America's inner cities in the 1980s. Another 14 percent believe in Bigfoot.

4. Fifteen percent of voters believe that the media or the government adds secret mind-controlling technology to television broadcast signals. They also believe the pharmaceutical industry is in league with the medical industry to "invent" new diseases for profit. A small percentage of these voters also believes the exhaust condensation trail behind airplanes is actually chemicals sprayed by the government to control people's minds.

5. Twenty percent of voters believe there is a link between childhood vaccines and autism.

6. Twenty-eight percent of voters believe extraterrestrials exist, and most of them believe a UFO crashed at Roswell in 1947.

7. Twenty-eight percent of voters believe that a secretive power elite with a globalist agenda is conspiring to eventually rule the world through an authoritarian world government, the "New World Order," but—fortunately—only 4 percent believe this elite to be shape-shifting reptilian aliens.

8. Thirty-seven percent of voters believe that global warming is a hoax.

On the surface, most conspiracy theories come and go, and there's a natural ceiling to the number of people who will buy into any particular one, but the truth is most can easily be traced back even hundreds of years and have constantly been adapted to the circumstances and issues of the day. Let's have a closer look at the most pervasive one, still slithering around in the world today . . .

BONUS FACT

Celebrating erections since 1969, the penis-themed *Kanamara Matsuri* ("Festival of the Steel Phallus") is held each spring at the Kanayama Shrine, in Kawasaki, Japan.

EVERYTHING IS ILLUMINATED

Next to "Satanism," few words conjure "secret cabal bent on ruling the world" notions like "Illuminati," but unlike made-up Satanic cults, 250 years ago the Illuminati were very real.

1. Originally a pejorative used since the fifteenth century to describe those claiming to be "enlightened," either via supernatural means (a prophetic connection to God) or plain human intelligence (nobody likes a smart-ass), the term was nonetheless co-opted in the mid-eighteenth century by Bavarian law professor Adam Weishaupt (1748–1830) when he founded his own secret society (originally called the Perfectibilists) within Bavarian freemasonry, as a means to spread the ideals of Enlightenment to its wider membership (most of them hardline royalists).

2. A "cult-within-a-cult" affair, the order was controlled through a system of mutual spying among three main member classes ("novices," "knights," and "regents"), recruited from the *crème de la crème* of German freemasonry. Its membership never exceeded two thousand people, and by the end of the eighteenth century the order began to crumble from within, its own members disregarding "the first rule of Fight Club" as the paranoid self-surveillance system became unsustainable. On March 2, 1785, a royal edict

banning all secret societies put the final nail to the real Illuminati coffin, if not its enduring legend.

3. Part of the legend is linked, of course, to the French Jacobin Club. Itself an ideological offshoot of the Bavarian Illuminati brand of Enlightenment, the *Société des Jacobins, amis de la liberté et de l'égalité* ("Society of the Jacobins, Friends of Freedom and Equality") was an open, and free-admission organization, its membership of five hundred thousand growing in political clout before and after the French Revolution, which they—partly— also orchestrated. Not unlike the Illuminati, but with terrible real-world consequences, the Jacobins' paranoia led to a Reign of Terror, which only ended when their leader, Maximilien Robespierre (1758–1794) and several prominent club members were executed, and the organization dissolved not long afterwards in 1794.

4. Meanwhile in America, fringe theories pinned Illuminati membership to the Founding Fathers and subsequent American presidents. As early as the nineteenth century, Christian fundamentalists like John Nelson Darby (1800–1882) were already accusing politicians of entering a Faustian arrangement to gain wealth and power, in order to lead people into a dystopian world empire ruled by Satan, the Antichrist, and the False Prophet (the Pope, of course) that would bring about the apocalypse.

5. Over in Russia, an anti-Semitic tract known as *The Protocols of the Elders of Zion*, alleging a Judeo-

Masonic conspiracy to reach total world domination, was published in 1903. Though it was clearly a hoax, ripped straight off lesser-known French political tract *Dialogue aux enfers entre Machiavel et Montesquieu ou la politique de Machiavel au XIXe siècle* ("The Dialogue in Hell Between Machiavelli and Montesquieu"; 1864), subsequent anti-Semitic and anti-Communist political movements all over the world—the Nazis among them—have appropriated its words to preach against "Jewish Bolshevism."

6. Then along came President Woodrow Wilson (1856–1924) touting a post-World War I "new world order" in which his proposed League of Nations would guarantee collective security, democracy, and self-determination. This concept fell out of use when the League did not live up to expectations and was used very little when establishing the United Nations after World War II. It was, however, still used occasionally in American political and presidential speeches throughout the twentieth and twenty-first centuries, as a naive reference to the *Novus ordo seclorum* ("New order of the ages") motto on the back of the Great Seal of the United States (itself nothing but an innocent nod to Roman poet Virgil; 70–19 BC).

7. Well, not according to conspiracy theorists who saw, and still see, patterns in every word and number, which to them do nothing but confirm previously established biases. For some the New World Order is a "white genocide" plot to promote miscegenation. For others on either side of the political aisle, it's a nefarious Communist or Capitalist scheme. Those with a religious bent see in it the hand of Satan, while a growing fringe group blames it on aliens ... which brings us to David Icke (b.1952).

8. In the years preceding the explosion of the World Wide Web, a former mid-level soccer player and sports broadcaster named David Icke found in New Age beliefs a way to reinvent his ailing career. When proclaiming himself the "Son of the Godhead" on national television did not pan out the way he had hoped, Mr. Icke took public rejection as proof that something was inherently wrong with the world; surely a conspiracy of vast proportions, which he elaborated on in his many books. So vast, in fact, that we are kept from knowing we live in a universe of infinite "vibrational" dimensions, which has been hijacked by a race of reptilian beings (alternatively named Archons or Anunnaki), and their evil offspring with humans (you guessed it, none other than the Illuminati!) manipulate history to keep us all in fear. By 1994, Icke was already endorsing the veracity of *The Protocols of the Elders of Zion*—apparently there's nothing more reptilian than a Jew—though he has since denied any anti-Semitism. According to him, the Jews are to be blamed for anti-Semitism as well!

9. As far-fetched as Icke's theories may be, the Internet helped him find a wide international fan base, inspiring New Agers, Ufologists, Neo-Nazis,

Christian Nationalists, White Nationalists, and every other counter-cultural movement with a chip on their shoulder against reality as it stands today.

10. An early sign that Icke's ideas could fuel practical, real-world domestic terrorism reared its ugly head back in 2016, when Hillary Clinton's (b.1947) campaign manager John Podesta's (b.1949) fairly boring emails were leaked online.

Of all things, conspiracy theorists focused on the many Comet Ping Pong pizza orders contained in them (not unusual during breakneck presidential campaigns). Naturally, the messages could only mean one thing—*deep breath*—that Clinton and Podesta were running a child trafficking sex ring from the aforementioned pizzeria. Then rumors began to circulate affirming a secret snuff film (code name: "Frazzledrip") had been taped showing Hillary and campaign staffer Huma Abedin (b.1976) flaying a girl's face to use her skin as a vitamin mask, as reptilians are known to do. This motivated not only the harassment of Comet Ping Pong owners and employees, but also made the restaurant (and several other pizza parlors in its vicinity) a target for several shootings.

11. Spreading through a series of vaguely cryptic, anonymous social media posts, the most recent iteration of the Illuminati-New World Order conspiracy (with a dash of 1980s "Satanic Panic" thrown in for good measure), the Qanon "movement" (remember, *not a cult*) believes former President Donald J. Trump (b.1946) is waging a

secret war against a cabal of cannibal, pizza-loving, Satanist pedophiles belonging to the highest echelons of United States government, business, and the media. These include some of Icke's favorite targets: the Rockefellers, the Rothschilds, the Windsors, the Bushes, and the Clintons. Sure enough, Trump *was*—and still is—waging a no-holds-barred war against the political establishment, which came to a head after his 2020 election defeat on January 6, 2021, when he rallied his supporters, QAnon included, into a failed putsch attempt against Congress, the infamous Storming of the Capitol, which claimed the lives of five people.

12. The latest iteration of the Illuminati-New World Order conspiracy—its name taken from the 2020 fiftieth annual meeting of the World Economic Forum (which did acknowledge the need to align with the United Nations 2030 Sustainable Development Goals)—stems from fear of a looming "Great Reset" in world affairs.

Allegedly caused by the Illuminati-manufactured Covid-19 pandemic, and its mind-controlling 5G aborted-fetal-tissue-made vaccines, this reset would finally trigger the establishment of the dreaded "New World Order," via the destruction of Capitalism, Socialism, Christianity, or the environment, depending on whoever's buying this nonsense behind a computer screen.

ONE FLEW OVER ICKE'S NEST

The best way to provide an overview of how David Icke's hate-mongering ideas connect to the current state of the western world's decay, is to quote the man himself.

"For you to believe that there is no major world conspiracy which involves a small number of people manipulating humanity through a hierarchical structure of control toward a New World Order, shows you have, in actual fact, not looked genuinely into the abundance of well-researched information on world conspiracy to see if there is one!"

"In the very late 1800s, a controversial document came to light called the *Protocols of the Elders of Zion*. I call them the Illuminati Protocols, and I quote many extracts from them in *The Robots' Rebellion*."

"The 'All-Seeing' Jews, however, and their non-Jewish conspirators, use the smokescreen of 'anti-Semitism' and the genuine suffering of real Jews to prevent investigation of their sinister activities. I am convinced that it was this clique which wrote and leaked the Protocols (of the Elders of Zion) and made it look like a plot by Jewish people as a whole."

"This Jewish/non-Jewish Elite used the First World War to secure the Balfour Declaration and the principle of the Jewish State of Israel (for which, given the genetic history of most Jewish people, there is absolutely no justification on historical grounds or any other). They then dominated the Versailles Peace Conference and created the circumstances which made the Second World War inevitable. They financed Hitler to power in 1933 and made the funds available for his rearmament."

"So, in effect, what I'm saying is that my research is very strongly pointing to the fact that the extraterrestrials are not coming, they're not going to invade, they've actually been controlling this planet, increasingly, for thousands of years."

"What we call the 'world' and the 'universe' is only one frequency range in an infinite number sharing the same space. The interdimensional entities I write about are able to move between these frequencies or dimensions and manipulate our lives."

"I prefer to speak of 'interdimensionals' rather than 'extraterrestrials' because the latter has connotations of 'little green men' and all the other cliché responses. Nor does it tell the full story."

"Humanity is actually under the control of dinosaur-like alien reptiles called the Babylon Brotherhood who must consume human blood to maintain their human appearance."

"The families in positions of great financial power obsessively interbreed with each other. But I'm not talking about one Earth race, Jewish or non-Jewish. I'm talking about a genetic network that operates through all races, this bloodline being a fusion of human and reptilian genes."

"It was these same families (Rothschild, Rockefeller, Harriman, Bush, etc.) who funded the eugenics movement which is pledged to remove the lower genetic blood streams and leave only those of superior stock. Eugenics today often goes under the title of 'population control.'"

"The Planned Parenthood Federation, which has been supported at every opportunity by George Bush and the manipulating elite, was actually founded in London, at the offices of the British Eugenics Society."

"Former US president, drug baron, and pedophile, George Herbert Walker Bush, incidentally, is mentioned more than any other person in my experience in relation to shape-shifting."

" . . . the plan is to engineer events, real and staged, that will create enormous fear in the countdown years to 2012. This includes a plan to start a third world war either by stimulating the Muslim world into a 'holy war' against the West or by using the Chinese to cause global conflict. Maybe both."

"The opening and closing ceremonies of the London Olympics are mass satanic rituals disguised as a celebration of Britain and sport."

"Humanity is at a fork in the road, and we can no longer stand there staring at the map pondering which direction to take. It is hardly a choice, after all. One road leads to a global fascist dictatorship that would control every aspect of our lives, including our thoughts. The other will open the door to freedom and potential on a scale never experienced in the 'world' as we have known it."

"I don't think I would use a gun, but who knows what a person would do in certain circumstances? My instincts are that I don't see the point of using violence to oppose violence, but many people would, and the Brotherhood knows that. For this reason they want an unarmed population."

Mea Culpa:
I originally considered interviewing Mr. David Icke for this book, and even reached out to him about it. While not everybody's cup of tea, he seemed harmless enough, and I wanted to stay open-minded. Though Mr. Icke politely declined on account of his busy schedule, my view on his ideas naturally changed upon further examination, not to mention the particularly bitter fruit his brand of vitriol bore on January 6, 2021, with the seditious Storming of the Capitol.

—Diego Jourdan Pereira

FROWNING ALL THE TIME

Apparently too pedestrian for conspiracy theorists to even notice, history is full of very real conspiracies which usually seek to conceal or disguise all-too-human misdeeds or mishaps, but exclude any alien dinosaurs. Some of history's most notorious real conspiracies include:

The Assassination of Julius Caesar: Lying in a pool of his own blood, spilled from twenty-three stab wounds, dictator Julius Caesar (100–44 BC) drew his last breath on March 14, 44 BC. Presented as an act of just tyrannicide by the sixty or more middle-aged senators involved in this conspiracy (young and elderly ones were left out) concocted by Marcus Junius Brutus (c.85–42 BC) and Gaius Cassius Longinus (c.86–42 BC), but which ultimately failed to avert the demise of the Roman Republic.

The Gunpowder Plot: Led by Robert Catesby (c.1572–1605), this Catholic conspiracy to blow up King James I (1566–1625) alongside the entire House of Lords, at the State Opening of Parliament ceremony on November 5, 1605, ended up blowing up in the conspirators' faces when an anonymous letter sent to Baron William Parker (1575–1622) revealed the plot, and the man in charge of lighting the match, Guy Fawkes (1570–1606), was found sitting on thirty-six barrels of gunpowder the day before the ceremony began. Fawkes's effigy has burned amid fireworks in the United Kingdom ever since, and his legend came to be canonized by popular culture which turned the man from terrorist to action hero in the course of the following centuries.

The Dreyfus Affair: Carried out by the French military, this plot to accuse Jewish artillery officer Alfred Dreyfus (1859–1935) of spying for Germany in place of the real culprit, Ferdinand Walsin Esterhazy (1847–1923), almost succeeded, as Dreyfus was quickly trialed and sentenced to a life in prison at Devil's Island, French Guiana, with the acquiescence of the French press and the political establishment of the era. Fortunately, through the efforts of the man's family and military investigator Marie-Georges Picquart (1854–1914), alongside the unwavering support of writer Émile Zola (1840–1902), who faced prosecution for his support, Dreyfus was exonerated and reinstated in the military, serving during World War I, and passing away at age seventy-two. Real culprit Esterhazy, on the other hand, ended up fleeing to England, where he died at age seventy-five.

The Tuskegee Experiment: If you're thinking red-tail Mustangs knocking Luftwaffe fighter planes out of the skies, think again. Better known as the "Tuskegee Study of Untreated Syphilis in the Negro Male," this unethical research program, which began in 1932, was conducted on six hundred poor Alabama African American sharecroppers for a period of forty years. While no men were *given* the disease, as is often erroneously stated, 399 of the men already had contracted it (the other 201, acting as a "control group," were healthy), and though they were promised treatment (which by 1947 had become available in the form of penicillin) they only got placebo shots, as the purpose of the study was to assess the long-term damage syphilis causes in men. Research only ended in 1972, when it was leaked to the press, but by then 128 men were already dead.

The Business Plot: In 1933, Wall Street conspired to remove President Franklin Delano Roosevelt (1882–1945) from office and establish a fascist government in America, with the former head of the National Recovery Administration, General Hugh S. Johnson (1882–1942), at the helm. Approached by conspirators to lead the putsch, the plot was instead denounced by retired Major General Smedley D. Butler (1881–1940). In the end, while a Congress investigation into Butler's allegations concluded in favor of their verisimilitude, no action was taken to prosecute the conspirators, Butler himself becoming subject to much media ridicule for his whistleblowing.

The Shelling of Mainila: The Russian town of Mainila, near the border with Finland, just couldn't catch a break. On November 26, 1939, the Red Army bombed it, while staging military losses as part of a plot to pin the blame on the Finnish Army—what is generally known as a "false flag operation"—to justify the launching of the Winter War four days later.

Almost two years later, however, the Finnish decided to shell Mainila on their own, and film it for propaganda.

Operation Valkyrie: Originally an emergency plan to ensure the continuity of German government during World War II, it was subverted by German Army officers, General Friedrich Olbricht (1888–1944), Major General Henning von Tresckow (1901–1944), and Colonel Claus von Stauffenberg (1907–1944), with the purpose of taking control of Germany, disarming the SS, arresting the Nazi leadership, and reaching a ceasefire with the Allies, after Adolf Hitler (1889–1945) had been taken out of the picture via a briefcase bomb explosion, during a June 20, 1944, conference. While the bomb did go off, Hitler spectacularly survived, which led to a massive purge, and the execution of thousands of Germans, plotters included, in the operation's aftermath. It should be noted this was the twenty-second, and most spectacular attempt to take Hitler's life, out of forty-two yet-uncovered plots, but in the end, it looks like only Hitler could kill Hitler, as the beleaguered genocidal maniac ended up shooting himself on April 30, 1945.

Project Sunshine: A series of studies conducted between 1953 and 1956, the purpose of the project was to ascertain the effect of nuclear radiation on the biosphere due to the dispersion of the Strontium-90 isotope, a byproduct of the many nuclear bomb testings of the era. One study in particular sought to understand the effect of nuclear fallout on human tissue and bone, particularly from young people, achieved by the gathering corpses and body parts of babies and children from Australia and Europe (1,500 of them!) without bothering to secure proper parental consent! As it was revealed in 1995, scientists taking part in the study knew their methods posed an egregious ethical breach, but carried on regardless, procuring bodies from poverty-stricken town hospitals less subject to serious scrutiny.

MK Ultra: Running from 1953 to 1973, this secret CIA operation sought ways to manipulate people's brain functions by any means necessary, be they psychoactive drugs, electroshocks, hypnosis, sensory deprivation, isolation, sexual abuse, or "enhanced interrogation techniques"—a fancy name for torture! In 2018, declassified documents also revealed that dogs were also experimented on via brain implants for remote control, while a side project code-named "Acoustic Kitty" engaged the mad endeavor of training cats as spies.

The Conqueror: Back in 1956, this epic film produced by Howard Hughes (1905–1976) saw John Wayne (1907–1979) grossly miscast as none other than Genghis Khan (1158–1227), and the plains of Mongolia equally mis-recreated on Utah's irradiated soil, which sent forty-six members of its cast and crew to an early cancer grave. In a fatal case of "attention to detail," Hughes even went as far as shipping sixty tons of fallout-enriched Utah dirt to Hollywood in order to lend realism to studio re-shoots. Despite studio-paid experts' constant denial of any connection between residual ground radiation and the deaths, reasonable doubt persists to this day, and Hughes himself is said to have been left an emotional wreck out of sheer guilt over the issue.

The Mars Bluff Incident: Dubbed a "weapon loss incident" by the military, the accidental 1958 release from a B-47 of an unarmed nuclear bomb over Mars Bluff, California, could have ended in a much larger tragedy had the bomb carried its intended payload; but this "Little Boy" did fall near a family of six, its conventional explosives leaving all injured, and a seventy-foot-wide, thirty-five-foot-deep crater in their backyard to be remembered by—some "bluff!"

The Dyatlov Pass Incident: On February 26, 1959, the remains of nine Russian hikers, college students from the Ural Polytechnic Institute, were found on the slopes of the ominous "Dead Mountain" after being reported missing. Three died as a result of severe trauma (skull and chest), while the other six died from hypothermia. As reported in lurid detail, some bodies were found almost naked, two of them were missing their eyes, one was missing its tongue, and one was missing its eyebrows.

With the Soviet Union's penchant for secrecy, which included sealing off the area for three years, theories abounded as to the cause of the "incident," which ranged from ultrasound weapons testing, military involvement, and even UFOs. Yet in 2020 a new investigation by Russian authorities confirmed what the Soviet ones had guessed back in the day: the hikers ran from an avalanche which engulfed and tossed them around like rag dolls, while nature did the tissue mauling in the weeks that followed.

Lost Cosmonauts: When the young Judica-Cordiglia brothers, Achille (1933–2015) and Giovanni Battista (b.1939), set up their own salvaged ham radio station in the outskirts of 1950s Turin, little did they realize they'd become radio-astronomy pioneers. On November 28, 1960, pointing their antennas to the skies, they picked up the SOS Morse code signal of a Soviet cosmonaut moving away from Earth. Over the course of the next four years, they'd hack several other suffocating transmissions, all of which were quickly disavowed by the Soviets. After a 1964 trip to NASA, the brothers dropped amateur radio for good, and went on with their lives (Achille became a cardiologist, while Giovanni worked for the Italian Police).

The Three Mile Island Accident: Considered the most significant accident in American commercial nuclear power plant history, this 1979 averted meltdown at the Three Mile Island Nuclear Generating Station (TMI-2) in Pennsylvania resulted in the release of massive amounts of nuclear reactor coolant, radioactive gasses, and iodine into the environment.

While the full extent of the damage and the danger it posed was originally kept from government agencies and the public alike by Met-Ed (Metropolitan Edison), eventually the evacuation of 144,000 civilians in a twenty-mile radius was implemented. The subsequent billion-dollar closure and cleanup operations took until 1993 to be finished.

The Bhophal Disaster: Buried under layers of mutual accusations of mismanagement or sabotage (not to mention the usual corporate scapegoating and later mergers), disaster hit the Union Carbide India plant in Bhopal at the end of 1984, when deadly pesticide *methyl isocyanate* fumes leaked from a broken pipe into neighboring towns, killed almost four thousand people instantly, and scarred at least 520,000, not counting those children born with birth defects in the decades following the disaster.

The Chernobyl Disaster: A 1986 Chernobyl Nuclear Power Plant (Prypiat, Ukraine) reactor safety test gone wrong, which resulted in a Level 7—worst of the worst—reactor meltdown, and a massive blast of radioactive materials, which blanketed part of Europe, the ensuing fallout affecting three hundred thousand people in Belarus, Ukraine, and Russia alone. Thanks to the selfless sacrifice of Soviet Army conscripts and civilian volunteers, less than one hundred deaths may be directly linked to the disaster, as the population was evacuated in a 1,200-square-mile Exclusion Zone. While an initial government cover-up was attempted, the impossibility of keeping a disaster of this magnitude under wraps, coupled with the necessity to contain its effects, led to a request for international help in order to build a multi-layered shelter, dubbed the "sarcophagus," to encase the reactor and its deadly contents (200 tons of melting corium, thirty tons of radioactive dust, and sixteen tons of uranium and plutonium). Nuclear deterioration demanded a new structure, the Chernobyl New Safe Confinement, had to be built by an international coalition to encase the sarcophagus itself in 2017. Cleanup operations of the surrounding areas are calculated to conclude around 2065.

The Rwandan Genocide: Planned for over a year and started the day after President Juvénal Habyarimana's (1937–1994) plane was shot down with missiles, the killing of five hundred thousand to six hundred thousand Tutsi tribesmen (as well as moderate Hutu who opposed the plan) was carried out by gangs armed with machetes between April and July of 1994. An estimated 250,000 to 500,000 Tutsi women were also raped during this modern-era atrocity. Despite being fully aware of the looming genocide, neither the United Nations nor the United States chose to intervene militarily. In the UN's case, this was due to absurd office politics, while the Clinton administration feared another Mogadishu; so the former chose to focus on creating refugee camps, while the latter dealt with evacuating their own citizens and called it a day.

The Srebrenica Massacre: According to *The Week: How to Be Really Well Informed in Minutes* (Ebury Press; 2012), this symphony of destruction perpetrated by genocidal maniac Ratko "The Butcher of Bosnia" Mladić (b.1942) on that eastern Bosnian town in 1995, was enabled by UN General Bernard Janvier (b.1939) who, after dining with Mladić the night before, denied Dutch peacekeepers their request for an airstrike that could have prevented Mladić's forces from entering the town, and slaughtering 8,373 people in cold blood, later bulldozing their corpses into mass graves.

The FEAR Militia: A far-right, American paramilitary terrorist organization within the Army, it got as far as purchasing $87,000 worth of guns and bomb materials, while conspiring to take over Fort Stewart, destroy a dam, and assassinate President Barack Obama (b.1961) in 2012. They also killed two teenagers they suspected had revealed their plot. Their main leader, nineteen-year-old Private Isaac Aguigui, got sentenced to life imprisonment, while his many accomplices got up to thirty-year prison sentences.

The Boeing Fiasco: No one could have guessed upon the launch of its original 737 plane back in 1968, that a company as beloved as Boeing could fall into what the United States Department of Justice condemned as "fraudulent and deceptive conduct," by concealing information about its automated flight control system, known as MCAS, which overrides pilots, and forces planes to nosedive shortly after takeoff, resulting in over five hundred crashes over the years, and the deaths of around 5,600 passengers all over the world. Boeing even refused to cooperate with the Department of Justice for six months, but early in 2021 the company was finally forced to pay 2.5 billion dollars to settle what its management chalked down to a mere "falling short on expectations."

The Big Tech Manipulation: As former Apple and Google employee whistleblower Tristan Harris (b.1983) revealed to *60 Minutes* **back in 2017, smartphones and their entire app ecosystems—social networks chief among them—have come to be engineered with only one goal in mind: the hijacking of the human mind. Peddling on behavioral addiction, the Silicon Valley industrial complex (dubbed "tobacco farmers with t-shirts" by Bill Maher; b.1956), use intermittent positive reinforcement ("like" buttons galore!), and our pathetic-yet-helplessly-instinctive need for social approval to turn us into sugar-high-clicking Pavlovian dogs, while they mine our data and sell it to the highest bidder. Harmless? Not by a long shot. As author Cal Newport (b.1982) succinctly puts it: "They want you, therefore, to think of their offerings as a sort of fun ecosystem where you mess around and interesting things happen. This mind-set of general use makes it easier for them to exploit your psychological vulnerabilities." (***Digital Minimalism***; 2019).**

CAMELOT HAS FALLEN

The mother of all political conspiracies, the assassination of John Fitzgerald Kennedy (1917–1963) continues to both fascinate and horrify people, as 80 percent of Americans still believe a yet unidentified plot was behind it. Was there? Let's give it a closer look.

1. Heir to a wealthy and influential Massachusetts family, JFK graduated from Harvard, served in the Pacific during World War II (United States Navy Reserve), became a representative for Massachusetts' eleventh district, and then a junior senator, also for Massachusetts. While at the Senate, his ghost-written nonfiction book, *Profiles in Courage* (1956), won the Pulitzer Prize.

2. Narrowly defeating Richard Nixon (1913–1994) in the 1960 election, he became America's thirty-fifth president, and one of its youngest. Under his leadership the United States locked horns with Communism via several botched attempts at assassinating Cuban dictator Fidel Castro (1926–2016), invading Cuba itself (the infamous Bay of Pigs Invasion of 1961), and finally deploying Operation Mongoose, an extensive JFK-directly-approved terrorist campaign against Cuban civilians, leading to Castro asking for Soviet aid, which arrived to the island in the form of missiles. Needless to say, this resulted in the Cuban Missile Crisis which put the world on the brink of an

all-out atomic war, until an agreement was finally—and fortunately—reached with the Soviet Union.

3. It should be noted that there was an early attempt at Kennedy's life, right after winning the 1960 election, in the form of a mentally ill New Hampshire postman—*more on him in our "The Postman Always Shoots Twice" section!*—by the name of Richard Paul Pavlick (1887–1975), who planned to ram his dynamite-filled car against the president-elect's, but changed his mind upon seeing JFK's wife and small children waving him goodbye. Later caught by the police, he confessed his intentions, and was committed to a mental hospital.

4. After signing the world's first nuclear treaty, the Partial Test Ban Treaty, in October of 1963, Kennedy's attention shifted from his disastrous foreign policy moves (which were also embroiling the nation into the growing Vietnam reunification conflict) toward the domestic, including the national space program, the civil rights movement, and Democratic Party squabbles in Texas. The latter would prove his undoing.

5. Embarking on a political trip to Dallas on November 22, 1963, the presidential motorcade came under fire while riding through Dealey Plaza at 12:30 p.m. One bullet missed, a second pierced through both Kennedy and Texas Governor John Connally (1917–1993), and the third one finally blew the president's brains out.

6. Spotted by a witness at the sixth-floor window of the Texas School Book Depository, the shooter found himself on the run from the Dallas Police Department. Killing the officer who spotted him on the street below, he was finally caught as he tried to hide at a local movie theater. It was a disgruntled former Marine by the name Lee Harvey Oswald (1939–1963).

7. The year before, Oswald (a disturbed man who had once defected—briefly—to the Soviet Union) had unsuccessfully tested the 6.5 by 52-millimeter Italian Carcano M91/38 bolt-action rifle he had purchased under a false identity on another politically motivated victim, retired Major General Edwin Walker (1909–1993), an outspoken anti-communist. He had also campaigned in favor of Cuba during the months prior to the Missile Crisis.

8. Interrogated by law enforcement the next day, Oswald would deny it all, and not just his involvement in the Kennedy assassination, but also ever buying the rifle, his now-famous photos holding it, the fake ID, etc. He also turned down legal representation as it was offered to him by the president of the Dallas Bar Association, and even by his own brother.

9. The following comedy of errors would see Oswald being escorted through the basement of Dallas Police Headquarters on the way to county jail the next morning (November 24, 1963), when a nightclub manager named Jack Ruby (Jacob Leon

Rubinstein; 1911–1967) shot and killed him. The murder took place under camera flashes, and amid scores of police officers, FBI agents, and journalists. It was even transmitted on live national television by NBC! Ruby would be quickly sentenced to death for Oswald's killing, but died from lung cancer three years later, while awaiting a new trial date to be set under appeal.

10. Established by President Lyndon B. Johnson (1908–1973) five days after Oswald's killing, the President's Commission on the Assassination of President Kennedy, known as the "Warren Commission," established both the sequence of events, the shots fired, and the type of wounds sustained by the president and the governor. It concluded Oswald and Ruby acted on their own volition, and neither were part of any conspiracy. It also condemned the security inefficiencies which led to Oswald's death, regretting it put an end to normal, judicial investigation into Kennedy's death.

11. However, during the following decades it surfaced that not all members of the Commission agreed with its conclusions, in part because they had been "shepherded" by the FBI and the CIA, shielding them from relevant information concerning their Cuban operations (which may have given Castro a clear motive to have Kennedy killed). Plus, others were just not sold on the "magic bullet" theory, which established the bullet fired in Oswald's second shot as the one responsible

for wounding both Kennedy and Connally. Not to mention two mysterious calls (one to a news service in England, the other to an Oxnard, California, telephone operator who contacted the FBI) which warned about the assassination that would take place minutes later.

12. And so, a second inquiry into the crime was launched by Congress in 1976, the United States House of Representatives Select Committee on Assassinations. Their controversial twelve-volume 1979 report concluded that Lee Harvey Oswald had indeed fired the three shots, including the "magic bullet" which cut through Kennedy and Connally in the manner specified by the Warren Commission, and the one that finally killed the president. However, it also established the presence of a fourth shooter at the scene who fired a single shot from the infamous grassy knoll, but missed. And while ruling out the participation of Cuba, the Soviet Union, American intelligence agencies, and the mob, the Committee also acknowledged the assassination to be part of a larger conspiracy. Whose? Nobody really knows.

13. On one hand, there's plenty of evidence of many a witness being cajoled by both the Warren Commission and the FBI, with any testimony not aligned with the "single shooter" hypothesis being quickly dismissed. The fact that someone impersonating Oswald had tried to fly to Cuba via the Soviet Union embassy in Mexico was also carefully concealed from the public. A number of

"convenient deaths," which included witnesses, organized crime figures, and even a skeptical reporter (Dorothy Mae Kilgallen; 1913–1965), also obscured the whole investigative process.

14. On the other hand, hundreds of articles, books, and films, each pointing fingers in a different direction, like some mad game of CLUE, didn't help either. Those conclusively discarded by the 1976 Committee notwithstanding, "Kennedy killers" at this point include LBJ, Texan oilmen, peculiar bystanders, Israel (ah, *ze Jews!*), one of the president's Secret Servicemen (sigh), and even the limo driver—guess the White House butler wasn't available!

BONUS QUOTES

"The eagle may soar, but the weasel never gets sucked into a jet engine."
—John Benfield

"Being a hero is about the shortest-lived profession on earth."
—Will Rogers

"The ideal form of government is democracy tempered with assassination."
—Voltaire

WILE E. COYOTE AND THE ROAD RUNNER

Needless to say, JFK hasn't been the only American president ever assassinated. Far from it, with firearms becoming widely available since the early nineteenth century, and no shortage of nut jobs willing to take a shot—pun intended—assassination attempts pretty much come with the territory for Commanders in Chief.

Andrew Jackson (1767–1845): The seventh president of the United States faced the first attempt on the life of any American president on January 30, 1835, when a deranged house painter called Richard Lawrence (c.1800–1861) came at him, guns swinging, but got the beating of his life from the battle-hardened Jackson when the weapons misfired. It took legendary frontiersman Davy Crockett (1786–1836) himself to restrain the cane-wielding president and save Lawrence's life!

Abraham Lincoln (1809–1865): At 7:22 a.m., on April 15, 1865, America's sixteenth president died after being shot in the head the previous night by stage actor John Wilkes Booth (1838–1865), while attending the play *Our American Cousin* at Ford's Theater, in Washington, DC.

Originally a plot to kidnap President Lincoln by Booth, and eight other conspirators, the idea soon evolved into a plan to murder him alongside Vice President Andrew Johnson (1808–1875) and

Secretary of State William H. Seward (1801–1872). The latter survived being stabbed in the face and neck five times, while the former's would-be assassin lost his nerve and never carried out the plan. Booth was killed after a two-week manhunt, while four of the remaining conspirators were executed by hanging. The rest were sent to prison—one of them would die behind bars, but the rest were pardoned years later.

It should be noted that Lincoln survived two previous attempts on his life, the "Baltimore Plot" of 1861, which was dismantled by the Pinkerton Agency, and a lone, unidentified sniper taking a shot at him nine months before the assassination.

James A. Garfield (1831–1881): The twentieth president of the United States, and the second to be killed, only got to serve from March to September 1881. A moderate, self-effacing man, Garfield volunteered to serve in the Civil War, where he became a Union major general, and landed a presidential nomination he never really sought, but went on to win the election anyway via a quiet front porch campaign. By contrast, his assassin, Charles J. Guiteau (1841–1882), a failed office-seeker with delusions of grandeur, was so upset the new administration rejected his applications for a consul position, he purchased a gun on borrowed money (he was, by then, destitute), and on July 2, 1881, went to the Baltimore and Potomac Railroad Station, where he cowardly shot president Garfield twice from behind, as the latter was about to leave with his two sons on a vacation. It would be the second bullet, lodged behind the president's pancreas, that would cause the infection which ultimately killed him seventy-nine days later. In spite of his evident insanity, Guiteau was executed by hanging the following year.

William McKinley (1843–1901): Like Garfield, McKinley was also shot twice and killed by the ensuing infection. The twenty-fifth president of the United States was known as a moderate, who nonetheless raised import tariffs to protect American industry and labor. Well, not according to former steelworker-turned-anarchist Leon Czolgosz (1873–1901), who deemed the man an "enemy of the people" and shot him in the stomach on September 6, 1901, at the Temple of Music in Buffalo, New York, during the Pan-American Exposition. McKinley died eight days later, while Czolgosz was quickly tried and executed the following month.

Theodore Roosevelt Jr. (1858–1919): A towering figure of exceptional intellectual talent and physical stamina, Mr. Roosevelt remains the youngest American president ever, the twenty-sixth, taking office upon the death of McKinley. While campaigning for a third term under his very own Progressive "Bull Moose" Party, Roosevelt was shot in the chest once by John Flammang Schrank (1876–1943), a former barkeeper with Messianic tendencies (he had been visited upon by the ghost of McKinley, who pinned his own demise on Roosevelt) on October 14, 1912. The length of the speech saved his life, as the folded copy in his breast pocket slowed the bullet down, his glasses case finally deflecting it into his right pec, where it remained for the rest of the man's life. After making sure Schrank was properly taken into custody by the police (he would remain committed to an insane asylum for the rest of his life), "Teddy" proceeded to deliver his full speech to the astonished Milwaukee crowd, while blood dripped from his chest and soaked his shirt!

William Howard Taft (1857–1930): On October 16, 1909, America's twenty-seventh president was greeting Mexico's own Porfirio Díaz (1830–1915) in El Paso, Texas, when an unnamed man holding a concealed palm pistol was caught only a few feet away from Taft and Díaz, by the president's private security detail and a Texas Ranger.

Herbert Hoover (1874–1964): Despite a successful career in public service, which included leading the United States Food Administration and the American Relief Administration, and becoming Secretary of Commerce for two sitting presidents, Hoover's policies as America's thirty-first president fared poorly against the Great Depression. Before he faced that particular challenge, however, he would face another while on a good will tour through Central and South America, where an Argentinian anarchist—*them again!*—plot to bomb his train would be prevented by local authorities.

Franklin Delano Roosevelt (1882–1945): FDR would fare much better in the battle against the Great Depression, but would also have to face powerful enemies in a second World War, and his own walking disability.

A first attempt on his life would come early in his long presidential career, on February 15, 1933, when bricklayer Giuseppe Zangara (1900–1933) fired five shots at the president in Miami, Florida, during an impromptu speech from the back of a car. While FDR came away unscathed, Chicago mayor Anton Cermak (1873–1933) was killed, and five other people trying to restrain Zangara were also wounded. Zangara would be sentenced to die on the electric chair the following month, but much continues to be speculated about the reason behind his actions.

Roosevelt's life (alongside Joseph Stalin's and Winston Churchill's) was also the target of an elaborate 1943 Nazi assassination plot, Operation Long Jump, thwarted by Soviet super-spy Gevork Vartanian (1924–2012).

Harry S. Truman (1884–1972): In many ways, America's thirty-third president both created the modern world (atomic bombings, the Marshall Plan, NATO), and suffered its new threats, in the form of two very particular assassination attempts.

The first attack on his life happened around 1947, when the White House received letter bombs from Zionist paramilitary group Lehi which were promptly defused by the secret service.

The second was the November 1, 1950, armed

attack by two Puerto Rican nationalists, Oscar Collazo (1914–1994) and Griselio Torresola (1925–1950) at the Blair House, which ended with one police officer dead, Leslie Coffelt (1910–1950), and another gravely injured. Coffelt took Torresola with him to the grave, while Collazo's initial death sentence was commuted by Truman to life in prison. Truman would end up allowing a plebiscite in Puerto Rico in 1952, to self-determine its relationship to the United States; it's stayed a Free Associated State since.

Richard Nixon (1913–1994): Lots of people wanted America's thirty-seventh president dead during his time in office, but only a few came close to accomplishing the deed.

On April 13, 1972, Arthur Bremer (b.1950), an unemployed busboy, brought a gun to an event in Ottawa, intending to kill the president, but got kicked out by security instead. So he went to his second-favorite target, Alabama Governor George Wallace (1919–1998) in Maryland and shot the man, leaving him in a wheelchair for the rest of his life. Sentenced to sixty-three years in prison, he was released after only thirty-five, in 2007.

A month after the Ottawa incident, during a state visit to Iran, Marxist terrorists (the "People's Mujahedin of Iran") planted a bomb in a mausoleum Nixon was scheduled to visit, but they detonated it forty-five minutes before the president's arrival.

Then on February 22, 1974, a clinically depressed man named Samuel Byck (1930–1974) attempted to hijack a plane flying out of Baltimore/Washington International Airport, in order to crash it into the White House, but ended up taking his own life after being wounded by the police.

Gerald Ford (1913–2006): Not counting staircases, America's accidental thirty-eighth president had to face off against equally formidable enemies: raving Charlie Manson (1934–2017) follower "Squeaky" Fromme (b.1948), and a batshit-crazy divorcee, Sara Jane Moore (b.1930). "Squeaky" tried gunning Ford down on September 5, 1975, while Ms. Moore pulled a gun on him three weeks later. The first attempt was thwarted by Secret Serviceman Larry Buendorf (b.1937), while the second would be stopped by a heroic bystander, gay Vietnam veteran Oliver Sipple (1941–1989). Both women would spend three decades in jail for their crimes.

Jimmy Carter (b.1924): America's thirty-ninth president and all-around nice guy, Mr. Carter apparently came close to dying at the hands of two mentally ill vagrants by the names Raymond "Lee Harvey" and "Osvaldo"—Oswald?— Espinoza Ortiz. On May 5, 1979, they were arrested after "Lee Harvey" was found carrying a starter pistol with blank rounds around the Los Angeles Civic Center Mall before a planned Carter speech. Deeming these drifters crazy and intoxicated, the police let both go with a warning, and they simply vanished from sight since.

Another would be "Carter-killer," the Jodie Foster-obsessed John Hinckley Jr. (b.1955) would lose his "Taxi Driver" mojo after stalking the president all around the country, but would return to haunt the next president on this list.

Ronald Reagan (1911–2004): On March 30, 1981, as he was about to board his limousine after speaking at the Washington Hilton Hotel, the fortieth president of the United States was seriously wounded by a ricocheting bullet fired by John Hinckley Jr., which went into his left underarm, breaking a rib, and puncturing a lung. Hinckley's gunshots also hit White House press secretary James Brady (1940–2014), Secret Service agent Tim McCarthy (b.1949), and policeman Thomas Delahanty (b.1935).

Reagan and all three men ultimately survived the attack, but Brady was left brain damaged, Delahanty suffered permanent spinal damage which left his left arm paralyzed, and McCarthy, who had shielded Reagan with his own body, got his right lung, diaphragm, and right lobe of the liver pierced. John Hinckley Jr., who was found "not guilty by reason of insanity," remained institutionalized until his release in 2016.

George H. W. Bush (1924–2018): In 1993, Kuwaiti authorities claimed to have stopped an Iraqi Intelligence Service conspiracy to kill America's outgoing forty-first president. While this motivated the swift shelling of the Iraqi Intelligence building in Baghdad, the CIA later concluded the plot to be a Kuwaiti fabrication.

Bill Clinton (b.1946): While America's forty-fourth Commander in Chief loved to do his own "shootings," he also became target practice for three "stooges," none of them former interns, in 1994: unemployed limousine driver Ronald Gene Barbour (b.1955) who never carried out his threats, depressed truck driver Frank Eugene Corder (1956–1994) who died trying to crash a stolen Cessna into the White House; and Francisco Martin Duran (b.1968), who fired twenty rifle rounds at the White House from the perimeter fence, but was subdued by tourists and is currently serving a forty-year prison sentence.

Then in 1996 Clinton almost got killed in Manila on account of a bomb planted under a bridge by a young Osama Bin Laden (1957–2011), but the president's motorcade had been fortunately rerouted in the last minute by the Secret Service.

George W. Bush (b.1946): A lot of things were hurled at the forty-third president of the United States, but bullets, planes, a grenade, and shoes stand out.

Two weeks after his first inauguration, a disgruntled former IRS accountant named Bob Pickett unloaded several shots in the White House's direction and was sentenced to three years at the Federal Medical Center in Rochester, Minnesota.

Seven months later, on September 11, 2001, the al-Qaeda-hijacked United Airlines Flight 93 crashed on the way to the White House, due to the heroic sacrifice of its passengers.

In 2005, amateur terrorist Vladimir Arutyunian (b.1978) threw a handkerchief-wrapped grenade at Bush and Georgia's president Mikheil Saakashvili (b.1967), which fortunately did not detonate. When finally caught, Arutyunian got a life without parole sentence.

Then on December 14, 2008, the president barely dodged two shoes symbolically thrown at him by Iraqi journalist Muntadhar al-Zaidi (b.1979). Whether the gesture struck any chord in the president is another matter.

Barack Obama (b.1961): America's first African American Commander in Chief, her forty-fourth, was the target of a number of assassination threats and plots, some of which were extended to the man's family as well, both before and after he came to sit in the Oval Office.

Two bespoke "skinheads" from Tennessee, twenty-year-old Daniel Gregory Cowart, and eighteen-year-old Paul Michael Schlesselman, plotted to kill a symbolic eighty-eight African Americans, fourteen by beheading, and then go out with a bang by ramming their car into Obama himself. Arrested after firing rounds at a Brownsville church in 2008, they were sentenced to fourteen and ten years in prison respectively.

In 2011, twenty-one-year-old criminal Oscar Ramiro Ortega-Hernandez fired shots at the White House from his car parked on Constitution Avenue, using a semiautomatic rifle. Ortega-Hernandez believed Obama to be the Antichrist and was sentenced to twenty-five years in prison.

The infamous 2013 ricin-laced letters sent by actress Shannon Richardson (b.1977) to the president and the mayor of New York, as well as her hare-brained attempt at framing her ex-husband, are also worth mentioning. Richardson was sentenced to eighteen years in 2014.

Donald J. Trump (b.1946): Deeply embroiled in many scandals of his own making, it is nearly impossible to separate fact from fiction regarding attempts made on the life of America's forty-fourth president. That said, credible ones from 2017 include a forty-two-year-old, mentally ill Dakota man named Gregory Lee Leingang trying to flip the presidential motorcade limousine with a stolen forklift (which got stuck in a gated area, forcing him to jump out and flee the scene), while months later an unnamed man affiliated with the Islamic State was arrested in the Philippines for plotting to assassinate the president as well.

Of course, according to conspiracy theorists, there have been at least fifty-five assassination attempts on the president's life, which failed because the president has—*brace yourselves*—clones! Apparently, you can tell who the real Don is by the color of his necktie, but would-be assassins are not in on this.

BONUS FACT

Elton John's biopic film, *Rocketman* (2019), was partially financed by the Vatican.

STAYING ALIVE

If previous chapters prove anything, it's that nobody can live forever. But for some reason or another, instead of accepting its own planned obsolescence, humanity has continued its mad pursuit of immortality through the ages.

1. "Immortality" means different things for different people, which reminds us of the stark warning posed by the Greek myth of Eos, goddess of the dawn, who asked Zeus to make her human lover Tithonus immortal, but forgot to ask for eternal youth as well, so the poor man ended in a constant state of aging, dementia, and decay, but incapable of dying, though he begged to be put out of his misery.

2. On the other hand, while putting a stop to aging would provide us with physical immortality, it wouldn't make us invulnerable to death via trauma or disease. Case in point, *The Picture of Dorian Gray* (1890) by Oscar Wilde (1854–1900) reminds us of the ethical price to pay for biological immortality, which isn't to say it isn't achievable . . .

3. Some species of jellyfish, also known as medusae, may revert to the polyp stage of their development after becoming sexually mature, which means in essence that they can go back to being a baby, and grow again, repeating the cycle as many times as they please, effectively "cheating death."

Male lobsters also present a curious case. Apparently, they do not get weaker, nor lose fertility with age, and the older they become, the stronger and most fertile they get! That said, their shell does get more fragile with age, its shedding and regrowing process alone capable of killing them.

4. Religious immortality also remains a source of hope for many, taking the form of a "life after death," and usually comes in two flavors:

The first one, a transcendent supernatural abode for the human soul, which traditionally was no heaven but a cold, hellish landscape where the dead dwelt (*kur*, *sheol*, *hades*, etc.), while the heavens were reserved for gods alone. It should be noted that until the late Middle Ages Christians did not believe in a spiritual "heaven" or a "hell" as espoused today, but rather the Jewish belief of a merging ("coming") of heaven (God's kingdom) and Earth, which would result in the ensuing resurrection of the faithful dead.

The second, which became the dominant view of the afterlife in the far east, is known as reincarnation, rebirth, or transmigration. According to this view, after death our essence will undertake new physical or spiritual forms (some of which inhabit heavenly planes) in a constant cycle. Hence, these religions focus on mental enlightenment (*nirvana*), rather than moral transcendence (faith, behavior, etc.).

5. Esoteric beliefs and folk legends, on the other hand, focus their quest of physical immortality on

different types of youth elixirs (including the western "philosopher's stone" and "fountain of youth," and the eastern "*amrit*" and "peaches of immortality"), while modern science puts its faith in extending life beyond its current limits via technologies which include tissue rejuvenation, stem cell treatment, gene therapy, pharmaceuticals, bionics, and organ transplant. However, despite heterodoxy, science, and anti-aging movements' wildest claims and hopes, the fleetingness of human life on this world remains.

6. **The longest documented human lifespan is 122 years and 164 days, reached by the "super-centenarian" Jeanne Calment (1875–1997). Of course, women live longer than men on average, the longest male lifespan on record being Jiroemon Kimura (1897–2013), who lived to age 116 years and fifty-four days. Also from Japan, 118-year-old Kane Tanaka (b.1903), is the oldest living person in the world as of the writing of this book.**

BONUS QUOTES

"For all sad words of tongue or pen,
The saddest are these: 'It might have been.'"
—John Greenleaf Whittier

"The real excitement is playing the game."
—Donald J. Trump

FLATLINERS

Despite falling in and out of favor through the ages, the idea of physical immortality, as well as the notion of bringing the dead back to life (ditched by many a belief-system and replaced with a harder-to-disprove "spiritual" resurrection) remains a popular part of our collective culture. Some of most popular semi-legendary immortals include:

Ziusudra: A part of both the Sumerian flood myth (similar to that of Noah) and the Gilgamesh epic (about a failed quest for immortality), this legendary king is said to have reigned for 3,600 years (likely a cuneiform mistake).

Zalmoxis: A still-debated Thracian divine being mentioned by classical historian Herodotus (c.484-425 BC) and others, Zalmoxis is rumored to have once been a Greek slave who, after gaining his freedom and amassing a fortune, moved to Thracia (modern day Bulgaria, Romania, and Moldova) where he taught his guests they would never die, but instead go to a great dining hall where they would all live forever in a complete happiness. Ceremonially buried in an underground tomb, he is rumored to have come back from the dead after three years, converting the Thracians who witnessed the event—sound familiar?

Aristeas: A seventh-century BC Greek poet who claimed the power of astral projection, Aristeas is said to have turned into one of Apollo's sacred ravens, until miraculously reappearing in southern Italy, 240 years after his death, to command the construction of a temple in Apollo's honor.

Elijah (c.900-∞): This powerful Israeli prophet technically never died, but hitched a ride to the heavens aboard a fire chariot. While Elijah resurrected the son of the hospitable woman of Shunaam, his protégé, Elisha, was so powerful that after his death his bones resurrected a dead Moabite man accidentally buried atop that prophet's remains.

Jesus Christ (4 BC-∞): Arguably the most famous of all, Jesus of Nazareth needs no introduction. A historical figure revered by many peoples and religions, whether sharing the tenets of Christian faith—as the author of this book does—or not, His story inspired a number of other immortals, historical or imagined, listed below.

John the Apostle (6–100 AD): The youngest of Jesus's twelve apostles, and the only one to have died of natural causes while exiled in Patmos, according to tradition he was the author of both the fourth gospel and the book of Revelation. In his lifetime, however, rumors began to circulate regarding the man's apparent immortality, which he pointedly disclaimed.

Lazarus of Bethany: The brother of Mary and Martha, all close friends of Jesus, according to the

Gospel of John, was resurrected by the Messiah four days after his burial. Lazarus would be the third person on record resurrected by Jesus, after Jairus's daughter, and the widow's son at Nain, before His own resurrection.

The Wandering Jew: According to Anti-Semitic medieval lore, after mocking Jesus on His way to the cross, this Jewish cobbler was cursed by Christ to wander the Earth until His return.

Sir Galahad: Part of the Arthurian legend, the miraculous and chaste illegitimate son of Sir Lancelot and Elaine of Corbenic is granted immortality by the Holy Grail (Jesus's cup from the Last Supper), or rather death at a time of his own choosing, which would come in the form of an angel-guided ascension into heaven, upon being visited by Joseph of Arimathea himself, the immortal keeper of the Grail.

The Three Nephites: In the Book of Mormon, while caught up into heaven around 34 BC, three Nephite disciples of Jesus were blessed to never taste death and continue to minister until Christ's Second Coming. Latter Day Saints also maintain John the Apostle's immortality, though his current whereabouts remain unknown.

Nicolas Flamel (c.1330–1416): Don't let the date of his death (November 22, 1416) fool you! According to several seventeenth-century sources, this fourteenth-century scribe and bookseller learned the secrets of alchemy from a Jewish *converso* during a pilgrimage to Santiago de Compostela, which he used to make gold out of lead, and grant himself and his wife, Perenelle, immortality. While official records disavow any notion of Flamel dabbling in alchemy, pharmacy, or medicine, nor of any huge wealth attributed to a purported philosopher's stone, his old home at 51 rue de Montmorency remains the oldest in all of Paris, the man himself achieving immortality through this unlikely legend.

BONUS FACTS

Argentinian nurse and ocean liner stewardess Violet "Miss Unsinkable" Jessop (1887–1971) notably survived the RMS *Olympic* collision of 1911, and the sinking of both the RMS *Titanic* in 1912, and the HMHS *Britannic* in 1916.

According to legend, Austrian portrait painter Joseph Matthäus Aigner (1818–1886) was saved twice from committing suicide, and once from the gallows by the same unnamed Capuchin monk who presided over his funeral mass in 1886.

The city of Colon, MI, with its magic convention, Magician's Walk of Fame, magic museum, and a Magic Capital Cemetery (twenty-eight magicians are buried there) is considered the Magic Capital of the World.

THERE CAN BE ONLY ONE

Actually, make that four theatrical films, one TV film, two live-action TV series, an animated show, and an anime film, alongside a tepid flash animation series, original novels, and comic books. One of the most underrated fantasy franchises of all time, Highlander put the quest for immortality back on the map when the first movie was released in 1986.

1. The 1982 brainchild of UCLA undergrad and part-time firefighter Gregory Widen (b.1958), who was tasked with writing a feature-length screenplay for his Theater Arts class. Encouraged by his teacher's positive reaction to it, he sent the script to six agents, one of whom managed to sell it for $200,000 to production company Panzer-Davis.

2. Inspired by a visit to the Tower of London, the dark story about a race of immortal sword-fighters bent on claiming a mysterious "Prize" by beheading each other in one-on-one clandestine matches collectively known as "The Game" (which in turn enables them to absorb each other's "Quickening," or life-force, but renders them infertile) gained traction in Hollywood, where star Kurt Russell (b.1951) was offered the title role, but was convinced to turn it down by his partner Goldie Hawn (b.1945), and went on to shoot kung-fu cult-classic *Big Trouble in Little China* (1986) instead.

3. Connor MacLeod's part then went to the spectacularly near-sighted French actor

Christopher Lambert (b.1957), who had to learn English while trying not to slice his co-stars (hence, his strange accent); while the role of his mentor, Spaniard Juan Sánchez-Villalobos Ramírez, was nabbed by none other than the late Sean Connery (1930–2020), an actual Scotsman, who netted a nifty $1 million for his seven-day filming schedule (not counting the film's opening narration he ostensibly recorded in his own bathtub, while practicing his character's Spanish accent). The main villain, Kurgan, was played by an imposing Clancy Brown (b.1959), who agreed to work for free in order to land this career-defining role.

4. Rock band Queen, originally contracted for just the one song, liked the early film footage so much they decided to compose more songs for its soundtrack. Notably, Brian May (b.1947) confessed he was inspired to write "Who Wants to Live Forever" during a taxi ride home, after seeing some unedited scenes.

5. Despite being directed by ground-breaking Australian director Russell Mulcahy (b.1953), who delivered a bombastic romp filled with iconic characters and some impressive visual effects (which included hooking the swords to car batteries for some sparkling action), *Highlander* fared poorly both with critics, and at the box-office of the day, grossing around $13 million against a $19 million budget. That could have been the end of the story, were it not the 1980s, when video reigned

supreme; rentals turned it into a runaway hit well into the age of DVDs—*in your face, Goldie!*

6. The franchise's fortune turned around by home entertainment, fans were screaming for a sequel, until 1991's *Highlander II: The Quickening* made them regret their wish.

Filmed in Argentina, it delivers some interesting eye-candy despite its troubled budget cuts, but it would be its editing room cuts that doomed it (not to mention choosing to depict immortals as extraterrestrials from a planet called "Zeist"). Perhaps Roger Ebert's (1942–2013) words summarize it better: "This movie has to be seen to be believed. On the other hand, maybe that's too high a price to pay."

7. Despite *The Quickening*'s fiasco, it is a testament to Panzer-Davis's mad business acumen that in 1992 they managed to strike a deal with Gaumont in France, and Filmline International in Canada, to co-produce *Highlander: The Series* (each of the show's half seasons would henceforth be set in Canada and France respectively), in partnership with several international backers including RTL Plus (Germany), Rysher Distribution (United States), Reteitalia Productions (Italy), and Amuse Video (Japan). The six-season series went on to become a massive international hit, the first of the Internet era in which rabid fans networked, and adult merchandising (including sharp replica swords) blossomed.

8. *Highlander: The Series* owed its success not only to its well-oiled distribution machine, but also to the efforts of producer David Abramowitz keeping the expanding continuity in check, as well as its very charismatic cast, including the occasional overpaid cameo by Lambert himself. However, this time around the titular hero (Duncan MacLeod, a distant relative of Connor) would be played to perfection by British choreographer and martial artist Adrian Paul (b.1959), picked for the part over 400 other hopefuls on account of his confident attitude, and "Sean Connerish" good looks. He would continue to portray the character for the next fifteen years, and these days teaches stage sword-fighting.

9. *Highlander III: The Sorcerer* (also known as *Highlander: The Final Dimension*, or *Highlander III: The Final Conflict*), is a 1994 sequel that measures poorly against the original, but does its story a great service by resetting the franchise continuity, effectively erasing *The Quickening* but also doing away with MacLeod winning the Prize (seen as a measure to integrate the TV series canon). It squares Connor MacLeod against evil Mongol immortal Kane (played by Mario Van Peebles, b.1957) who kidnaps MacLeod's adoptive son. While faring as poorly with critics as all the previous theatrical installments, this Canadian production finally managed to break even at the box-office, and also performed well in the rental and cable markets, propelled by *The Series'* success.

It's not a great movie but, as mentioned, paves the way for both MacLeods to meet again on the silver screen. Before that could happen, however, two other shows were produced.

10. Never shy on capitalizing success, Gaumont sought to make inroads into the youth market as well, by producing two seasons of *Highlander: The Animated Series* (1994–1996), a French cartoon in line with other popular adventure cartoons of the day like *Batman: The Animated Series*, and Disney's *Gargoyles*. Set in a decaying post-apocalyptic future, it echoes the ill-fated *The Quickening*, but centers around yet another MacLeod, Quentin MacLeod, and a new Ramírez. It spawned a card game and a video game, among other merchandise.

11. After the conclusion of *Highlander: The Series*, in 1998, producers also tried to keep the franchise alive via a twenty-two-episode spin-off, the underrated *Highlander: The Raven*, starring Elizabeth Gracen (b.1961), reprising her breakout role as Amanda Darieux, a witty immortal jewel thief. An unconventional, urban fantasy "cop show," *The Raven* never quite struck a chord with audiences but it's still fun to watch.

12. It was time to bring the most popular Highlanders, Connor and Duncan, to the screen, in *Highlander: Endgame* (2000). Filmed in Romania, and firmly set within *The Series* continuity, it is regarded by in-the-know fans as the second-best *Highlander* picture, after the 1986 original, despite being a critical and box-office failure, perhaps due to general audiences not being familiar with the source material. Ironically, *Highlander: The Source* would be the franchise's fifth and final film installment. Fittingly described as a "bad dream" by producer Abramowitz, this 2007 Sci-Fi Channel TV movie (a direct-to-dvd release elsewhere) features Duncan MacLeod (Adrian Paul) seeking the "Source of Immortality" in a dark and grim future, clearly failing to learn the lessons gained from *The Quickening*. Not content with *The Source*, the Sci-Fi Channel also produced the *anime* film *Highlander: The Search for Vengeance* in 2007, also set in—you guessed it—a post-apocalyptic future—*sigh*.

13. While a much-announced Highlander reboot remains in *Quickening* hell, the franchise is far from beheaded, and has even inspired its own "immortals living among men" sub-genre, notable recent examples including television shows like *New Amsterdam* (2008) and *Forever* (2014–2015), and streaming services films *The Old Guard* (2020) and *Infinite* (2021), not to mention the outstanding 2007 indy film *The Man from Earth*.

BONUS QUOTE

"The worst part of success is to try to find someone who is happy for you."
—Bette Midler

BRIDE OF THE HIGHLANDER

Nothing we could glean on a show's inner workings
may match the live-in experience of a cast member, so
this author couldn't pass on the chance to interview
the kind and talented Ms. Elizabeth Gracen (b.1961),
whose breakout character, Amanda, made
Highlander: The Series and its Highlander: The
Raven spin-off something truly special back in the day.

What was your youth in Arkansas like?
I'm from a very small town called Booneville, AR.
We moved to another, slightly larger town when I
was around nine. Most towns in Arkansas are
small! Ha! My childhood was pretty rough. I had a
violent, alcoholic father and a monster of a
stepfather, so I spent a lot of time navigating
through some turbulent waters. I survived it
though—somewhat intact!

What was your original career of choice?
Before I won Miss America, I thought I would go
into corporate law. I was an accounting major up
until I won Miss Arkansas.

**What would you say drew you to risk pursuing an
acting career after winning the Miss America
contest in 1982?**
I traveled over 200,000 miles the year I was Miss
America and performed a twenty-minute show
every other day. The performing bug really grabbed

me and it felt like a logical step. Once I rested for a year back in AR, I moved to NYC to study acting. The scholarship money I won allowed me to move and start my studies.

Generally speaking, what was working in American television like in the 1980s, and what changed the most into the 1990s?
When I moved to Hollywood to really start pursuing a career, I was still relatively a fresh young thing who got to audition for so many projects. It was a slow build for me, just slogging away, trying to get a job. That never really stops for an actor unless you become famous. By the time I was offered *Highlander: The Raven*, my acting chops were in place. That last show, however, was still a syndicated production in a world of fewer channels—nothing like it is now. I think the series would have found a larger audience in this current climate.

What was playing Jasmine like, in *Death of The Incredible Hulk*?
Getting the role of Jasmine was a huge break for me. Bill Bixby was an early supporter and really gave me a terrific opportunity to play the part. I adored him. I loved playing that character, and I think she was indicative of the kind of parts I would get in the future.

At which point would you say your career in television took off?
There was a year when I landed a role on a short-

lived network series called *Extreme*. I played a psycho real estate woman. It was a big break because it was on a major network, but I made sure that my agents let the *Highlander* producers know the situation so that they could decide if they wanted to sign me for episodes for the next season—which they did—making Amanda a reoccurring character instead of simply a guest star. It was the first time I had multiple contracts going at the same time.

What series of events brought you to play Amanda on the *Highlander* show?
I don't know the answer to that exactly, but I do know that it had something to do with the work I had done on *Death of the Incredible Hulk*. There was some connection, but I'm not sure what it was.

What was the casting process like?
What was so great about the offer to play Amanda was that it was simply a phone call that I received out of the blue. They asked me if I had any interest in shooting an episode in Paris, France, playing an immortal jewel thief who was a thousand years old. You can imagine my reaction—"Yes!"

What was it like to work with Adrian Paul?
Adrian and I got along famously from the moment we met and started working together. He was always a terrific acting partner. We were also great friends off screen. We both have a similar work ethic and attention to detail. We like working hard and we like laughing a lot!

How long did production and post-production of each episode take?
It took about eight days to shoot an episode. I can't remember the post-production time frame.

On average, how many hours of work (including makeup, actual filming, and re-shoots, etc.) did you go through each day?
It sort of depended on where we were shooting. Because of the unions, there is always a required turn-around time between the end of each day's shooting and when it can begin the next day. However, if we were in Paris, our locations were usually out of the city, which necessitated an early pickup to drive to location. That part is usually pretty grueling, but it's what I call a "champagne problem."

What unique point of view, sensibility, and performance traits did you bring into the role?
If you're talking specifically about Amanda, all I can tell you is that she was a perfect fit for me. The writing and the character's traits brought out a very playful side in me—which, in turn, was necessary to play her. Kismet.

What would you say is your favorite episode? Why?
I loved the episode set in the 1940s with Roger Daltrey—"Stone of Scone." We all had such a fun time working on it. Lots of laughs. I also have an emotional connection with "The Lady and the Tiger," since that was my first episode!

The highlight for me, however, was dancing the tango on the Eiffel Tower with Adrian in one of the final episodes. You can't top that.

At which point in that show, would you say it became clear Amanda had become a fan favorite and a breakout character?
As much fun as I had working on that first episode, it came as quite a surprise to me when I got the call that the fan base for the show really loved Amanda. When you think about the fact that fan forums have changed and how different our lives are now—I'm trying to imagine how the producers of the *Highlander* garnered that information. At any rate, the fans loved Amanda, so I was invited back. Basically, after that, it was a slow build to keep bringing her back on the show. When you work on *Highlander*, the first thing you always do is check the back of the script to see if your character has kept their head!

What brought *Highlander* to an end? Was it abrupt or foretold?
You'd have to ask Adrian about the end of his *Highlander* run. I think that it just sort of ran its course for him and he wanted to move on. However, I'm not sure. We knew it was coming, but I think we all felt it was a great run and that we were incredibly lucky to have been a part of it.

Beyond action and special effects, which attributes and core values would you say contributed to the *Highlander* popularity?

What always set the show apart for me was the romance of the flash-back sequences and the writer's ability to create huge story arcs where you could really flesh out the morality lessons that can only be told through time. Lessons learned . . . life and death.

When did you learn about the plans for a spin-off series?
I had actually sort of given up acting for the most part and had moved back to Arkansas to set up a painting studio. I knew I would have a handful of *Highlander* episodes to shoot that year, but I was burned out on Hollywood and just really wanted a different life. Toward the end of the year when I left, I was offered *The Raven*. They had been trying out several actresses in that last year of *Highlander*, trying to find a spin-off character. I'm not sure why they chose Amanda, but they did.

Did you have any input on the development of *Highlander: The Raven*?
I didn't really have that much input on *The Raven*. I wish I had felt more confident to put in my two cents at the time. Amanda was an established character with a big personality. It was a challenge for us to find a way of maturing her enough to not be quite as childish and as selfish as she had been written for the *Highlander* years. We sort of pulled it off.

Did you have any concerns at the time, of being typecast into that character (say, the way Chris

Reeve was pigeon-holed as Superman)?
No! I loved playing Amanda. I would have played her forever!

What brought *The Raven* to end after only one season?
That's a complicated question. There were a lot of factors. My personal life was off the charts crazy at that time. Paul and I really didn't get along. There were multiple producers from three different countries. Everyone wanted something different. If we had been given another year of production, I think we would have figured it out. Such is life!

In retrospect, what lessons would you say you learned from your involvement in both *Highlander* and *The Raven* shows, and how did those shows help your career moving forward?
I have always said that those were the best jobs I've ever had. All productions after that just paled in comparison. I grew up and matured during those years—and learned some hard lessons—not necessarily because of those productions, but because they were the anchor in my life during some turbulent times. It's interesting that even though the shows were popular with a certain fan base, they didn't really help me that much going forward. Because the shows were syndicated, that meant that a lot of people in America didn't even know about them. As I mentioned before, I think it would be a very different case now.

Recent years have seen you diversify from acting, into directing, producing, and writing. What brought this change about?

I've given up my acting career a couple of times in my life. I do love the craft, but there is a certain aspect to the audition process that I have never enjoyed. Once I had a kid, I spent a lot of time trying to figure out what I really wanted to do with my life. When she was around four and in preschool, I finally had a few hours to myself to contemplate where I should focus my creative energy. I'm a painter and mixed-media artist, but I just couldn't see myself doing that as a profession. I used to walk this beautiful park near my kid's school when she was in class. I just walked and walked and meditated and contemplated. I decided, very specifically, that I wanted to create educational, inspirational, informational content that would help other people. Once that decision was made, it was just a matter of figuring out how to make films on a shoe-string budget. Fortuitously, at that same time, I met a wonderfully creative choreographer named Hilary Thomas who owned the Lineage Dance Company. Through our long-running collaboration, I have learned to develop my eye and become a filmmaker. I am constantly adapting her work to film or creating pieces that her work has inspired. I've also always written short stories and scripts. Right before I got pregnant, I contemplated writing romance novels, but quickly realized that I didn't really like those types of books. *Shalilly* came from an exploration of creating a romance in a different genre—YA Fantasy.

Which of all the creative aspects of your life do you enjoy the most these days?
That is a loaded question. My creative plate is full at the moment. I'm finishing up a documentary that I've been working on for the past couple of years about Lee Meriwether, and I've re-launched my Flapperpress.com website into a blog portal for eclectic perspectives from an international group of writers. It is all rewarding and challenging. I feel lucky that I get to do it all.

What did you love the most about writing *Shalilly*? Are you planning any new novels?
Writing that book was a real challenge, because it was a first for me. It was something I wrote and put on a shelf for many years until one day I woke up and realized that I wanted to illustrate it. Once I made that decision and found an amazing artist named Luca di Napoli—I was off and running with it. Since I knew I would self-publish, it was a lot of work to bring across the finish line. It was a rewarding experience. I do have plans to write another book, but I don't like to talk about such things. I believe that if you talk about it too much, you don't actually ever do it!

BONUS FACT

Blamed by many a murder in the local lore, The Baie Chaleur Fireship, a.k.a. the Phantom Ship, is a form of "ghost light" in the shape of an arc, often seen in Bathurst, Canada.

III

STRANGE SUBCULTURES

"I remember when we watched television without a hazmat suit, when the waves hit our brain unfiltered, and we were glad for it, not knowing that every second of screen exposure would turn us, slowly but surely, into mutants."
—Álex de la Iglesia

NERDS IN PARADISE

An obsession for every person under the sun, "fans" come in all shapes and sizes. The only common thread among them being the need to possess, collect, and even—in its most most unhealthy variant—hoard that which their heart desires, which results in them molding their life around it. What follows is a comprehensive list of the—generally harmless—"fandoms" out there.

Numismatists: Perhaps the oldest form of collecting, people have gathered coins, tokens or medals (*exonumists*), paper money (*notaphiles*), medals (*falerists*), and other minted objects since ancient times (the first Roman emperor, Caesar Augustus, was known for gifting odd foreign coins to friends during the *Saturnalia* festivities), be it for its material, historical, or artistic value. The hobby really took off during the early Renaissance, when authors like Petrarch (1304–1374) were regarded as experts in the field. Several national organizations, such as the American Numismatic Association (est. 1891), regulate and promote the activity around the world. Notable coin collectors include John Quincy Adams (1767–1848), James Earl Jones (b.1931), and Matthew McConaughey (b.1969).

Bibliophiles: Collecting books, be them in scroll, codex, printed, or even digital form, is yet another obsession coming to us from antiquity. Going from the inexpensive to the ostentatious, this hobby has been boosted in modern times by the advent of online sales, as well as new digital formats suitable for electronic gadgets. Condition, available print-run, and an elastic demand drive the price of books either through the roof, or down to the ground. Bibliophiles often join book clubs which sometimes coalesce into bigger organizations, such as the Fellowship of American Bibliophilic Societies. Founding Father Thomas Jefferson (1743–1826), philosopher Friedrich Nietzsche (1844–1900), and James Bond creator Ian Fleming (1908–1964) were all famous "bookworms" in their lifetime.

Sometimes run-of-the-mill bibliophilia may go off the rails, turning into bibliomania. Case in point, Stephen "Book Bandit" Blumberg (b.1948), arrested and charged in 1990 for stealing more than 23,600 volumes from 268 universities and museums in the United States and Canada. Since his release from prison in 1995, he has been arrested and imprisoned three more times in connection to similar crimes.

Philatelists: Technically, stamp collecting is only a small part of the art and science of *philately* and has existed ever since stamps have been printed and available for the most varied uses. The earliest stamp collector on record, Ireland's Earl John Bourke (1705–1790) got his collecting *mojo* fired up by embossed revenue stamps, which he gathered in a 1744 book, but it would be Sir Rowland Hill's (1795–1879) reform of the British postal system, and its 1840 issuing of the world's first postage stamp, the "Penny Black," that would unleash stamp collecting madness—originally labeled "timbromania"— upon the world.

Considered the most widespread field of amateur collecting, since 1926 its regulating body, the *Fédération Internationale de Philatélie*, organizes exhibitions around the world, and a championship every four years. Franklin Delano Roosevelt (1882–1945), John Lennon (1940–1980), and Freddie Mercury (1946–1991), were all devoted philatelists.

Ephemerists: All those who collect *ephemera* (items never meant to endure forever), such as postcards (*deltiologists*), phone cards (*fusilatelists*), matchbox labels (*phillumenists*), cigarette cards (*cartophilists*), toys (*plangonologists*), and stuffed bears (*arctophiles*). Comic-book collecting, in particular, has attracted a number of living celebrity *pannapictagraphists*, including America's forty-fourth President Barack Obama (b.1961), actor Nicholas Cage (b.1964), and rapper Eminem (b.1972).

Discophiles: Some people live for collecting sound recordings, be them of music, "spoken word," or ambient, and normally range from the *audiophile* (those in love with sound quality reproduction), to the nostalgic devoted to outdated formats such as vinyl or cassette. The largest record collection in the world (8 million vinyl albums, plus one hundred thousand CDs) belongs to Brazilian millionaire Zero Freitas (b.1955). Famous musicians Elton John (b.1947) and Dr. Dre (b.1965) eventually sold their own collections—of seventy thousand and eighty thousand albums respectively—for undisclosed sums.

SF Fans: When seminal pulp magazine editor Hugo Gernsback (1884–1967) started publishing reader mail in the 1920s, little did he realize it would create a grassroots movement of science fiction and fantasy aficionados which would network and eventually gather around the genres (and related products) that were becoming the object of their new affection, producing their own jargon ("fanspeak"), publications ("fanzines"), and organizations (clubs, societies, and conventions). Cells stemming from this "fandom," as it came to be called, would eventually include *Trekkies* (*Star Trek* fans), *Ringers* (*Lord of the Rings* fans), *RPG Fans* (fans of role-playing games), *Browncoats* (*Firefly* fans), *Bronies* (adult male fans of *My Little Pony*), *Superwholocks* (the collective fans of TV shows *Supernatural*, *Dr. Who*, and *Sherlock*), and many, many more! Celebrities who have confessed their allegiance to assorted "fandoms" include Patton Oswalt (b.1969), Joe Manganiello (b.1976), and Mila Kunis (b.1983).

Nerds: While sometimes used interchangeably with the term "geek" (first applied to eccentric people, then claimed by fans of pretty much anything), this term has come to denote a person specially preoccupied with computer technology and the digital world, rather than their formerly stereotypical interest in superheroes, fantasy, and science fiction, currently embraced by the masses.

Broadly speaking, computer nerds come in two forms: mainstream consumerists such as *gamers* (those who play video games), *influencers* (people using social media to peddle products), or *trolls* (gratuitous Internet bullies); and introvert experts like *developers* (people who write programs), or *hackers* (those who break into systems).

Hipsters: A loosely-defined, upper middle class youth subculture from the early twenty-first century, it is chiefly defined by its focus on the attires and hairstyles of yesteryear, including skinny jeans, plaid shirts, horn-rims, well-groomed facial hair, and their very name (borrowed from the 1930's jazz subculture) in a feeble scramble for "authenticity."

Beyond garments, hipsters do not discriminate, and are therefore prone to joining in the ranks of all of the above subcultures as long as their collections are certifiably "vintage" (even old electronics), but they also sprouted subgroups of their own, including *Lumbersexuals* (hipsters dressing up like lumberjacks), *Normcore* (hipsters wearing nondescript, functional clothes), *Cottagecore* (hipster pastoral escapists), *Seapunks* (hipsters with turquoise hair and clothing from the 1990s), and—most disturbingly—*Nipsters* (neo-Nazis ditching their post-punk wardrobe for a hipster one). Movie stars embracing the hipster lifestyle include Jared Leto (b.1971), Jason Schwartzman (b.1980), and Natalie Portman (b.1981).

MY GENERATION

Perhaps nothing says "subculture" like the many urban tribes rooted in music styles, particular lingo, and fashion statements. Generally purporting "uniqueness" (new generations always claim at reinventing the wheel), in the end, members of these groups mirror each other, the only variation being the number of people joining their ranks, as they temporarily fade and then "come back" at any moment in time.

Original Hipsters: From the 1930s through the mid-fifties, jazz, swing, and bebop aficionados (mainly white youngsters who frequented African American neighborhoods for their music and dance) ruled supreme. Embracing the bohemian lifestyle, hepcats (as they were also called) influenced the trends and fashions of every following subculture since (even punks!), in part due to the substantial existentialist literary oeuvre they produced, spearheaded by Jack Kerouac (1922–1969), Allen Ginsberg (1926–1997), and the rest of the Beatnik Generation.

Greasers: The post–World War II working-class answer to ivy-league contentment, as well as hipster cultural refinement, greasers emerged in the 1950s and have gone in and out of favor since. Originally fans of doo-wop (a vocal ensemble variation of rhythm and blues), they veered into rockabilly (itself an early form of Rock 'n' Roll) as performed by Carl Perkins (1932–1998), Elvis Presley (1935–1977), Johnny Cash (1932–2003), and others; adopting a combination of blue-collar clothes with leather boots and jackets, not to mention their trademark greased-back hairstyle, they need to constantly comb to maintain. Their lifestyle, long associated with tattoos, motorcycles, and hot-rods, has been imitated internationally in places like England (*rockers*), Holland (*nozem*), Sweden (*raggare*), Botswana (*renegades*), and even Japan (*bōsōzoku*).

Hippies: Stemming from the counterculture movement sparked by *hipsters*, and developed by *beatniks*, hippies took things in a radical new direction heavily swayed by recreational drug use and loose morals, which put them at odds with the prevalent culture of the day, which nonetheless embraced *hippie* aesthetics in an effort to appeal to the youth market. Drug-fueled psychedelia (in turn inspired by forgotten turn-of-the-century art and design) indeed permeated music, art, and society, becoming *the* cultural manifestation of the mid-1960s, until the consequence of substance abuse and unregulated communal lifestyle (embodied by the Tate-LaBianca murders of 1969—*more on them later!*) began rearing its ugly head. Despite waning from the spotlight, hippies never quite died out, leaving behind still-truckin' *deadheads* (Grateful Dead fans), and *New Agers*.

Punks: Something was brewing below all that late 1960s and early 1970s flower power and glitter, and it wasn't pretty. An undercurrent of disenfranchisement-fueled rage wanting not to reform the existing world but to burn it to the ground, and which expressed itself in assorted underground cultural expressions—music included—which finally exploded in the face of mainstream culture, first in Britain and then abroad.

Fashion-wise, *punks* may be spotted a mile away on account of their provocative T-shirts, leather jackets, military boots, mohawks, and tattoos, all stitched together with enough safety pins. Punk music doesn't leave anybody indifferent either. Still very much alive and generating punk-inspired urban tribes everywhere (including *goths, new romantics, straight-edge, anarchos, crusties, hardlines, emos,* and several others), the movement's greatest appeal is also its greatest drawback, as it rarely keeps its hold on those who do better and climb the mainstream social ladder.

Metalheads: Growing strong since the late 1960s, "heavy metal," a heavy-duty rock music subgenre, attracts its own brand of fans (traditionally lower middle-class white males), known for their *greaser-*inspired attire, loud *punk* attitude, and very, very long hair they're pleased to *bang* (hence the *headbanger* sobriquet) up and down at concerts. A tight-knit band weary of "posers," *metalheads* rarely venture beyond the boundaries of their chosen music style (which nonetheless has shown a degree of latitude over the years, including *glam metal, metalcore, industrial, mall-core, Christian* metal, *black metal*, *death metal*, etc.), which in turn has narrowed its appeal outside of wrestling events, and other examples of lowbrow culture.

Grunge: A short-lived hard rock and punk hybrid of the late 1980s to mid-1990s, *grunge rock* brought white middle-class garage bands like Nirvana, Pearl Jam, Soundgarden, Alice in Chains, and Stone Temple Pilots to the forefront of popular culture, its considerable following imitating the musicians' ragged fashion, hairstyles, and other disenchanted leftovers from the late 1960s counterculture. Becoming mainstream signaled the movement's doom, however, when its figurehead, Kurt Cobain, was brought to an early grave by his opioid addiction at age 27, in 1994.

Hip-hop: The unlikely replacement of suburban white *grunge*, this inner-city "black and brown" subculture has made a more lasting impact—thirty years and counting—than its predecessor. Originally emerging from 1970s block parties, over time the hip-hop subculture sublimated elements of rap music, break-dancing, turntablism (what DJs do!), beatboxing, trap, urban fashions, Ebonics (African American vernacular), and bespoke entrepreneurship which has kept it trendy for decades, well into the digital age. Going international since the 1990s, its Puerto Rican offshoot, *reggaeton*, and its fans, seem poised to take over hip-hop's spot as the dominant music subculture on Earth—in many countries it already has!

Juggalos: If there's a side to every coin, *Juggalos* and *Juggalettes* have come to be regarded as hip-hop's darkest subculture. The face-painted followers of Detroit's *horrorcore* (the most aggressive brand of hip-hop) duo Insane Clown Posse—normally neglected and impoverished white kids—are currently split between non-violent Juggalo "families" involved in community service, and criminal Juggalo gangs dabbling in drug-trafficking, burglary, and murder. However, both factions continue to assemble at the "Gathering of the Juggalos" every year, a four-day festival marred by the deaths of some of its attendants. Among various stars exclusive to the hip-hop scene, honorary Juggalos include Charlie Sheen (b.1965), and Elon Musk (b.1971).

BONUS QUOTES

"No man leaves before his time, unless the boss leaves early."
—Groucho Marx

"The reason people use a crucifix against vampires is because vampires are allergic to bullshit."
—Richard Pryor

"The meek shall inherit the Earth, but not its mineral rights."
—J. Paul Getty

BIG IN JAPAN

No other country in the world quite conjures "nutty subculture" like Japan does, and for good reason! Famed for its tolerance of eccentricity, the land of the rising sun takes urban lifestyles (like past favorites Sukeban and Takenokozoku) to the next level.

Otaku: Originally a term to describe those socially inept unfortunates with an all-consuming obsession, these days it refers to those socially inept unfortunates with an all-consuming obsession … for *anime* (Japanese cartoons) and *manga* (Japanese comics)! The *Otaku* subculture is considered a vital part of Japan's "soft" (as in cultural) industries promotion and export overseas, which explains why these days we find it firmly rooted almost everywhere. *Cosplay*, a portmanteau of "costume play," is one of the main subsets of *Otaku* culture and consists of dressing up as fan-favorite characters from anime and comics. It has become a mainstay in comic conventions around the world alongside *Furries* (those interested in, attracted to, or cosplaying as anthropomorphic animals), and harmless *Kigurumi* (people wearing anime mascot or stuffed animal inspired jumpsuits, a lesser form of cosplay).

Lolita Fashion: Japan's second biggest "soft" export after *Otaku* culture, it involves young women dressing in bespoke and highly elaborate Rococo or Victorian inspired gowns, complete with petticoats, bonnets, parasols, and other accessories, which makes them look like living China dolls. Popular *Lolita Fashion* themes include *punk*, *gothic*, *classic*, *sweet*, *sailor*, *ero* (erotic), *guro* (grotesque), *wa* (short kimonos), and *steampunk*, among many others.

Gyaru and Gyaruo: Rumored to be inspired by American TV show *Baywatch*, this subculture sees "gals" (*Gyaru*) and young men (*Gyaruo*) bleach their hair, get a matching tan, and wear a somewhat exaggerated late 1990s American wardrobe. As is usually the case with Japanese trends, members of this subculture compete to outdo each other, resulting in *Ganguro* (when their tan is so overdone it resembles "black face") and *Manba* (*Ganguro* in garishly bright outfits). Often *Gyaru* and *Gyaruo* will dress in their fanciest clothes and biggest hair to work as *Hostess* and *Hosuto* (host) respectively, meaning they will be hired to keep company to older ladies and gentlemen—and you may guess what follows ...

Visual Kei: Japan's answer to British glam rock (*kei* meaning style), this movement sees makeup-laden, anime hair–styled, flamboyantly costumed musicians and fans alike play (or cheer) music ranging from rock to electronica. Declining in the late 1990s, *Visual Kei* made an underground comeback locally in the 2010s, but the popularity of its greatest acts (Kamijo, Nocturnal Bloodlust, Versailles, Jupiter, etc.) remains undiminished among the genre's hardcore western fans.

Mori Kei: Pretty low-key by Japanese standards, this "forest style" is akin to western *Cottagecore*, but mainly involving girls who either live or wish to live in a cabin amid one of Japan's many enchanted forests. It includes wearing light or neutral shades of brown and green, as well as floral or nature-inspired patterns, and may go from the fairy-tale-elaborate, to the simple, understated, and chic. *Mori Kei* is the only subculture with a set guidebook, written by an author going by the pen name "Choco."

Decora: With a large worldwide following, the people belonging to this subculture may wear a simple, usually bright color-coded wardrobe under a plain hairstyle, but they more than make up for it in the sheer number of accessories they blanket their faces, heads, and bodies with, including pins, hairclips, hairbands, barrettes, stickers, toys, and even flashing lights. Like a breathing, walking Hello Kitty Store or Christmas tree, the goal is to look as *kawaii* (cute) as possible.

Dekotora, on the other hand, is the trucker version of this subculture, where drivers decorate their vehicles in neon or ultraviolet lights, fluorescent paints, adding useless stainless or golden parts to the chassis in an effort to make trucks look like something straight out of a Vegas casino or anime series (*Gundam*-based themes are currently very popular).

Zentai: A subculture of people, usually performers of all sorts, who wear full-body, silky nylon-spandex tights (*zenshin taitsu*) that make them look like faceless henchmen in Saban's *Power Rangers* episodes. As absurd as it sounds, and in spite of its sexual fetishism streak—or maybe *because* of it—this trend has been commercially and artistically adopted all over the west as well (Scotland's Morphsuits, Canada's Green Men, and America's Body Poets come to mind).

BONUS FACTS

According to record, different British men by the same name, Hugh Williams, have alternatively survived shipwrecks in 1660, 1767, 1820, and 1940.

Working for the Kennard Novely Company, Confederate veteran Elijah Bond (1847–1921) patented the "Ouija" parlor game in 1891, which gained its current creepy reputation as a *séance* tool only decades later.

According to PETA, *Game of Thrones* fans' obsession with the show's "direwolves" made the number of abandoned huskies in Riverside County, California, rise from 351 in 2013 to a staggering 1,027 in late 2017.

At the unlikely forefront of space exploration since 1914, Italy has its own space agency and spaceport, the Broglio Space Center, in coastal Kenya (Africa).

LE FREAK C'EST CHIC

Forget neurotic collectors and hysterical fashion trends; the time has come to take an unflinching look at the seedy underbelly of subcultures active in the world today.

Living Dolls: Also known as "maskers," this movement involves thousands of cross-dressing men who wrap themselves up in full-body PVC bodysuits ("femskins"), masks, and wigs in order to become some grotesque version of Mattel's Barbie via "Buffalo Bill" from *The Silence of the Lambs* (1991). Insane as it sounds, their motivation isn't always sexual, nor do they represent a danger to others.

Otherkin: The living proof there should be laws preventing nutjobs from networking, this thriving subculture sprung from *Ringer* and fantasy role-play Internet communities in the 1990s. Its dysphoric members identify as not fully human, be them *Fictionkin* (those who identify as fictional characters), *Animalkin* (identify as animals), *Conceptkin* (identify as abstract concepts), and *Weatherkin* (weather systems), some even claiming physical, mental, or spiritual *shapeshifting* abilities!

Godspouses: For those with a mystical streak—and an ancient mythology fetish—there's a subgroup of people, mainly women, who claim to have intimate relationships with deities from the Norse, Hellenic,

Egyptian, or Hindu pantheons. Whether harmless *New Agers*, Christians, or simpletons who have watched *Xanadu* (1980) one time too many, *godspouses* are clearly a consequence of our western world's ongoing divorce from reality.

Pro-Ana: The kind of "movement" that needs to be seriously scrutinized—and punished—by authorities, pro-Ana engages in the promotion of *anorexia nervosa* (the lesser known "pro-Mia" refers to bulimia) under the guise of non-judgmental understanding, disseminating photos of skinny models as "thinspiration," while sharing tips on suppressing hunger, concealing vomit-breath, and other harmful content.

Columbiners: A growing worldwide community of young, mainly female bloggers sharing their obsession with suicide, self-harm, and ... the Columbine High School massacre. In 2019, one of these young bloggers, Sol Pais (b.2001), bought a shotgun, a black T-shirt, camouflage pants, and black boots, and traveled from Florida to Colorado intending to finish what Eric Harris (1981–1999) and Dylan Klebold (1981–1999) started in 1999. Her threats forced the closure of several Colorado schools; the ensuing FBI manhunt ending with Ms. Pais found dead from a self-inflicted gunshot wound. Unfortunately, as "Columbiners" continue to make pilgrimages to the aforementioned high school, a lot of people in town think it's not a matter of *if*, but rather *when* another Columbiner will give mass murder another try.

Incels: In a nutshell, this is an online hate group of frustrated, straight, white men unable to find a romantic or sexual partner despite desiring one. Lashing out against women both within the "manosphere" (a network of websites, blogs, and forums promoting toxic masculinity), and in real life. "Involuntary celibates" have perpetrated several mass-murders, including the 2020 Toronto Machete Attack, and the 2021 Atlanta Spa Shootings.

Apotemnophiliacs: The word refers to those suffering from a psychological pathology known as BIID (Body Integrity Identity Disorder), who fantasize about missing a limb and seek amputation (say, as opposed to psychiatric care) in order to achieve this "ideal" picture of themselves. Some will go about it the civilized way, like Belgian author Alex Mensaert (b.1970) who bribed a doctor to have both legs and one arm surgically removed, but others will *Texas Chainsaw Massacre* their own limbs off, like Americans Jewel Shuping (poured drain cleaner on her eyes to blind herself) and George Boyer (blew his own arm off with a shotgun).

BONUS QUOTE

"One seldom recognizes the devil when he is putting his hand on your shoulder."
—Albert Speer

MASTERS OF THE UNIVERSE

Move over, DUNE! Step aside, Game of Thrones! The spot for the biggest, roughest, most exciting modern "sword and planet" saga, complete with its own sprawling 25,000-member subculture, has been claimed by John Norman's Chronicles of Counter-Earth, and it won't relinquish it without beating you into submission . . . literally.

1. Professor John Frederick Lange Jr., PhD (b.1931) had a secret. Beneath his respectable higher-education persona lay risqué author John Norman, author of the 1974 BDSM (as in "bondage and submission") precursor *Imaginative Sex* ("With Fifty-three Detailed Scenarios for Sensual Fantasies . . . "). Norman would best expound his male-female domination philosophy, in his thirty-six volume *Chronicles of Counter-Earth*, as well as in a few other non-related novels, but it would be this saga that made him famous—or *infamous*, depending on who you ask.

2. The swashbuckling novels are set on the fictional Solar System—yet perpetually hidden from us behind the Sun—planet of Gor, a low-gravity-yet-habitable planet not unlike Earth, except it's ruled by insect Priest-Kings who impose restrictions to the technological development of Gorean human civilizations, which in many ways are equivalent to

Earth's own ancient cultures. While mainly focused on the adventures of "John Carter-ish" Tarl Cabot of Earth, the plots generally involve proud women of Earth who get abducted, stripped, abused, and branded as slaves (known as *kajira* in Gor), but eventually come to *enjoy* it.

3. Described by many as clever social satire disguised as epic fantasy or space opera, the GOR saga was enormously popular from the "sexual revolution" years of the late 1960s to the more prudish 1980s, when its contents began to trouble some in the embattled American publishing landscape of the era—as well as the occasional overzealous feminist—which eventually got the series canceled, and its author effectively blacklisted by the end of that decade.

4. The author's misfortune, however, did not prevent his followers from embracing the ideas he espoused; a *Gorean* fandom soon formed and gathered with the coming of the Internet age, not only to collect out-of-print paperbacks (or stage their digital comeback in the early twenty-first century), but also to willingly enact some of the fantasies portrayed within them.

5. Ironically derided by the "mainstream" sadomasochism Norman's writings took great, er, pain in validating, the Gorean community (alongside its more radical *Kaotian* splinter group) comprises online sexual role-playing gamers, as well as real-life ones. These "*LARPers* from hell" have occasionally made the news in America and abroad, when explaining to confused police officers they had actually allowed themselves to be tied up, beaten, and branded with the *kajira* "kef" symbol, in order to properly serve their new master … all *consensual*, you know.

6. Largely ignored and forgotten by SF, film, and general 1980s retro *fandoms* alike, the *Chronicles of Counter-Earth* first novel, *Tarnsman of Gor* (1966), was adapted into a 1987 film, GOR, directed by Fritz *Children of the Corn* Kiersch (b.1951), and starring Urbano Barberini (b.1961), Rebecca Ferratti (b.1965), Jack Palance (1919–2006), and Oliver Reed (1938–1999). Campy and low-budgeted as it was, it did well enough to fast-track a sequel, *Outlaw of GOR* (1988), based on the 1967 *Tarnsman* follow-up, and directed by John *Kingdom of the Spiders* Cardos (1929–2020). Unfortunately, the book series publisher's refusal to do any tie-in editions, coupled with the demise of Cannon Films, buried any chance of GOR ever reaching a wider audience.

BONUS FACT

On August 29, 1979, fifteen-year-old Eddie Seidel Jr., of Saint Paul, Minnesota, killed himself over the cancellation of the *Battlestar Galactica* (1978–1979) TV show.

ADAMITES À GOGO

Anatomically modern humans roamed the world buck-naked for ninety thousand years until newly formed agrarian societies saw the need to differentiate people by status, class, and individual identity. Despite being pushed to the sidelines, Adam and Eve "cosplay" has been staging comebacks for centuries, modern-day naturist subculture being its latest iteration.

1. Back in ancient north Africa, the Middle East, and the far East, well-to-do members of society inherited or came to own a single, valuable item of clothing. Nudity, therefore, came to be associated with poverty, indebtedness, crime, and slavery; hence, its rather shameful reputation in Judeo-Christian and Islamic traditions, while the Chinese deemed it unseemly and highly disrespectful.

2. By contrast, no such associations were made by the western Hellenistic culture, where nudity was considered a celebration of freedom and beauty, the very root word for gymnastics and gymnasium, *gymnosis*, meaning nudity. On the other hand, the Italic peninsula heirs of the Greek culture, Romans, were slightly more prudish, reserving nudity for public bathing alone, but even that would come to an end as the empire embraced Christianity.

3. Adult and infant Christian Baptism, however, was celebrated naked. Oftentimes, pictorial representations of the Crucifixion would also be of an accurately naked Jesus (criminals were crucified naked in Roman times). Conversely, it would be a second-century north African Christian sect, the *Adamites*, that proclaimed that mankind's freedom from sin through Christ's resurrection meant going back to Adam and Eve's Biblical nudity, and a restoration of the Garden of Eden.

4. There would be several Adamite revivals throughout Europe between the thirteenth and eighteenth centuries, including those Dutch Anabaptists known as *Naaktloopers* ("naked walkers"). It should be noted that public, if segregated, baths were still much in use until the Renaissance. The unearthing of classical Greek and Roman art also helped Adamites gain some degree of acceptance during this period, which began to wane when the discovery of the New World linked the practice to savagery, and the struggle between Reformed and Catholic Christianity drove both to become fiercely modest.

5. While people in western countries continued to bathe and swim naked in rivers and lakes (as well as in public baths, saunas, and swimming pools), since the end of the nineteenth century, public nudity has been stripped from religious aspects to become a political, social, or environmental statement.

In Germany and Switzerland, the proto-naturist Freikörperkultur (FKK), a part of the larger anti-industrialization Lebensreform movement, was instrumental in the changing of attitudes toward the naked body. They organized the very first naturist Olympics in 1939 Swizerland.

6. The many strands of naturism which emerged from the aforementioned FKK continue to seek harmony with nature, as well as optimal physical performance, rather than "nudism" for its own sake. These days, the *Deutscher Verband für Freikörperkultur* ("German Association for Free Body Culture" or DFK; est. 1949) is a member of the German Olympic Sport Federation, and the largest member of the International Naturist Federation (INF).

7. The counter-culture movement of the 1960s also embraced nudity as a form of protest against the established order and values, and part of the "sexual revolution." During the following three decades, naturist clubs and organizations around the world allowed for the establishment of nudist camps and beaches almost everywhere in the world. While they continue to grow strong in Europe, in America their numbers have dwindled, in part due to the aging of their membership, but also due to a recent regression into a curious form of secular prudishness, which has caused "up-and-coming" organizations like the Young Naturists America to close their doors for good. On the other hand, the perennial American Association for Nude Recreation (est. 1931) stays strong with thirty thousand members, and around two hundred affiliated clubs.

8. For the past three decades, American photographer Spencer Tunick (b.1967) has specialized in staging massive naked *tableaux vivants* around the world. Starting with twenty-eight nude people in front of the United Nations New York headquarters, Tunick portrayed three thousand at the *Place des Arts* in Montreal (2001); four thousand people in Santiago de Chile's *Parque Forestal* (2002); 1,800 at the old Buffalo Central Terminal (2004); a staggering eighteen thousand at Mexico City's Zócalo square (2007); 5,200 at the Sydney Opera House (2010); 1,200 in the Dead Sea (2011); and 3,200 in Kingston upon Hull, United Kingdom (2016).

BONUS QUOTES

"So, in the interests of survival, they trained themselves to be agreeing machines instead of thinking machines. All their minds had to do was to discover what other people were thinking, and then they thought that, too."
—Kurt Vonnegut

"Vampires are make-believe, like elves, gremlins, and Eskimos."
—Matt Groening

"If you let go of fart jokes, you've let go of a piece of humanity."
—Andy Samberg

SOMEBODY SAVE ME

Diametrically opposed to nudism, the Real-Life Superhero subculture, a form of cosplay gone wrong, actually seeks to add layers of clothing to a person's body, to conceal their identity in order to "fight for justice" outside of the latter's regular channels, though time has proven none of them to be particularly capable at the concealing, nor the fighting.

1. If nineteenth-century Bald Knobbers and Klansmen are any indication, masked vigilantism (enforcement or punishment without legal authority) in America is far from a new phenomenon. Early vigilantes, however, found strength in numbers rather than seek individual glory.

2. A direct consequence of the fear and impotence of working-class people against violent crime during the Prohibition years saw vigilantism idealized in fiction (*Superman* co-creator Jerry Siegel's father, a tailor, died during a robbery), with individual characters given "super-powers" to fight crime. Most of these "superheroes" fell out of favor immediately after World War II (after all, America was fighting the ultimate "super-villains"), but were revived by publishers in the 1960s, as television gained footing in popular genres like western, crime, or soap opera.

3. From the mid-1970s, and all throughout the 1980s, the alarming increase in destitution,

poverty, and drug use led to a rise in violent crime unseen since the Depression. A similar sense of impotence again bred both community and individual inner-city vigilantism. The former was perhaps best represented by the Guardian Angels Safety Patrol, which spread to over 130 cities despite generating wide controversy. The latter was embodied by New Yorker Bernhard Goetz (b.1947), a private citizen who shot and wounded his would-be muggers in 1984, being upheld—and subsequently torn-down—as a local hero.

4. During this era, fictional vigilantes and superheroes alike got rougher too. Crime novel *Death Wish* (1972) by Brian Garfield (1939–2018), in particular, spawned not only a film franchise, but also served as inspiration for Curtis Sliwa (b.1954) when founding the Guardian Angels, as well as shifting superheroes toward the "grim and gritty," in comic-book classics such as *Daredevil: Born Again*, *The Punisher*, *Watchmen* and *The Dark Knight*.

5. Most ironically, as crime rates fell dramatically during the 1990s and onward, taking vigilantism down with them, both politicians and mass media (with the comic-book world in tow) failed to take notice; the misguided public convinced, against all statistical evidence, that crime was "worse than ever," while turning a blind eye on the industrial prison complex (which currently has incarcerations for misdemeanors at an all-time high).

6. Meanwhile, the Internet changed the cultural landscape in unforeseen ways, leading to the exponential growth of these communities (a.k.a. *subcultures*), and bringing formerly fringe-genres of fiction, like the superhero, to the forefront. Long an industry of adaptation, Hollywood quickly took notice, plunging into "the new westerns" with gusto, and pouring money into ever-growing comic-book events and conventions, which in turn imported a strange custom from Japan: *cosplay*.

7. Real Life Superheroes, RLSH for short, were thus brought about by the conflation of all of the above. While in the past, Napoleonic or Civil War *re-enactors* would have been swiftly committed to the loony-bin if they chose to take their hobby too far, post-modern "anything goes" culture cares not to keep deluded adult *cosplayers* from taking their chances at becoming their own superhero personas, despite lacking any actual superpowers other than some mad tailoring skills.

8. Truth be told, most RLSH do not pose a danger to themselves or others, their "heroic deeds" amounting to community outreach activities they could well engage while under civilian clothes. Some RLSH, like the Japanese *rōkaru hīrō* ("local heroes") are basically mascots, performing for a given company or regional government campaigns. A few RLSH, however, have strayed into full-blown madness …

9. Distraught over a set of alleged grievances, mid-level mixed martial artist Benjamin Fodor (b.1988) made himself a black and gold rubber "muscle suit," and went on to "fight crime" as "Phoenix Jones." Walking around Seattle while waiting for crimes to happen, he caught the eye of the news-hungry media for a short while, after engaging in unprovoked fights with strangers—*crime, it seems, is hard to come by these days.* These incidents got him reportedly pepper-sprayed, hit with a woman's shoe, beaten, and stabbed, not to mention arrested by the police (his entourage never stayed around). Rendered irrelevant by the Covid-19 pandemic, in 2020 he was arrested while attempting to sell drugs to, ironically, a police officer in disguise.

10. One of the earliest RLSH on record was also one of the most dangerous. A former Marine, who worked as a Six-Flags Park "Batman," Richard McCaslin (1964–2018) went *bat-shit crazy* over a number of conspiracy theories in 2002. Donning his "Phantom Patriot" outfit and skull mask and armed to the teeth, McCaslin attempted to raid the Monte Rio's Bohemian Grove campsite to stop the Club's secret reptilian cabal of Satanist pedophiles from sacrificing any more children—sound familiar? Setting the banquet hall on fire, he brandished his MK at the caretakers before fleeing the grounds, finally being arrested and imprisoned until 2008. Opting for less-violent forms of protest under the "Thoughtcrime" guise, he ended up shooting himself in 2018.

11. Long abandoning any semblance of social responsibility, Hollywood too would pander to the

RLSH subculture for a while, via films like *Kick-ass* (2010) and its 2013 sequel, and TV reality shows like *Stan Lee's Superhumans* (2010–2014), but quickly reverted to the more successful and harmless comic-book franchises when the fad had run its course. Many a Real Life Superhero dropped his or her tights as they belatedly entered adult life or engaged in other hobbies.

12. While in the contest of reality versus fantasy, reality usually wins the upper hand, scientific and technological progress may be verging mankind toward working super-powers and, like space flight and computers before them, may one day turn our superhero fantasies into reality.
    Years ago, reports confirmed that, not unlike the amphetamine-fueled Nazi *Wehrmacht*, the armies of the world's greatest superpowers happened to be looking for ways to enhance their soldiers (as announced with great fanfare by Barack Obama in 2014), but their plans at developing "the next Iron-Man" were also run aground by plain old reality. The technology just isn't there yet, and maybe that's for the best.

BONUS FACT

In 2021, American scientists announced they had successfully cloned a formerly extinct black-footed ferret from a specimen frozen since 1988.

KICK-ASS

Real-life superhero wannabes may be nothing but a sad joke, but the four-color counterparts that inspired them continue to fetch exorbitant prices. Here are twenty-five of the highest-valued superhero comic books ever sold as of 2021.

1. Title: Action Comics #1 | Description: First appearance of Superman | Year: 1938 | Publisher: DC Comics | Max. Value: USD 3,200,000 | Min. Value: USD 125,000

2. Title: *Batman #1* | Description: First solo Batman comic. First appearance of the Joker and Catwoman | Year: 1940 | Publisher: DC Comics | Max. Value: USD 2,220,000 | Min. Value: USD 15,000

3. Title: *Detective Comics #27* | Description: First appearance of Batman | Year: 1939 | Publisher: DC Comics | Max. Value: USD 2,100,000 (Ebay) | Min. Value: USD 100,000

4. Title: *Marvel Comics #1* | Description: First appearance of the original Human Torch. | Year: 1939 | Publisher: Marvel Comics | Max. Value: USD 1,260,000 | Min. Value: USD 25,000

5. Title: *Amazing Fantasy #15* | Description: First appearance of Spider-Man | Year: 1962 | Publisher: Marvel Comics | Max. Value: USD 1,100,000 | Min. Value: USD 3,000

6. Title: *All-Star Comics* #8 | Description: First appearance of Wonder Woman | Year: 1941 | Publisher: DC Comics | Max. Value: USD 936,000 | Min. Value: USD 10,000

7. Title: *Captain America Comics* #1 | Description: First appearance of Captain America and Bucky | Year: 1941 | Publisher: Marvel Comics | Max. Value: USD 915,000 | Min. Value: USD 25,000

8. Title: *X-Men* #1 | Description: First appearance of the X-Men | Year: 1963 | Publisher: Marvel Comics | Max. Value: USD 492,000 | Min. Value: USD 450

9. Title: *Superman* #1 | Description: First solo Superman comic | Year: 1939 | Publisher: DC Comics | Max. Value: USD 456,000 | Min. Value: USD 25,000

10. Title: *Flash Comics* #8 | Description: First appearance of The Flash (Jay Garrick) | Year: 1940 | Publisher: DC Comics | Max. Value: USD 450,000 | Min. Value: USD 9,000

11. Title: *Sensation Comics* #1 | Description: First Wonder Woman cover appearance | Year: 1942 | Publisher: DC Comics | Max. Value: USD 450,000 | Min. Value: USD 5,000

12. Title: *The Incredible Hulk* #1 | Description: First appearance of the Hulk | Year: 1962 | Publisher: Marvel Comics | Max. Value: USD 375,000 | Min. Value: USD 2,500

13. Title: *Tales of Suspense #39* | Description: First appearance of Iron Man | Year: 1963 | Publisher: Marvel Comics | Max. Value: USD 375,000 | Min. Value: USD 700

14. Title: *Action Comics #10* | Description: Third Superman cover appearance | Year: 1939 | Publisher: DC Comics | Max. Value: USD 325,000 | Min. Value: USD 8,000

15. Title: *Detective Comics #31* | Description: Third Batman cover appearance | Year: 1939 | Publisher: DC Comics | Max. Value: USD 325,000 | Min. Value: USD 18,000

16. Title: *Whiz Comics #1* | Description: First appearance of Shazam! | Year: 1940 | Publisher: Fawcett Publications | Max. Value: USD 300,000 | Min. Value: USD 12,000

17. Title: *Fantastic Four #1* | Description: First appearance of the Fantastic Four | Year: 1961 | Publisher: Marvel Comics | Max. Value: USD 300,000 | Min. Value: USD 1,000

18. Title: *Wonder Woman #1* | Description: First solo Wonder Woman comic | Year: 1942 | Publisher: DC Comics | Max. Value: USD 291,000 | Min. Value: USD 2,500

19. Title: *Detective Comics #29* | Description: Second Batman cover appearance | Year: 1939 | Publisher: DC Comics | Max. Value: USD 280,000 | Min. Value: USD 5,000

20. Title: *Journey into Mystery #83* | Description: First appearance of Thor | Year: 1962 | Publisher: Marvel Comics | Max. Value: USD 275,000 | Min. Value: USD 500

21. Title: *The Avengers #1* | Description: First appearance of the Avengers | Year: 1963 | Publisher: Marvel Comics | Max. Value: USD 274,000 | Min. Value: USD 500

22. Title: *Spider-Man #1* | Description: First solo Spider-Man comic, and Fantastic Four crossover | Year: 1963 | Publisher: Marvel Comics | Max. Value: USD 262,000 | Min. Value: USD 8,000

23. Title: *Fantastic Comics #3* | Description: "Samson versus the Iron Monster" | Year: 1940 | Publisher: Fox Features Syndicate | Max. Value: USD 243,000 | Min. Value: USD 5,000

24. Title: *Detective Comics #33* | Description: Origin of the Batman | Year: 1939 | Publisher: DC Comics | Max. Value: USD 225,000 | Min. Value: USD 8,000

25. Title: *All-American Comics #16* | Description: First appearance of the Green Lantern (Alan Scott) | Year: 1940 | Publisher: DC Comics | Max. Value: USD 215,000 | Min. Value: USD 10,000

SAINTS AND SINNERS

South of the border, Mexico has always had its real-life costumed superheroes, only they know its theater, or rather, wrestling!

1. Mexican strongman and wrestler Enrique Ugartechea (1881–1963) is considered the Founding Father of *lucha libre* ("freestyle wrestling"). Dubbed "Mexico's Strongest Man," and made a Spalding spokesman, Ugartechea toured the United States, and was greatly impressed by circus sideshow wrestling, which provided him the inspiration necessary to invent his own brand of staged sports entertainment.

2. By the 1920s, three circus companies from Italy, Spain, and Belgium, led by strongmen-turned-impresarios Giovanni Reselevich, Antonio Fournier, and Constant le Marin (1884–1965), had established themselves as the biggest *lucha* shows in Mexico. Fournier, in particular, would bring in the first Japanese wrestlers (along with their high-flying antics) into the sport, including *judoka* Mitsuyo Maeda (1878–1941), a.k.a. "Count Koma," the grandfather of Brazilian Jiu-Jitsu.

3. But it would be showman Salvador Lutteroth González's (1897–1987) foresight that turned *lucha libre* from a regional touring circus show into a mainstream spectacle in 1933, when he founded the *Empresa Mexicana de Lucha Libre* (modern-day

Consejo Mundial de Lucha Libre), the longest-running professional wrestling company in the world. Considered the *padre* of *lucha libre*, Lutteroth González first established fixed performing arenas, a unified fighting style, and big-name "superstars" like El Santo (Rodolfo Guzmán Huerta; 1917–1984), who drew crowds into the arenas on a weekly basis. Lutteroth González would also pioneer bringing wrestling events to television, as well as the introduction of one of *lucha libre's* most distinctive features.

4. According to *lucha* lore, Lutteroth González would be so impressed by the commanding performance of Canadian wrestler Frank Valois (1921–1998), a.k.a. the Masked Marvel, that he made masks an integral part of Mexican wrestling "mystique." Iconic *luchadores* like Blue Demon (Alejandro Muñoz Moreno; 1922–2000), Mil *Máscaras* (Aarón Rodríguez Arellano, b.1942), and the aforementioned *Santo* (buried with his silver mask on), henceforth making face-concealing an integral part of their in-the-ring personas.

5. Masks carry such symbolic weight, having one torn off as part of a *lucha de apuestas* betting match (meaning a bet is made on who will lose theirs) is seen as an emasculating experience, and may radically alter the future of *luchadores*. Popular *apuestas* after masks include *cabellera* ("hair"; losers will be shaved bald), *nombre* (winners get to keep their wrestling names), and *carrera* (losers must retire from the sport).

6. One of the features that sets *lucha libre* apart not only from other national wrestling styles but from most sports as well is its diversity. Alongside its two main categories, *técnicos* (faces, the good guys) and *rudos* (heels, the bad guys), you will find foreigners of every ethnicity (sometimes playing "anti-Mexico" *rudos*), female *luchadoras*, *minis* (short and little people), and *exóticos* (straight cross-dressing *luchadores* as well as LGBT+ *luchadores*, like the iconic Saúl "Cassandro" Armendáriz; b.1970), and in many instances they will all fight each other in inclusive matches where the only segregation allowed may or may not be determined by a weight class system not unlike the one found in boxing.

7. *Lucha libre* being such an integral part of Mexico's culture, and its second-favorite sport after soccer, it isn't unusual to see it become a family trade, wrestlers intermarrying and having children who follow into their parents' ... er, masks. Some, like El Hijo del Santo, or El Hijo del Perro Aguayo ("El Hijo de" meaning "The Son of") will go on to have successful careers of their own. Younger *familia* relatives, such as nephews or younger brothers, will add "Jr." to their uncle's ring name, like Stuka Jr. or Rey Mysterio Jr. (Óscar Gutiérrez; b.1974), also making their mark, both locally and abroad, particularly in Japan and the United States, where Mexican wrestlers have become a staple.

8. It comes as no surprise then, that *lucha* would generate its own superheroes outside of the ring.

Equal parts El Santo and Superman, the yet-unidentified Superbarrio Gómez donned his red and yellow outfit and mask to fight for affordable housing in Mexico City, after it had been devastated by a 1985 earthquake, and has since been featured in comic books, stage, and screen.

9. Inspired by Mexican film *El Señor Tormenta* (1963) and its sequel *Tormenta En El Ring* (1964), about a poor Catholic priest who supported the children of his orphanage by fighting as a *lucha libre* wrestler at night, Father Sergio Gutiérrez Benítez (b.1945) wrestled as *Fray Tormenta* ("Brother Storm") for thirty years in order to fund an orphanage of his own. Currently retired, Father Gutiérrez still wears his mask in processions, and during mass. His life would inspire the American film *Nacho Libre*, starring Jack Black (b.1969), in 2006.

10. Unfortunately, *lucha libre* also originated the world's first, real-life super villain: *Mataviejitas* ("Old-Ladies-Killer"). Originally going by the ominous ring name *La Dama del Silencio* ("The Lady of Silence"), Juana Barraza (b.1957) preyed on elderly lone women, whom she befriended, often posing as a welfare agent or caregiver, in order to kill them with her bare hands later on and steal their belongings. Remorseless, she later claimed to be doing society a favor by getting rid of these frail women. With an estimated body-count reaching up to almost fifty victims, in 2008 she was sentenced to 759 years in prison on account of twenty-seven confirmed casualties.

DIAL H FOR HEALER

He played the world's greatest hero but gave acting up to help others. John Haymes Newton (b.1965) graciously allowed the following interview to take place in between his busy schedule at Health Beyond Belief.

What geared you toward acting as a young man?
I did my first when I was in preschool, about the Apollo 11 moon landing. It was more improv than anything else, but I did theater also in high school, and caught the bug there. Moved to New York City when I was nineteen to study full time and pursued that. Did a lot of theater, mostly really small venues, but learned to exercise the techniques and finish the two-year program that was the Sanford Meisner study. That really is what got me into the world of acting. I feel that it was part of my journey in life, it's not what I do now. If you go to HealthBeyondBelief.Com, you can see what my other work is—I help train doctors and therapists in outside-the-box techniques to support patients in their quality-of-life issues (addiction, chronic pain, stress, things like that), and also have a private practice. That's what I feel my calling is, the acting was a *step* in that direction.

Generally speaking, what was working in American television like in the late 1980s?
Superboy was a syndicated show, sold to individual markets around the country and, of course, the

world. It was my first TV series; I had already joined the Screen Actors Guild before that, and had worked, but that was my first launch into the world of acting. I really enjoyed the show, it was a great opportunity for me. Felt like a big responsibility to wear that suit, and I even wore Christopher Reeve's suit to the audition, which was quite intimidating.

What series of events brought you to *Superboy*? What was the casting process like?
It involved me going to visit the studios in North Carolina while I was on vacation, and *synchronistically* the casting director, Lynn Stalmaster (1927–2021), happened to be there. This was my first audition after my two-year program in New York City had ended. It was for a movie called *Weekend at Bernie's* (1989), that's what he was there to cast, and after the audition Lynn said I did really well, and would I be interested in a TV series, so he had me read the *Superboy* material, and then flew me to Florida, I believe, for the screen test, and I ended up getting the job.

Did you have any concerns at the time, of being typecast into the role, as was the case with other superhero actors in decades past (Reeve, West, Ferrigno, etc.)?
Yes, I did have, not just because of superheroes in the past, but also just so many actors on TV who play such a distinct character tend to not move on beyond that. So that was a big concern of mine, and probably played into my decision to not go back for the third series pick-up. We did thirteen, then got

picked up for another thirteen, and then the third pick-up was for twenty-six, and that's when I left the show.

What was working for the Salkinds like?
The Salkinds were great. Alexander didn't really come to the set. I don't remember meeting him, but Ilya was very hands-on, and had a real passion for the Superman franchise. He was very European in a lot of ways, and we became great friends.

How long did production and post-production of each episode take?
With a half-hour live action, the shooting on film at the time was five days, so we had five days of production for each episode. Most hour-long series have seven to eight days for shooting. When you consider the writing, pre-production, location scouting, and then of course post-production, editing, polishing, music, and all of that can take up to a few weeks to produce one episode. There's obviously overlap, and that's why they have different directors each week for almost every series.

On average, how many hours of work (including makeup, suiting up, actual filming and re-shoots, etc.) did you go through each day?
Since I played two characters that means I was also working pretty much all the time, which was also another bargaining chip for, you know, issues I had when they asked me to come back for the third pick-up. Usually, a SAG work day is eight hours,

sometimes ten hours, it has to do with whether you're on location or at the studio as far as getting overtime. We usually ended up filming mostly ten hours, rarely sometimes twelve hours, but you go into what's called "golden time," when you make twice your salary per hour, which shows don't like to pay, especially lower-budget ones.

What unique point of view, sensibility, and performance traits did you bring into the role of Superboy?
I felt I didn't want to bring what Chris Reeve had brought to the character. I had concerns about doing what he had done, so I went to make Clark insecure as opposed to nerdy. I definitely feel that I fell more into the *comfortability*, the organic process with the character at the second pick-up of thirteen. If you look at the first thirteen, the second thirteen are of much higher quality. They put more time and energy into developing characters, and I think it showed. And also, that Clark was the alien, not Superboy. I wanted to get that across; Superboy is who the character really is, while Clark Kent is the *alter ego*.

What would you say is your favorite episode? Why?
I'd probably have to say, probably *Revenge of the Alien Part 1 and 2*, which was when production quality shifted to a higher caliber.

What brought your involvement with the show to an end? Was it abrupt or foretold?

They had promised me a raise several times, due to me doing most of my own stunts and wire work, and we had a couple of mishaps and things like that occur. When it came to going back for the third pick-up I questioned them about the raise and they said, "No, we can't, we don't have the money," so no one was willing to come up with the money. There were multiple people—Viacom and the Salkinds—and I had received a moving violation on private property, which was dropped by the sheriff's department in Florida, and at that time I wrote a letter to the sheriff's department which was published in the paper, and the producers used that against me saying that was something I shouldn't have done as it reflected badly on the character I was representing. So they said I needed to come back and was lucky to have my job, but I decided not to go back. In retrospect, I wish I had stuck to my contract. I was young and wish I hadn't written that letter to the sheriff's department. It wasn't a bad letter, just not the appropriate thing to do. Even though they dropped the ticket, it was still not the right way to go about that. So, long story short, they recast the character.

What did you learn from this experience, and what did you bring from it, moving forward with your acting career?
I was relieved in a lot of ways to be off the show for many reasons, but at the same time I also had regret around my behavior, and wish I had stuck to my contract, because that was the right thing to do.

In your view, what changed most in television between the late 1980s and late 1990s?

I think audiences have become more and more sophisticated—reality TV not included in that comment. As we see, shows evolve, and as audiences become more savvy they're not willing to be spoon-fed just traditional formulaic work, and so a lot of shows have become more and more creative to get audiences on board. Obviously, another change in that time period is seeing more film actors doing television. It became more accepted, whereas before that it was kind of taboo for a feature film actor to do television, it was a sign their career was going down. But, because of the changes in media, the payoff—what production companies can make, their profit margins—has gone down, so there's been less work available, so you have more film actors doing television, and now it's more common to go back and forth.

Which would you say are the main differences between starring on *Superboy*, and a hit show such as *Melrose Place*?

I wouldn't even put them in the same realm. *Melrose Place* was a good job but not something that I'd say I loved. I enjoyed the work, but the quality of what the show was about and all that is not what I am about, but I'm grateful *for* the work, and it was a fun experience; a definitely well-oiled machine by the time I came on at the seventh season. It was an "easy" job because I would work two to three days a week, as opposed to every day of the week on *Superboy*.

What was your journey as a healer like, all those years? How did you balance both activities?
I don't call myself a "healer" because I feel like the Creator or Higher Power of our understanding does the work, and I also teach and share what I do so that people don't think I have some special gift. I don't balance both activities, because I have really put acting aside, probably after *The Christmas Card* (2006), which was a very successful Hallmark production I did. That's when I shifted to full-time helping people in the work that I do now. If I could find a project that's profound, and reflective of my heart, I might be open to it, but I don't *pursue* acting at all anymore.

How did reconnecting with the Superman character feel, when starring in Robb Pratt's excellent *Superman* Classic and *Bizarro* Classic animated short films?
Yes, Robb is a talented director with a passion for Superman. I enjoyed working with him as he tried to cast voice talent from related productions (like *Flash Gordon*). It was fun for me to play Superman characters plus Ming the Merciless and to be involved in related projects, but outside of *Superboy*. Robb is someone who will be doing great things in the animated world in the future, and I would be open to working with him again for sure. He's become a good friend since we met close to ten years ago.

SAVE YOURSELF

Let's face it, "survivalism" made the bulk of what we now call "life," until the twentieth century wrapped some in a cozy safety blanket where an almighty government took care of their needs from cradle to grave, everybody was nice to each other, and nothing ever went wrong; but, as with every bubble, the illusion of safety—or control, or kindness—sooner or later always bursts. If you're not the kind of person who waits for somebody else to save you, you might be a member of the survivalist subculture all along . . .

1. A term dating from the 1970s, survivalism gathers individuals or communities who prepare for emergencies (hence, the term "prepper") large and small. From buying candles in the event of a blackout, to building your own nuclear shelter, survivalists gather the stuff they think might come in handy in the event an emergency, a crisis, a natural disaster, or even the apocalypse strikes—all in direct proportion to their fears, or the issues of the day.

2. Those who have suffered financial distress or unemployment are likely to safekeep hard currency or stockpile food "for a rainy day." Someone who has been robbed or *mugged* will likely spend money on home security measures, take self-defense lessons, or at least entertain the notion of buying a gun, just as parents concerned for the well-being of their children will have a first-aid kit at hand.

Others with an overly political or religious stance will prepare for an awaited "end of days" by building shelters or retreats where they will keep their supplies. The list is endless!

3. The importance of the Scouting movement's influence in the formation of the *preparedness* mentality cannot be overstated. A subculture in itself, this private, non-political, educational organization with a paramilitary bend was founded in 1910 by British Army Lieutenant General Robert Baden-Powell (1857–1941) as the Boy Scouts, while his sister Agnes (1858–1945) established the Girl Scouts, both of which put into action the ideas expressed by Baden-Powell's seminal *Scouting for Boys: A handbook for instruction in good citizenship* (1908). Since 1910, the Boy Scouts of America in particular have indoctrinated an estimated 110,000,000 children in those same principles of self-reliance (including basic wilderness survival tactics), and is currently joined by around 2,500,000 young recruits, and another million adult volunteers.

4. Survivalists—many formerly scouts in their youth—began to coalesce around a number of publications (including books, magazines, and newsletters) during the mid-1970s, when socio-cultural malaise began to grip a world still recovering from the "summer of love" hangover, and the fallout of the Oil Crisis (a vengeful oil embargo conducted by Arab nations on Israel supporters) which drove formerly staunch western nations to their knees.

5. Authors with a survivalist streak would initially cash in on their particular areas of expertise. These included economist Howard Ruff (1930–2016), who prodded people to invest in gold, silver, and other hard valuables, and USMC pistol expert John "Jeff" Cooper (1920–2006), who focused on defending your home or bunker against small-arms fire; but it would be generalist *homesteader* Donald E. Sisco (b.1932) who named the burgeoning movement from its fringes via his newsletter, *The Survivor*, as well as his much-sought-after *Granddad's Wonderful Book of . . .* series and *The Poor Man's James Bond* series of—you bet!—self-published books, written under the pseudonym "Kurt Saxon."

6. As with many other subcultures, survivalists have developed their own specialized military-inspired abbreviations jargon, including BOB ("Bug-out bag," containing everything needed to leave home during an emergency); EDC ("Everyday carry"); G.O.O.D.("Get out of Dodge," as in leaving town); YOYO ("You're on Your Own"); and the quaint TEOTWAWKI ("The end of the world as we know it"). On a humorous note, unprepared and in-denial people are often referred to as "zombies" and "pollyannas," respectively.

7. Purchasing and stocking up a convenient BOL ("bug-out location") is considered an integral part of survivalist preparedness. These refuges, ranging from urban safehouses or shelters to rural *retreats*, have to be self-sufficient and easy to either defend or escape from should the need for evasion arise.

8. If Cold War nuclear holocaust fears fueled survivalism during the 1980s, and the Y2K "computer-bug" scare did so in the late 1990s, terrorism, global warming, and pandemic disease have given the subculture a renewed push and global adherents during the first two decades of the twenty-first century. With renewed interest, however, comes heightened scrutiny both from the media and the government, an unholy complex which has painted survivalists as a whole as "extremists" prone to domestic terrorism.

9. Survival has been portrayed in fiction since ancient times. Eighth-century BC *The Odyssey* isn't just a "hero's journey" but one of the earliest stories of survival at sea, while Daniel Defoe's (c.1660–1731) *Robinson Crusoe* a thousand years later would set the "lone survivor" template, somewhat followed by mid-twentieth-century authors George R. Stewart (1895–1980) and Richard Matheson (1926–2013) on *Earth Abides* (1949) and *I Am Legend* (1954) respectively. On the silver screen, no other production would capture the survival zeitgeist than *First Blood* (1982), based on the 1972 novel by David Morrell of the same title, which would kick-start the whole "Rambo" franchise. A year later, *The Survivors* (1983) would go a step further by painting an unflattering picture of the survivalist movement as a whole. Long stepping up where the movies left off, television would later bring survivalism to the forefront with popular shows like LOST (2004–2010), and the enormously successful *Doomsday Preppers* (2011–2014).

BONUS FACTS

In addition to being embroiled in the abduction and rape of a Mormon missionary (the infamous "Manacled Mormon Case") in 1977, stalking the same man in 1984, and cloning her pit-bull dog in 2008, former Miss Wyoming, and all-around tabloid queen Joyce Bernann McKinney (b.1949) was charged with the vehicular manslaughter (hit and run) of Holocaust-survivor Gennady Bolotsky (1928–2019) in 2019.

Delight led to astonishment when American novelist Anne Parrish (1888–1957) found an old edition of *Jack Frost and Other Stories* while perusing secondhand books in the stalls along the Seine (Paris, France) and it turned out to be her own childhood copy of that book.

Richard Nixon (1913 – 1994) had mad music skills, excelling at five different instruments—piano, saxophone, clarinet, accordion, and violin!

In 2021, an unused 1936 *The Blue Lotus* graphic novel cover illustration by Herge (born Georges Remi; 1907 – 1983) was sold at auction $3,100,000.

Invented in 1938 by Sylvan Nathan Goldman (1898–1984) to induce bigger sales, the shopping cart was initially rejected by his store customers.

EVEREADY

Perhaps it's time to remind everyone of FEMA's Emergency Supply List (www.ready.gov), if only to be on the safe side, and keep a BOB readily available for a quick escape ...

- **Water:** one gallon of water per person per day for at least three days, for drinking and sanitation
- **Food:** at least a three-day supply of non-perishable food
- **Battery-powered or hand crank radio**, and a NOAA Weather Radio with tone alert and extra batteries for both
- **Flashlight** and extra batteries
- **First aid kit**
- **Whistle** to signal for help
- **Dust mask**, to help filter contaminated air and plastic
- **Sheeting** and **duct tape** to shelter-in-place
- **Moist towelettes**, **garbage bags**, and **plastic ties** for personal sanitation
- **Wrench** or **pliers** to turn off utilities
- **Can opener** for food (if kit contains canned food)
- Local **maps**
- Prescription **medications** and **glasses**
- Infant **formula** and **diapers**
- **Pet food** and **extra water** for your pet
- Important family **documents** such as copies

of insurance policies, identification, and bank account records in a waterproof, portable container

- **Cash** or **traveler's checks** and **change**
- **Sleeping bag** or **warm blanket** for each person
- Complete **change of clothing** including a long-sleeved shirt, long pants and sturdy shoes
- Household **chlorine bleach** and **medicine dropper**—when diluted nine parts water to one part bleach, bleach can be used as a disinfectant. Or in an emergency, you can use it to treat water by using sixteen drops of regular household liquid bleach per gallon of water. Do not use scented, color safe, or bleaches with added cleaners.
- **Fire extinguisher**
- **Matches** in a waterproof container
- **Feminine supplies** and personal hygiene items
- **Mess kits, paper cups, plates** and **plastic utensils, paper towels**
- **Paper** and **pencil**
- **Books, games, puzzles** or other activities*

*Author's note: I swear I did not make this up, but if you're searching for puzzle books, look no farther than page 472!

THE PLACE NOT TO BE

According to the US Army, the 120 American towns at most risk for an NBC attack—that's nuclear, biological, and chemical, folks, not Will & Grace reruns—are:

Akron, OH	Dayton, OH
Amarillo, TX	Denver, CO
Albuquerque, NM	Des Moines, IA
Anaheim, CA	Detroit, MI
Anchorage, AK	El Paso, TX
Arlington, TX	Fort Lauderdale, FL
Arlington, VA	Fort Wayne, IN
Atlanta, GA	Fort Worth, TX
Aurora, CO	Freemont, CA
Austin, TX	Fresno, CA
Bakersfield, CA	Garland, TX
Baltimore, MD	Glendale, CA
Baton Rouge, LA	Glendale, AZ
Birmingham, AL	Grand Rapids, MI
Boston, MA	Greensboro, NC
Buffalo, NY	Hialeah, FL
Charlotte, NC	Honolulu, HI
Chattanooga, TN	Houston, TX
Chesapeake, VA	Huntington Beach, CA
Chicago, IL	Huntsville, AL
Cincinnati, OH	Indianapolis, IN
Cleveland, OH	Irving, TX
Colorado Springs, CO	Jackson, MS
Columbus, OH	Jacksonville, FL
Columbus, GA	Jersey City, NJ
Corpus Christi, TX	Kansas City, MO
Dallas, TX	Kansas City, KS

Knoxville, TN
Las Vegas, NV
Lexington-Fayette, KY
Lincoln, NE
Little Rock, AR
Long Beach, CA
Los Angeles, CA
Louisville, KY
Lubbock, TX
Madison, WI
Memphis, TN
Mesa, AZ
Metairie, LA
Miami, FL
Milwaukee, WI
Minneapolis, MN
Mobile, AL
Modesto, CA
Montgomery, AL
Nashville, TN
New Orleans, LA
New York, NY
Newark, NJ
Newport News, VA
Norfolk, VA
Oakland, CA
Oklahoma City, OK
Omaha, NE
Orlando, FL
Philadelphia, PA
Phoenix, AZ
Pittsburgh, PA
Portland, OR
Providence, RI

Raleigh, NC
Richmond, VA
Riverside, CA
Rochester, NY
Sacramento, CA
Salt Lake City, UT
San Antonio, TX
San Bernardino, CA
San Diego, CA
San Francisco, CA
San Jose, CA
Santa Ana, CA
Seattle, WA
Shreveport, LA
Spokane, WA
Springfield, MA
St. Louis, MO
St. Paul, MN
St. Petersburg, FL
Stockton, CA
Syracuse, NY
Tacoma, WA
Tampa, FL
Toledo, OH
Tucson, AZ
Tulsa, OK
Virginia Beach, VA
Warren, MI
Washington, DC
Wichita, KS
Worcester, MA
Yonkers, NY

STEAL LIKE A HIPPIE

If you think survivalism is just for extreme right-wingers, think again. Abbie Hoffman (1936–1989) was a hero of the hippie counterculture who achieved notoriety as the most vocal of the "Chicago Seven," and yet, somehow managed to write not one but two of the best inner-city survival guides ever, Fuck the System (1967), and Steal This Book (1971). Short of reading the latter, the following quotes should give a—yes, free—glimpse into Mr. Hoffman's own heart.

Politics:
"Smoking dope and hanging up Che's picture is no more a commitment than drinking milk and collecting postage stamps."

"I think we are constantly faced with the same decision. The decision to be blindly obedient to authority versus the decision to try and change things by fighting the powers that be is always, throughout history, the only decision."

"You are talking to a leftist. I believe in the redistribution of wealth and power in the world. I believe in universal hospital care for everyone. I believe that we should not have a single homeless person in the richest country in the world. And I believe that we should not have a CIA that goes around overwhelming governments and assassinating political leaders, working for tight oligarchies around the world to protect the tight oligarchy here at home."

Free Stuff:

"A&P stores clean their vegetable bins every day at 9:00 A.M. They always throw out cartons of very good vegetables. Tell them you want to feed your rabbits. Also recommended is picking up food in a supermarket and eating it before you leave the store. This method is a lot safer than the customary shoplifting. In order to be prosecuted for shoplifting you have to leave the store with the goods. If you have eaten it there is no evidence to be used against you."

"Self-service restaurants are usually good places to cop things like mustard, ketchup, salt, sugar, toilet paper, silverware and cups for home use. Bring an empty school bag and load up after you've cased the joint."

" . . . consider demolition and construction sites as a good source for building materials to construct furniture. The large wooden cable spools make great tables. Cinderblocks, bricks and boards for bookcases. Doors for tables. Nail kegs for stools and chairs."

Panhandling:

"Panhandling nets some people up to twenty dollars a day. The best places are Third Avenue in the fifties and the Theater District off Times Square. Both best in the evening on weekends. Uptown guys with dates are the best touch especially if they are just leaving some guilt movie like *Guess Who's Coming to Dinner?*"

"Panhandle at the rectories and nunneries on the side of every Catholic Church. Contrary to rumor the brother and sister freeloaders in black live very well and will always share something with a fellow panhandler."

"If you notice people moving from an apartment or house, ask them if they'll be leaving behind clothing. They usually abandon all sorts of items including food, furniture and books. Offer to help them carry out stuff if you can keep what they won't be taking."

Writing:
"Structure is more important than content in the transmission of information."

"If you don't like the news, why not go out and make your own? Creating free media depends to a large extent on your imagination and ability to follow through on ideas."

"It's embarrassing when you try to overthrow the government and you wind up on the Best Seller's List."

BONUS QUOTE

"We have convictions only if we have studied nothing thoroughly."
—Emil Cioran

SUCKERS

The ultimate survivors, as part of mankind's oral tradition since time immemorial, vampires have come a long way since, from the depressing reanimated corpses of yesteryear to the cultured, sexy vampires of today, to … a whole subculture of people actually pretending to be them!

1. Revenants (from the Old French *revenant*, meaning "returning") come in all shapes, attitudes, and sizes. Mesopotamian chimera Lamashtu had the head of a lioness, the body of a donkey, and bird talons, and was known for stealing babies in order to suck their blood and eat their flesh raw down to the bone. Only monkey-faced demigod Pazuzu would defend newborns from this threat (which, if you have seen *The Exorcist*, proves how Hollywood cares not for accuracy).

2. Meanwhile in Greece, Polyphonte and her sons, Agrios and Oreios, were transformed into bloodthirsty *strix* creatures as punishment for their cannibalism. Around the world, in south-east Asia, the Philipino *manananggal* is the bat-winged severed torso of a woman with fangs who sucks the blood of the sleeping, while the Malay *penanggal* does the same, only as a floating, severed head with dangling entrails—yuk!

3. However, it would be in plague-ravaged eleventh-century Eastern Europe where the reanimated, nocturnal, shape-shifting, contagious vampires (partly influenced by the Scandinavian *daugr* undead) we know today came into existence, leading to mass collective hysteria and impromptu exhumations of suspected vampires during the 1720s. The investigations that followed would be collected in the bestselling, if long-titled 1751 *Traité sur les apparitions des esprits et sur les vampires ou les revenans de Hongrie, de Moravie, & c.* ("Treatise on the Apparitions of Spirits and on Vampires or Revenants of Hungary, Moravia, et al") by noted eighteenth-century Bible scholar and author Abbot Antoine Calmet (1672–1757), which provided all the research fodder many a western European writer of popular fiction would need to conjure his own vampires.

4. Starting with *The Vampyre* (1819) by John Polidori (1795–1821), which introduced romance and erotica elements into the vampire myth *and* the English-speaking public, Victorian readers couldn't get enough of the mysterious bloodsucking monsters of Eastern folklore. Popular "penny dreadful" series *Varney the Vampire* (1847), as well as lesbian vampire tale *Carmilla* (1872) would keep the blood of the genre pumping, until the advent of the definitive vampire masterpiece, *Dracula* (1897), by Irishman Bram Stoker (1847–1912), a full-time theater manager and part-time writer.

5. Modern even by our standards, and not only due to its provocative undertones of sex, blood, and death (there is no evidence the character itself was ever based on Vlad "the Impaler" Tepes III; 1428–1476), *Dracula* is an epistolary novel, meaning it purports to be a collection of letters, diary entries, newspaper articles, and other documents which, like a literary "found footage" film, not only gives it an air of plausibility, but also sways the reader's mind into assembling the narrative by itself.

6. Despite its novelty, *Dracula* would have faded into relative obscurity had it not been brought back under the spotlight well after its author's passing, thanks to a copyright infringement lawsuit brought against Prana Film by Stoker's widow, Florence Balcombe (1858–1937), for making the—unofficial—adaptation of her husband's novel, *Nosferatu, eine Symphonie des Grauens* (1922). Balcombe did more than force Prana into bankruptcy, she also preemptively tasked family friend Hamilton Deane (1880–1958) with creating a stage version. It would be the latter's 1927 Broadway production and its 1931 Hollywood "talkie" film adaptation—shot simultaneously in English and Spanish—that ensured everlasting life not only for Dracula and its author, but also Hungarian actor Bela Lugosi (1882–1956), who would be typecast into similar roles until his death.

7. Without Dracula, we wouldn't have any of the vampire fiction that followed—not even the *Buffy, the Vampire Slayer* franchise! Without Lugosi's seductive charm, on the other hand, there would be no *Interview with the Vampire* (1976) by Anne Rice (b.1941), nor any of the darkly sexy fiction *Interview* inspired the following decades, be it HBO's *True Blood* (2008–2014), the *Twilight* (2008) film series, or even *Fifty Shades of Gray* (2015). Of course, the grisly *Nosferatu* also had its modern children, namely *'Salem's Lot* (1975) by Stephen King (b.1947), and *The Strain* (2009) by Guillermo del Toro (b.1964) and Chuck Hogan (b.1967), both of which were ostensibly adapted to television.

8. Both stemming from and overlapping with *goth*, BDSM, and *otherkin* subcultures, *vampyre lifestyle* adherents take their obsession with the genre a bit too far, by pretending to be actual vampires (or rather, their sexy iteration) and living as such, coffin naps and nightly blood-drinking orgies included! Not unlike the Real Life Superhero movement, these cosplaying *vampyres* go off the rails too, finding their own "Fodors" and "McCaslins" along the way.

9. In an early example of what the *vampyre lifestyle* delusion leads to, with the help of four neo-Feminist friends, Tracey Wigginton (b.1965), the infamous "Lesbian Vampire Killer," lured a drunk middle-aged Australian councilman from a bar to a nearby park, where she stabbed him twenty-seven times, chopping his head off in order to drink his blood. Convicted alongside three of her friends, Wigginton was unfortunately released in 2012.

10. Albert "Jonathon Tepes" Sharkey (b.1964), is a former professional wrestler and self-professed *Satanist*, who became known for embracing the lifestyle, dressing for the part, drinking pig and cow blood, and, unsurprisingly, harassing teenage girls. The latter earned Sharkey a number of restraining orders from concerned parents, but apparently didn't prevent him from repeatedly running on congressional, gubernatorial, and even presidential elections. He was also the subject of a Secret Service investigation after claiming his desire to impale then-president George W. Bush (b.1946), but it would be similar threats made to an Indiana judge, as well as the discovery of the rifles and wooden spikes he had amassed to carry them out, that finally got him jailed ... for a while.

11. Luke Woodham (b.1981) was a disciple of The Kroth, a "vampire clan" (misreported as a "satanic cult") founded by double-murderer Rod Ferrell (b.1980). In 1997 he gathered his "courage" and tortured his dog "Sparkle" to death, then fatally bludgeoned and stabbed his mother before driving in her Toyota to Pearl High School in Mississippi, where the black trench coat-wearing *vampyre* teen gunned down his ex-girlfriend and another teen and wounded several others. Detained at gunpoint by the school principal, he was trialed, and is currently serving three life terms plus an additional 140 years in prison.

12. Fresno's own paraphilic mass-murderer, Marcus "Vampire Jesus" Wesson (b.1946), subjected his entire family to the *vampyre* lifestyle, including rape and sleeping in coffins, before a standoff with the police resulted in this real-life monster's 2004 arrest after executing several of his young children in cold blood. Convicted of nine counts of murder and fourteen counts of rape, Wesson was sentenced to death in 2005, and currently awaits the stake—*that would be fitting, wouldn't it?*—at San Quentin.

13. A year after Wesson's conviction, a gruesome crime shook the province of Alberta, in Canada. The murder of Marc Richardson, his wife Debra, and their eight-year-old son Tyler Jacob was soon pinned on their twelve-year-old daughter Jasmine, who planned the massacre in order to run away with her beau, Jackson May (born Jeremy Steinke; b. 1983), a *vampyre* lifestyle follower (he claimed to be 300 years old and drink blood, but some news outlets described him as a wannabe "werewolf" instead). Presumably "rehabilitated," Richardson was fully released from psychiatric care in 2016, while May sits in prison still, serving three life sentences, but could be eligible for parole in four years.

BONUS QUOTE

"Don't be so humble—you're not that great."
—Golda Meir

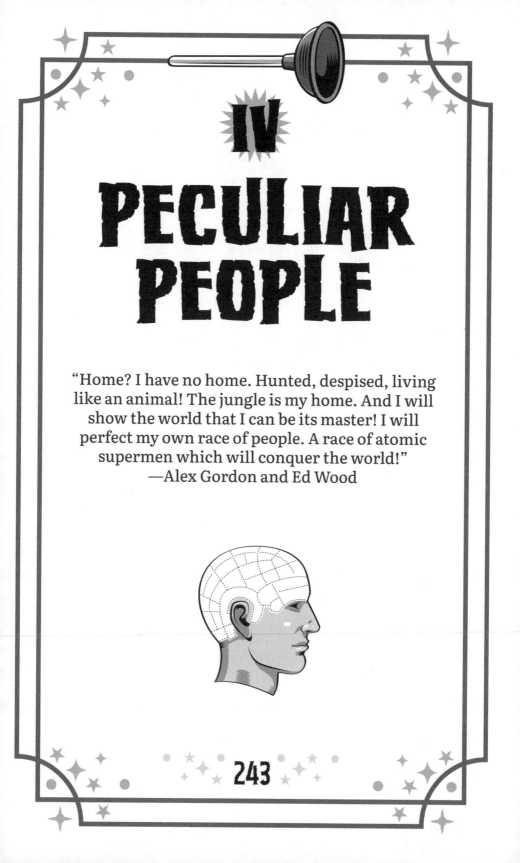

IV

PECULIAR PEOPLE

"Home? I have no home. Hunted, despised, living like an animal! The jungle is my home. And I will show the world that I can be its master! I will perfect my own race of people. A race of atomic supermen which will conquer the world!"
—Alex Gordon and Ed Wood

THE KATZENJAMMER KIDS

Pure evil has to start somewhere. For some it begins as early as the cradle, with the first temper tantrums. For others it's a work in progress which reveals their sadistic nature gradually until they reach their early teens and decide to put their dark thoughts in action. While for the most part child protection laws ensure underage killers remain largely unnamed worldwide, let's have a look at those who, for one reason or another, have been identified.

Carl Newton Mahan (1922–1958): At six, he gunned down his friend, eight-year-old Cecil Van Hoose, over a piece of scrap metal, and got a fifteen-year sentence—things were different back then—but was acquitted on appeal on account of his young age, and a press campaign carefully designed to make "sweet pea" look as cute and innocent as possible.

Amardeep Sada (b.1998): Arrested at eight, this "cheese weasel" got his killer groove on by strangling his baby sister to death as well as two other babies. Tried and sentenced to three years at a juvenile prison, presumably followed by being institutionalized for a while, but India being the chaotic melting pot it is, it is safe to assume Amardeep is now free, and—hopefully—finds himself working as a software developer now.

Peter Barratt (1855-?) and James Bradley (1855–1920): One hundred and thirty-two years before Jon Venables (b.1982) and Robert Thompson (b.1982) committed a similar crime, these eight-year-old truants savagely beat and drowned a two-year-old named George Burgess. Convicted to one year in prison for manslaughter, and a five-year reformatory stint, they were never heard from again.

Carroll Edward Cole (1938–1985): Starting young at age eight, by drowning a school mate and getting away with it, fifteen strangled women later this irredeemable American sociopath was finally caught, convicted, and executed by lethal injection in 1985.

Kyle Alwood (b.2010): In 2019, this little firecracker allegedly set his family's Woodford County mobile home on fire, smoking five people to death (grandmother Kathryn Murray, sixty-nine; his mother's fiancé Jason Wall, thirty-four; and children Rose Alwood, Daemeon Wall, and Ariel Wall, all under three years of age). Charged with first-degree murder and aggravated arson, he was declared unfit for trial in 2020; news media outlets seemingly lost interest in the case.

Cayetano Santos Godino (1896–1944): The infamous *Petiso Orejudo* who scared the daylights out of Buenos Aires in his teens got off to an early start. As a toddler he would kill cats and birds for fun, throw babies into ditches or stone them, but would often be caught in the act by the police. By the time he was ten, however, "little cookie ears" killed his first victim, three-year-old Maria Rosa Face by burying her alive. Her body was never found. By the time Godino was fifteen, he had brutally killed three other kids before being arrested and sent to a reformatory and then to prison ... where he proceeded to kill his fellow inmates' pet cats.

Jon Venables (b.1982) and Robert Thompson (b.1982): In 1993 then-ten-year-old truants Venables and Thompson kidnapped two-year-old James Patrick Bulger (1990–1993) from a shopping mall in Britain. After taking him around town, they tortured and sexually abused the little boy (nobody knows which of the forty-two gruesome injuries caused the child's untimely death), before dropping his corpse across the railway tracks where a coming train chopped it in half. Found guilty and sentenced to fifteen years of juvenile detention, they were finally given new identities and released earlier in 2001. Now a man, Venables has since been arrested twice, in 2010 and 2017, for possession and distribution of child pornography, while Thompson has basically vanished from the public eye.

Mary Bell (b.1957): Yet another British "angel face," Bell celebrated her impending eleventh birthday by strangling a four-year-old boy, followed by the murder of a three-year-old boy she carved her initials on with scissors. In-and-out of institutions until the age of twenty-three, and pursued by tabloids since, Bell finally won a 2003 court battle for her and her daughter to remain anonymous.

Jesse Pomeroy (1859–1932): With two confirmed kills, and suspected of at least another nine, Pomeroy astounded the people of Massachusetts as its youngest killer (he had begun his "career" at eleven), not unlike Argentina's own *Petiso Orejudo*. Arrested, trialed, and sentenced to death at fourteen, his sentence was commuted to life in solitary confinement, finally dying a frail, old man at the Bridgewater Hospital for the Criminally Insane in 1932.

Christopher Pittman (b.1989): Driven manic by a sudden change in his prescribed antidepressants, in 2001 twelve-year-old Pittman shot both his grandparents, stole their car, and ran away in a frenzy. Caught two counties away, he confessed, and was finally trialed as an adult three years later, given thirty years to life in prison. His sentence commuted to twenty-five years after a plea-bargain; he will be released in 2023.

It would take an entire book to list all unrepentant "underage" fiends aged thirteen and up, from the Hamamatsu Deaf Killer, Seisaku Nakamura (1924–1943), to Pedrinho "Matador" Rodrigues (b.1954). Suffice it to say, juvenile delinquency laws need a serious upgrade worldwide that forcefully punishes violent teenage crime, while keeping those same teens segregated from hardened criminals.

SITTING DUCKS

Either educating future sociopaths, or offering plenty of opportunities for terrorist target practice, nothing beats a school massacre, the top ten of which are listed by body count below.

10. Virginia Tech (2007): Wielding two semi-automatic pistols— a Walther P22 and a Glock 19—troubled student South Korean Seung-Hui Cho (1984-2007) killed thirty-two fellow students and injured seventeen others before taking his own life in what has been deemed the deadliest school shooting in US history.

9. Yobe State Secondary School (2013): The first attack by the infamous Boko Haram Islamic insurgency came on June 16, killing seven children, two teachers, and two soldiers guarding this public high school in Mamudo, Nigeria. The next day, the militants came back and shot nine students who were taking exams. On July 4, another attack murdered the school headmaster and his family. Two days later a new raid killed at least forty-two people, between students and staff. One hundred students also went missing that day.

8. Bath Consolidated School (1927): Schools became a target for psychos early in American history, with this massacre perpetrated by mass murderer Andrew P. Kehoe (1872–1927). Upon losing reelection as treasurer of the Bath Township,

Michigan, school board, with his wife terminally ill from tuberculosis, and about to see his farm foreclosed, Mr. Kehoe simultaneously bombed the school, shot his wife, and firebombed his property. Then he drove his dynamite-rigged, shrapnel-filled truck to the site of the school explosions and detonated it, killing himself and four rescuers, for a total of forty-five deaths (thirty-eight of which were schoolchildren), and fifty-eight injured.

7. Thammasat University (1976): Thailand's "October 6 event" saw that country's police crack down on left-wing demonstrators at Thammasat University with extreme prejudice. According to official reports, forty-six leftists were lynched, and another 167 were alternatively assaulted, sexually abused, shot, and burned alive, by police, right-wing militias, and even bystanders. With over three thousand people arrested on campus, the country would soon sink back into military rule during the following decades.

6. Kyanguli Secondary School (2001): Burning their school dormitory and its occupants to the ground, teenage students Davis Onyango Opiyo and Felix Mambo Ngumbao used arson and a padlocked main door to accomplish the killing of sixty-seven of their schoolmates, in an incident since remembered in Kenya as the Kyanguli Fire Tragedy. While Opiyo and Ngumbao were both given life sentences, the school principal and his deputy were also given jail time, eight months each, for failing to prevent the fire. Families of the sixty-seven dead kids were compensated financially by the state, but the crime remains a senseless one.

5. Garissa University College (2015): Another Kenyan school massacre, this one was carried out by four Islamic extremists belonging to Al-Shabaab, an Al-Qaeda splinter group, which took responsibility for the planning and execution of the attack. Taking hundreds of students hostage, they went shooting those identifying as Christians, until 142 students and three staff members were dead. Security forces finally surrounded and killed the men, but three soldiers also died in the ensuing shootout.

4. Army Public School (2014): The year before the Garissa University Islamist attack was carried out, another radical Muslim group, the TTP (Tehrik-i-Taliban Pakistan), entered this school in Peshawar, Pakistan, killing a total of 149 people, including 132 young schoolchildren, before Pakistani special forces took them down and rescued almost a thousand survivors.

3. Eastern University (1990): The Vantharumoolai campus massacre was genocidal attack carried out by the Sri Lankan Army. It saw 158 minority Sri Lankan Tamil refugees between the ages of twelve and forty arrested on campus grounds, then brought to a military camp where they subsequently "disappeared" in a state-sanctioned act of mass murder that remains unpunished.

2. Walisongo School (2000): Part of the violent Poso riots between Indonesian Christians and Muslims taking place from 1998 to 2000, this particular bloodbath took place when Christian militias surrounded the Javanese cacao farming village of Sintuwu Lemba. After cutting the power, they proceeded to raid homes and alternatively shoot, hack, torch, or rape everybody in sight, including the seventy teens and adults who took refuge in the town's boarding school. Between 165 and 191 people were killed before the Army sent in 2,200 soldiers to battle and subdue the militia, capturing its leaders, who were tried and executed by a firing squad six years later.

1. School Number One (2004): When an unknown group of Muslim Chechen separatists occupied this school in Beslan, North Ossetia (Russian Federation), taking 1,100 people hostage, the majority of which were children, the ensuing battle with Russian security forces left 385 dead, including 186 children, in what is considered the deadliest school shooting in modern history. According to the UN another 753 people were injured, with many children left permanently disabled. Chechen guerilla commander Shamil Basayev (1965–2006), who claimed responsibility for organizing the attack, was killed two years later during an arms deal gone wrong. Two other ranking members of Basayev's militia were also killed, while another two were eventually captured and imprisoned.

WE DON'T NEED NO EDUCATION

It should come as no surprise that every country has its share of low-performance schools, nor that the worst school systems can be found in Third World countries, but what about those schools that don't even try to match any standard academic criteria?

Charming School: Instead of being taught sight-words, young children of the nomadic Indian tribe of Vadi are traditionally taught the far more dangerous art of snake charming between ages two and twelve. At first, both boys and girls learn to play with and around cobras, but then the boys are taught to play snake-charming flute music, while girls learn to handle and care for the snakes on the side, as snake charming is usually a family affair, with strictly divided labor.

Elf School: Álfaskólinn, the Icelandic Elf School is a Reykjavík-based organization established in 1991 by founder and director Magnús Skarphédinsson (b.1982), a former artist, musician, and ufologist. Offering borderline-fraudulent lectures and guided tours about Icelandic folklore, including the different kinds of conveniently "hidden" elves that over half the Icelandic population believe inhabit their sparsely populated island, Skarphédinsson also teaches "aura readings" and "past-life explorations" to the spiritually adventurous and affluent tourist.

Santa School: Surprisingly unrelated to the Elf School, the Charles H. Howard Santa Claus School was founded in 1937. A farmer who portrayed Santa in department stores and parades as a seasonal job, Howard (1896–1966) saw a need to train better Santas, starting the school at his home in Albion, New York. Currently run by International Santa Claus Hall of Fame—yes, that's actually a thing—inductee Tom Valent and his wife Holly in Midland, Michigan, the school trains an average of three hundred Santas per year.

Witch School: Teaching Wicca, Paganism, Divinatory Arts, and the like to 240,000 students since 2003, this school with campuses in Illinois and, appropriately, Salem, Massachusetts, was founded by self-styled "Reverend" Edward Hubbard—wait, *Hubbard*?!— a con-man who, at best, scams people into courses in esoterica or, at worst, flirts with Satanism, all the while playing victim to "religious intolerance."

Parkour School: Founded by the creator of free running, Sébastien Foucan (b.1974), it teaches future *traceurs* (free runners) the basics of this discipline which combines military obstacle course training and martial arts to find a person's way fluidly through any environment ... which sounds very cool until we find out about the many, many gruesome deaths of free runners since the fad began.

Marriage School: Established in Tokyo, Japan, in 2010, a thriving Infini School offers classes that will turn anyone into eligible marriage material. This includes those having trouble finding a suitable partner, or being found as one, as well as current brides and grooms looking to impress their future spouses and in-laws. For two hundred thousand yen, students go out on simulated dates, to be instructed into matters related to wardrobe, posture, and even the way to cross your legs in a given social setting.

Hooking School: APROSEX, the Spanish government-funded *Asociación de Profesionales Sexuales* (Sex Workers Union) based in Barcelona offers affordable "intensive" courses in prostitution open to men, women, and trans people. These include marketing, and foreign language lessons since 2012. No wonder an estimated four hundred thousand people in Spain currently dedicate themselves to "the world's oldest profession!"

BONUS FACT

Bullying at school and the harassment of *Star Wars* fans and the press due to his role as a child Anakin Skywalker (the future Darth Vader) in prequel film *The Phantom Menace* (1999) drove Jake Lloyd (b.1989) not only to quickly quit acting in 2001, but sadly also into paranoid schizophrenia.

IT TAKES A VILLAGE

Fiction, of course, presents us with a great variety of evil in addition to reality's run-of-the-mill underage serial killers. According to Grady Hendrix's modern classic Paperbacks from Hell: The Twisted History of '70s and '80s Horror Fiction (2017), the most common types include:

Slow-growing adults: Benjamin Button (*The Curious Case of Benjamin Button*; 2008) and Oskar Matzerath (*The Tin Drum*; 1979) notwithstanding, this category includes crafty midgets like North Korean terrorist "Pygmy" in the eponymous 2009 novel by Chuck Palahniuk (b.1962); and Esther from the film *Orphan* (2009), which was partly inspired by the strange story of Ukranian teen Natalia Grace Barnett (b.2003). Due to her dwarfism, Natalia's adoptive American parents came to believe she was much older than she claimed, and ended up frightfully fleeing to Canada without her.

Chemically altered: Referring not only to chemicals, but also the victims of radioactive and genetic tampering; in essence, not the product of anything "supernatural" as we understand it. As Hendrix puts it, " . . . should be destroyed immediately because they cannot be reformed." The murderous mutant babies in Larry Cohen's *It's Alive* (1974) saga is a prime example of the category, and so is cult-film *The Children* (1980), with its irradiated, black fingernailed, school bus zombies.

Possessed: *The Exorcist*—both the 1971 novel by William Peter Blatty (1928–2017), and the 1973 film adaptation by William Friedkin (b.1935)—pretty much defined this particular evil children subset with its many sequels and prequels, not to mention countless knock-offs of lesser quality, with perhaps one notable exception: *Hereditary* (2018), a disturbing, gut-wrenching film that took all of the genre's cliches and turned them on its collective 180-degree-twisted head.

Not possessed, but certainly *perverted* by a demonic presence lurking in the cornfields—"He Who Walks Among the Rows"—Isaac, Malachi, and their minions ritually murder adults around Gatlin, Nebraska, in Stephen King's *Children of the Corn* (1984).

Reincarnated: If you're thinking *Chances Are* (1989) or *Kundun* (1997), think again. In a template set by the 1898 novella *The Turn of the Screw* by Henry James (1843–1913), incestuous duo Miles and Flora may be controlled by two dead servants—or it may all be in the head of their increasingly hysterical governess! *Screw* found a more than dignified big screen adaptation in *The Innocents* (1961). Far more innocently, *Audrey Rose* (1975) and its 1982 sequel, *For Love of Audrey Rose*, both by Frank Paul De Felitta (1921–2016), dealt with Audrey reincarnating into the body of another girl, Ivy, which makes her more unnerving than evil. With no place for 1970s subtlety, however, modern film *The Prodigy* (2019) sees newborn Miles being gradually and irreversibly taken over by a dead Hungarian criminal.

Poorly parented: These are all textbook cases for "sparing the rod" on the wrong child, which leads to some very spoiled munchkins, as budding psychopaths Rhoda Penmark (*The Bad Seed*; 1954), Frank Cauldhame (*The Wasp Factory*; 1984), Joffrey Baratheon (*A Game of Thrones*; 1991), and Kevin Khatchadourian (*We Need to Talk About Kevin*; 2003) remind us both in print and on the screen.

Violent for no good reason: Sometimes neither the parents nor the school system can be blamed for a child's wicked ways, and even Satan wouldn't want to take credit for William Golding's wild Jack Merridew (*The Lord of the Flies*; 1954), Doris Lessing's troublesome Ben Lovatt (*The Fifth Child*; 1988), or Ian McEwan's truly wicked Henry Evans (*The Good Son*; 1993).

Gifted with psychic powers: If innocence and powerlessness are children's traits, what happens when they suddenly find themselves wielding enormous power? Actor-turned-writer Thomas Tryon's (1926–1991) debut novel *The Other* (1971) explores the issue when identical twins Holland and Niles Perry discover the power to psychically inhabit other creatures. Following in Bram Stoker's *Dracula* stylistic footsteps, Stephen King's 1974 epistolary novel *Carrie* (and its subsequent adaptations) revolves around Carrie White, a bullied high-school girl with the power of telekinesis, which she uses to indiscriminately exact revenge on anybody and everybody that crosses her path (and some who don't).

Two years later, Spanish horror movie *¿Quién puede matar a un niño?* (*Who Can Kill a Child?*; 1976) filled an entire island with telepathic children bent on destroying mankind. In a town of their own, the mind-reading alien children of *The Midwich Cuckoos* (1957), a novel by British novelist John Wyndham (1903–1969), were just incapable of human feelings. This book was adapted to film twice—in 1960 and 1995—as the unforgettable *The Village of the Damned*.

Satan spawn: When the devil decides to sire a kid all hell ensues, as well proven by Damien Thorn's antics, a silent-but-deadly Antichrist in the making we see grow up—satanic Rottweilers and nannies in tow—throughout *The Omen* (1976), and its many sequels. Unfortunately, no movie or book dealing with Satan's usually neglected or left for adoption offspring could ever escape the template set by *The Omen*, but at least one tried to subvert it. Netflix's *Little Evil* (2017) went beyond a mere spoofing of the original, to pit nature versus nurture, and make a point in favor of the latter.

BONUS QUOTES

"If they can make penicillin out of moldy bread, they sure can make something out of you."
—Muhammad Ali

"You only die once, but you will be dead for a very long time."
—Molière

WE SHOULD ALL BE MURDERERS

Evil knows no gender, but it certainly has made many a female psycho feel empowered or liberated throughout history.

Countess Elizabeth Báthory de Ecsed (1560–1614): Wielding no political power of her own didn't prevent Countess Báthory from behaving like a tyrant in her own Hungarian fiefdom; in fact, that probably even *motivated* her to become the world's most prolific serial killer between 1590 and 1610. Luring around 650 girls into her castle with job promises, she tortured and killed them instead. Protected by her family from capital punishment, she was imprisoned at the Castle of Csejte, in modern-day Slovakia, where she passed away four years later.

Marie-Madeleine d'Aubray (1630–1676): As opportunistic as they are narcissistic, psychopaths like this French Marquise often *rehearse* on weaker prey, be it animals, children, the elderly, or disabled people. Madame d'Aubray surreptitiously tested her poisons on the Parisian Hôtel Dieu Hospital patients, thirty of which she killed, before trying them on her own father and two brothers in order to inherit their states. She probably never would have been found out, had it not been for a chain of events starting in 1672 with the death of her lover and fellow poisoner, an officer by the name of Godin de Sainte-Croix, who left behind a box filled with incriminating evidence, which ended in the hands of the police. Sending her henchman, a shady character known as Jean Hamelin, a.k.a. *La Chaussée*, to retrieve the box, the police immediately arrested Hamelin, who confessed d'Aubray's involvement in the deaths of her kin. Fleeing to England, and then Belgium, to avoid capture, the Marquise was finally caught in 1676, and sentenced to be beheaded after the customary four-hour torture session. Her death motivated a royal purge, known as the "Affair of the Poisons," which saw a number of prominent French women either executed or exiled on similar charges.

Darya Saltykova (1730–1801): Not content with being heir to proud and ancient Russian nobility and wealth, like Countess Báthory before her, *Saltychikha* decided to become a notorious mass murderer instead, killing around 140 serfs in the process. Going unpunished for a long time on account of her political clout, her luck eventually ran out and she was finally arrested in 1762. Tried and found guilty of the torture and murder of a confirmed thirty-eight girl servants, Saltykova was publicly shamed in a Moscow square, and then imprisoned for the rest of her life in a local convent's cellar.

Hélène Jégado (1803–1852): Another serial poisoner from France, only this time not a noble-woman but a house maid, Madame Jégado discovered the joy of arsenic, which she used to kill an estimated thirty-six people over eighteen years. Her first seven kills were the town priest and his family, as well as Jégado's own sister, all of which were attributed to the cholera outbreak of 1832. Going back to her hometown to replace her recently deceased—by her own hand—sister as caregiver, she killed three elderly people including her aunt. Going from town to town, "The Pious Poisoner" left a trail of corpses, including boarders and employers, as well as their respective families. Caught stealing, she laid low from 1841 to 1851. That's when she came under the roof of French politician Théophile Bidard (1804–1877) and killed two "rival" house maids, their deaths suspicious enough to demand a thorough investigation which eventually led to the woman's death under the guillotine's blade.

Mary Ann Cotton (1832–1873): Putting the "black" next to the "widow," this enterprising Victorian murderess used arsenic to kill her own mother, three of her four husbands (husband #3 became suspicious and divorced her in time), two lovers, and eleven of her thirteen children, in order to collect various inheritances. Found out over an insurance inquest, Cotton was tried and sentenced to hang on March 24, 1873. Due to the rope shortness, however, she slowly choked to death instead of dying instantly from a broken neck.

Belle Gunness (1859–1908): Born Brynhild Paulsdatter Storset, this imposing Norwegian American woman took a page off Cotton's book, poisoning between fourteen and forty people in her lifetime, including two husbands, several of their children, and many suitors she lured to her farm in La Porte, Indiana, via personal ads in the newspaper. She also had a well-known history of arson to collect insurance payouts, and as the net of public suspicion closed in on her, Gunness supposedly killed herself and three of her still-surviving children by setting fire to her farmhouse in 1908 . . . except the headless body that was assumed to be hers didn't quite match the woman's six-foot-tall, two-hundred–pound frame. It should be noted that the ensuing inspection of her scorched property also revealed countless hacked corpses and body parts.

Leonarda Cianciulli (1893–1970): Distraught over the deaths of thirteen of her children (three through miscarriage, the rest to sickness), which she blamed on family curses, the superstitious Signora Cianciulli was determined not to lose her remaining four. Finding her eldest and dearest son, Giuseppe, had enlisted to go to war, she decided to magically keep him safe by any means necessary, and that meant *human sacrifices*. Between 1939 and 1940, la *Saponificatrice di Correggio* ("The Soap-Maker of Correggio") killed three middle-aged women from her neighborhood, turning their remains into soap bars she gifted family and friends with, as well as crunchy tea cakes she fed anyone that came to visit with, *including* Giuseppe. Caught and tried, the unrepentant—after all, her son survived the war, so the magic worked—

Mrs. Cianciulli was finally sentenced to thirty years in prison, and three years in an asylum where she passed away from a brain aneurysm at age seventy-seven.

Ilse Koch (1906–1967): The devious "Witch of Buchenwald" started as a guard and secretary at the Sachsenhausen concentration camp, and soon married her evil soulmate, camp Commandant Karl-Otto Koch (1936–1945). The happy couple would be posted to the Buchenwald death camp, where the Oberaufseherin (female guards chief) Koch and her hubby engaged in all manner of depraved shenanigans, including the wanton torture and murder of prisoners in order to stock their body part "trophies" collection. Apparently, this was too extreme, even by Nazi standards, so the couple was tried and imprisoned by the Reich. Karl-Otto was executed by an SS firing squad before the war was over, while Ilse would taste freedom briefly, only to be jailed again by the Allies in 1945. Given a life sentence, she hanged herself in a cell at age sixty, fifteen years before the release of the Canadian cult film her life inspired, *Ilsa, She Wolf of the SS* (1975).

Irma Ida Ilse Grese (1923–1945): With her cold, defiant stare, Grese quickly became known for her Nazi leather boots, as well as a penchant for prisoner abuse, and gas-chamber executions. Alternatively known during her lifetime as the "Beautiful Beast of Belsen," and the "Hyena of Auschwitz," at fifteen *Frau* Grese became an assistant SS nurse, and worked her way up the sadism ladder to become a full-time concentration camp Rapportführerin (warden) at Auschwitz-Birkenau, Ravensbrück, and Bergen-Belsen. She was trialed and sentenced to be hanged at the young age of twenty-two.

Myra Hindley (1942–2002): Together with her lover, Ian Brady (1938–2017), a young criminal with a Nazi fetish, during the early 1960s "the most evil woman in Britain" raped and killed five children "for the fun of it" (the hellish couple also took sadistic pornographic photos and made audio recordings). Technically, they were trying to accomplish the "perfect crime," and in fact two of their young victims' corpses were found only decades later, after Brady "spilled the beans" to a reporter while serving his three life sentences. Hindley received two of those and, her every appeal denied by courts, died behind bars.

Marybeth Tinning (b.1942): If ever there was a warning against blind-dating, Ms. Tinning would be its poster child. After meeting her husband this way, many children, both biological and adopted, would come shortly afterwards, and then leave this world in quick succession, their deaths attributed to either natural, genetic, or undetermined causes, including the occasional "sudden infant death syndrome." It would only be the passing of four-month-old Tami Lynne in 1985 that rose suspicion of foul play, as the autopsy revealed she had been smothered. The following investigation (which also surfaced a 1974 attempt at lacing her husband's grape juice with barbiturates) would land Ms. Tinning a "twenty years to life" imprisonment conviction over Tami Lynne's death. She was finally released on parole in 2018.

Piedad Martínez del Águila (b.1953): Hailing from Murcia, in south-eastern Spain, this twelve-year-old girl killed four of her younger siblings in quick succession using rat poison, during the first half of the 1960s. When found out, she quickly blamed her mother, but ended up confessing she was tired of helping around her working-class home and wanted to go out and play with her friends, so she decided to drastically "reduce her workload." As a minor, Piedad was consigned to the *Monasterio Para Jóvenes Descarriadas De Las Oblatas De Murcia* (Monastery for Wayward Young Women Of The Oblates Of Murcia), where she professedly found God, took up knitting, finally becoming a cloister nun and vanishing from sight.

Rosemary West (b.1953): Now firmly established as a "British thing," from the late 1960s to the early 1990s, Mrs. West raped, tortured, and killed at least twenty adolescent girls, including her own daughter Heather, working in tandem with her husband Fred (1941–1995). The disappearance of the daughter led to increased scrutiny over the West's lifestyle, the revelation of the couple's depraved acts against their own children (who have repeatedly attempted to kill themselves since), and finally, after Fred's confession, the search for human remains at their 25 Cromwell Street "House of Horrors," exposing what had become of Heather, and many of the couple's victims. Fred killed himself while in custody, but Rose was sentenced to deservedly rot in prison without the possibility of parole.

Beverley Allitt (b.1968): If "angels of mercy" are a category of their own, nurse Allitt deserves a place in its podium. Killing three babies and one eleven-year-old, and attempting to murder another nine children, all via insulin or potassium overdoses (as well as the occasional air bubble injected into the bloodstream). In 1991 she was sentenced to thirteen life sentences for the crimes, but will be eligible for release in 2023.

Griselda Blanco (1943–2012): Born to poverty in Colombia, and quickly turning to crime in order to survive, La Madrina ("The Godmother") would rise among the ranks of the Medellín Cartel, becoming the world's first billionaire female criminal. She set up shop in Miami in the 1980s, where she ruled the cocaine trade with an iron fist and was directly involved in at least two hundred murders, until assassinated while on a trip to her native Colombia in 2012. Though Blanco's real-life exploits would put *Scarface* **(1983) and** *Queen of the South* **(2016–2021) to shame, they also inspired the underrated 2017 film** *Cocaine Godmother*, **starring none other than Catherine Zeta-Jones (b.1969).**

GOOD-NIGHT STORIES FOR EVIL GIRLS

Malevolent and black-hearted fiction has its own female villains we all love to hate, seduced as it may be under their devilish prowess. Despite modern attempts at justifying their evil deeds via trendy prequels, here's some of the most iconic evil women ever created for the screen or the printed page.

Medea of Colchis: It doesn't get any more justifiably evil than this character from ancient Greek myth. The magically gifted daughter of King Aeëtes (she's the granddaughter of sun god Helios) falls for hero Jason, helping him in his quest for the Golden Fleece, and finally marrying the guy and settling in Corinth for a "happy ever after" ending. Well, not according to Greek dramatist Euripides (c.480–406 BC), who expanded the story to show us Jason's infidelity, and Medea's descent into murderous madness, which struck not only Jason's lover, but her own children as well—hell hath no fury like a powerful witch's scorn!

Lady Macbeth: A pivotal character in William Shakespeare's (1564–1616) *Macbeth* (1604) tragedy, she goads her husband, ambitious Scottish general Macbeth, into murdering King Duncan in his sleep, pinning the deed on his servants, and taking the throne for himself. Driven by guilt and paranoia, King Macbeth soon starts murdering those who suspect him of regicide, dragging his wife along in a downward hallucinatory spiral that would finally make her kill herself, mercifully off-stage. The play has been brought innumerable times to other media, meaning there have been equally countless portrayals of the character, including Marion Cotillard's in 2015.

Thérèse Raquin: An Émile Zola (1840–1902) creation for the eponymous serialized novel about this young woman who, tired of her hypochondriac husband and overbearing mother-in-law, starts a fiery love affair with unsuccessful painter Laurent. They will manage to get the husband out of the way via drowning, and get away with it too, but don't get away from their conscience. Like the Macbeths before them, Thérèse and Laurent will both be driven by guilt to their untimely end.

The Wicked Witch of the West: The epitome of evil witches everywhere, the aquaphobic, umbrella-wielding, shoe-obsessed sorceress was created by L. Frank Baum (1856–1919) for his seminal children's novel *The Wonderful Wizard of Oz* (1900). The original stout, pigtailed, and one-eyed appearance would forever be altered by the iconic black-clad, green-skinned, broom-wielding technicolor version, the amazing Margaret Hamilton (1902–1985), in the 1939 film. It would be this version of the Wicked Witch that misguided—and idle—revisionists have sought to "redeem," starting with the 1995 novel *Wicked: The Life and Times of the Wicked Witch of the West*, adapted into a

Broadway musical in 2003, or the 2013 Disney prequel film *Oz the Great and Powerful*.

Phyllis Nirdlinger: Not the original *femme fatale*, but certainly one of the category's most conniving, Phyllis emerged from the pages of 1943 novel *Double Indemnity* by James M. Cain (1892–1977), who, if *The Postman Always Rings Twice* (1934) and *Mildred Pierce* (1941) are any indication, was already an expert on the tropes of the genre. Adapted to film by yet another master of the genre, Raymond Chandler (1888–1959), the *Double Indemnity* movie would give Phyllis a new last name, Dietrichson (played by a ravishing Barbara Stanwyck; 1907–1990), but the same predatory lust.

Cruella de Vil: Presented in the original 1956 novel by Dorothy "Dodie" Smith (1896–1990), *The Hundred and One Dalmatians*, as the spoiled and very rich wife of a furrier, Cruella de Vil is—naturally—obsessed with wearing furs, and will stop at nothing to slaughter and skin all the spotless Dalmatian puppies she needs for a new coat. Turned single by the blockbuster Disney animated film from 1961, the spoiled British socialite would remain set on wearing puppy fur at whatever the cost. Cruella (as played by Glenn Close; b. 1947) would then run the "House of DeVil" *haute couture* firm for the inferior 1996 live action remake, an angle revisited by the 2021 *Cruella* prequel—*that word again!*—starring Emma Stone (b.1988), which presented the character as a sort of misunderstood anti-hero who *rescues* Dalmatians.

Mildred Ratched: Created by writer Ken Kesey (1935–2001) for his 1962 novel *One Flew Over the Cuckoo's Nest*, and unforgettably brought to life in an Academy Award–winning performance by Louise Fletcher (b.1934) for the silver screen, the "Big Nurse" in charge at the Salem State Hospital is as rigid and ruthless as a Nazi camp guard, serving as an allegory of the corrupting influence of institutional power and authority. Recently, a younger and far more twisted version of the character is interpreted by Sarah Paulson (b.1974) on the 2020 Netflix television prequel series *Ratched*.

Joan Crawford: Though film star Joan Crawford (born Lucille Fay LeSueur; c.1900–1977) was a very real—and controversial—Hollywood legend, it was her portrayal through the eyes of her adoptive daughter Christina (b.1939) in her bestselling *Mommy Dearest* 1978 exposé, as well as the splendid 1981 film adaptation starring Faye Dunaway (b.1941), that painted her as the narcissistic, alcoholic, and violent bisexual nympho character we all remember. This revisionist prequel-immune version of Crawford loves children like Cruella de Vil loves her puppies,and watch out for those wire hangers!

Baroness: Being the product of unbridled early 1980s commercialism, which turned Saturday-morning cartoons into half-hour ads for action-figure toylines, doesn't prevent this evil doll, introduced to the G. I. Joe toyline in 1984, from having a rich backstory. Not unlike many entitled college students of today, Anastasia Cisarovna would be radicalized on campus, turning into a full-blown terrorist, under the "Baroness" alias. Working for the Cobra organization, she would stand out for her deadly skills, all wrapped up in a tight black leather outfit that sparked many a young boy's fetishism back in the day. Sienna Miller (b.1981) was cast as Baroness in the live-action G. I. Joe: *The Rise of Cobra* (2009) movie, and the role is set to be reprised by Úrsula Corberó (b.1989) in the 2021 *Snake Eyes* spin-off.

Alex Forrest: Controversial even by today's standards, editor Alexandra "Alex" Forrest (Glenn Close, b.1947) becomes Manhattan lawyer Dan Gallagher's (Michael Douglas; b.1944) worst nightmare after a mutually consensual weekend affair, in the 1987 film *Fatal Attraction*. Refusing to let her lover go, Alex quickly devolves from clingy to psychopathic, harassing Dan at the office before going after his family at home with, er, fatal consequences for the family pet.

Annie Wilkes: This terrifying "angel of death" is the brainchild of horror's grand master Stephen King (b.1947), who brought her to life in the pages of his 1987 novel *Misery*. A serial-killer since early childhood, as her captive favorite novelist, Paul Sheldon, finds out, nurse Annie has killed many of her patients, including eleven children, and Paul is next. The only thing stopping her is the desire to see her favorite character from Sheldon's novels officially resurrected, going at great lengths to keep him writing. In the novel, she chops off Paul's foot and then cauterizes the stump with a blowtorch. In the gut-wrenching 1990 Rob Reiner (b.1947) film adaptation, she opts for a sledgehammer instead. Unforgettably portrayed in an Oscar-winning performance by Kathy Bates (b.1948), Lizzy Caplan (b.1982) was recently cast as Annie's younger version on the second and final season of *Castle Rock*.

Catherine Trammel: One "bunny boiler" apparently wasn't enough for Michael Douglas, as his character, detective Nick Curran, gets involved with a dangerous *femme* named Catherine Trammel (Sharon Stone; b.1958) in the torrid 1992 Paul Verhoven (b.1938) classic, *Basic Instinct*. A bisexual crime novelist, Trammel is so cool she apparently needs to keep an icepick always at hand, in this cocaine-sprinkled, "cat-and-mouse" neo-noir romp, where nothing's quite what it seems.

Harley Quinn: Created by writer Paul Dini (b.1957) and artist Bruce Timm (b.1961) for *Batman: The Animated Series* in 1992, and originally voiced by Arleen Sorkin (b.1955), Harleen Frances Quinzel is a former psychiatry intern at Gotham City's Arkham Asylum, where she fell in love with the Joker. A "Florence Nightingale syndrome" victim, she would be turned into a female version of the Joker himself, his lover and loyal minion, in a toxic relationship she's only recently been able to break from, ditching her black and red jester jumpsuit for top, shorts, fishnets, and boots. This iteration of the character is brought to life by Australian bombshell Margot Robbie (b.1990) in action blockbusters *Suicide Squad* (2016), *Birds of Prey and the Fantabulous Emancipation of One Harley Quinn* (2020), and the 2021 *The Suicide Squad* sequel.

Villanelle: The main character in a series of self-published e-book novellas by author Luke Jennings (b.1953), which in turn inspired the ongoing BBC TV show *Killing Eve* (where she's given more of a supporting role, as played by Jodie Comer; b.1993), her real name is Oxana Vorontsova (Oksana Astankova in the show), a Russia-born psychopath hired as a paid assassin by The Twelve, a secretive and all-powerful crime syndicate. Modeled by Jennings on former Spanish ETA terrorist Idoia López Riaño (b.1964), a.k.a. *La Tigresa*, Villanelle is a sadistic killer with no empathy, and a love for expensive living, but is nonetheless infatuated with the plain, middle-aged MI5 agent hot in her pursuit, Eve Polastri, played by Sandra Oh (b.1971) on the show.

The Colonel: Specializing in detached (*The Unbearable Lightness of Being*; 1988), seductive (*The Ninth Gate*; 1999), and scheming (*Alias*; 2001–2006) femme fatales, Swedish actor Lena Olin (b.1955) became The Colonel, the main antagonist in streaming series *Hunters* (2020). The evil leader of an underground "Fourth Reich," an evil cadre of infiltrated and home-grown Nazis bent on destroying America, she is revealed to be a fictional version of Eva Braun (1912–1945), who never died at the bunker, instead running way with Adolf Hitler (1889–1945) to Bariloche, Argentina—for more on *that theory*, go to page 296!

BONUS FACTS

Contrary to popular belief, it is highly unlikely aliens are currently enjoying *I Love Lucy* (1951–1957) fifty light-years away from us, on account of radio signal degradation over long distances.

Attacks on McDonald's restaurants and social networks carried out by fans of cartoon show *Rick and Morty* in 2017 led the corporation to re-issue their long-forgotten and discontinued "Szechuan Sauce."

The difference between manslaughter, murder, and assassination? Professionalism.

Crazy film theories concocted by fans include E.T. (the extraterrestrial) being a Jedi, Ferris Bueller being Cameron's second personality, *John Wick* being a training program inside *The Matrix*, Willy Wonka and his minions secretly cannibalizing children, and Don Draper, of the *Mad Men* TV show, eventually becoming D. B. Cooper!

HAIR-BRAINED

The quintessential evil cult leader, much has been told, written, and filmed about Charles Manson (1934–2017) and the perverse "Family" he famously set on a path of death and destruction. But what do we really know about it all? Let's find out!

1. Manson was the son of a sixteen-year-old prostitute, Kathleen Maddox (1918–1973), who originally registered the boy as "No Name Maddox" in Cincinnati, Ohio. He never met his biological father, who appears to have been a conman and occasional farmhand nicknamed "Colonel" Walker Henderson Scott Sr. (1910–1954). Kathleen would—briefly—be married to a dry-cleaner named William Eugene Manson (1909–1961), and though little Charlie would inherit William's last name, the man soon divorced her.

2. Growing up in extreme poverty, neglected by his alcoholic criminal of a mother, often skipping school altogether, and prone to setting other kids' toys on fire, at age nine Charlie would be sent off to reformatory after reformatory, all of which he promptly escaped, until finally placed at the hellish Indiana School for Boys in Plainfield, where he would be frequently beaten by guards, and gang-raped by other boys.

3. At age twelve he finally escaped from the Plainfield correctional with two other kids.

Set for California, they robbed a number of filling stations aboard several stolen cars all the way to Utah. When arrested there, their federal crime-spree meant Manson would be sent off to the National Training School for Boys, a juvenile facility in Washington, DC, where his psychological testing yielded an illiterate, aggressive, and yet extremely sensitive man with an above-average IQ of 109.

4. Sent to a minimum-security prison in 1951, four months later he was caught raping another boy at knifepoint, only a month before his parole hearing. Sent to the Petersburg, Virginia, Federal Reformatory he sexually attacked three other inmates there, which prompted authorities to transfer him to the maximum-security reformatory in Ohio, which he was released from in 1954.

5. In 1955, Manson would marry and move to California. Frequent parole violations and petty crime would land him three more years in prison and a quick divorce by 1958. Soon after his release, he would again be arrested for pimping a teenage girl and his own sweetheart (they would eventually marry for a while). He also forged US Treasury checks on the side, accumulating an ever-growing list of prison terms as a result.

6. Transferred to the United States Penitentiary of McNeil Island, Washington, Manson ended up learning how to play the guitar from former

"Public Enemy #1" inductee Alvin "Creepy" Karpis (1907–1979), who also introduced him to the music of The Beatles. To Karpis's own surprise, "Little Charlie" learned quickly and had a pleasant voice. In prison, he also read Dale Carnegie's *How to Win Friends & Influence People* (1932) which he took to heart. By age thirty-two, upon his 1967 discharge, he had spent most of his life in prison, and begged not to be set free.

7. Arriving in San Francisco during the "Summer of Love" and becoming acquainted with the hippie scene, Manson quickly changed his mind and began to entertain the idea of "making it" as a musician. He hooked up with UC Berkeley assistant librarian Mary Brunner (b.1943), and moved in with her. They soon brought Lynette "Squeaky" Fromme (b.1948) in, followed by dozens of other disillusioned middle-class teens who were sampling the hippie life. Alternatively squatting at abandoned properties, traveling the land aboard a bus, or freeloading at other people's homes (like the Beach Boys' own Dennis Wilson; 1944–1983), the commune they formed around Manson (and, to a lesser degree, Brunner) quickly gained cultish traction, as the now-magnetic leader (Carnegie's lessons weren't wasted) wouldn't hesitate to prostitute his nubile entourage to gain new adepts.

8. With a following, however, comes messianic expectations, as Manson was quick to grasp, fashioning himself a new Jesus, Brunner a new "Mother Mary," and his followers as the heralds of a

new age. Unbeknownst to them, guitar-playing and how to win friends wasn't the only quirks Manson had picked up in prison: he had been turned into a white supremacist too. Cleverly disguising this perverse ideology in borrowed pseudo-Christian philosophies popular at the time, he soon began preaching an impending doomsday scenario—named "Helter Skelter" after the Beatles song—where African Americans would rise up to kill all whites but would end up destroying themselves too. Then, out of the ashes, the Manson Family would emerge as the new master race, and . . . you get the gist.

9. Manson and the Family relocated at a former Hollywood westerns set called Spahn Ranch, in exchange for maintenance chores, and allowing its elderly owner, George Spahn (1889–1974), to "sample" the girls (that's how "Squeaky" Fromme got her byname). The Family supported itself legally by offering horseback rides in and around the ranch, but also "the Abbie Hoffman way," including the theft of Volkswagen Beetles they'd turn into dune buggies, while waiting for Manson's music stardom dreams to materialize.

10. Through Dennis Wilson, Manson had indeed become acquainted with producers in the music business, where his aura and devoted following caught the attention of "California Sound" mastermind Terry Melcher (1942–2004). After talks about a possible album and film release at Melcher's 10050 Cielo Drive home, the producer drove to Spahn Ranch to hear the family rehearse, but a lackluster performance, the white-supremacy ideology surfacing in the lyrics, and violence erupting at the Ranch, were enough to scare Melcher into moving away from the Cielo Drive home, and warning Wilson to sever all ties with the Family.

11. With a suddenly unreachable Melcher, Manson naturally went to Cielo Drive to find out what was going on, only to find new tenants on the premises, Roman Polanski (b.1933), Sharon Tate (1943–1969), and an unfriendly entourage that sent him on his way. Despondent and enraged, Manson dropped his original plan to unleash a racial apocalypse via his music, in favor of direct action. The new scheme contemplated the murder of blacks and whites to pit races against each other, and the opportunity presented itself early in 1969 via the Family's shady drug deals, which prompted it to take swift retaliation. First, they attempted to kill an African American drug dealer, and presumed—by Manson—Black Panther, known as Bernard "Lotsapoppa" Crowe, who survived the shooting. Then, they abducted and killed a white music teacher by the name of Gary Hinman, attempting to pin the murder on the Black Panthers, presumably to further hurt Crowe, which provided the template of what would come.

12. The evening of August 8, 1969, Manson would launch "Helter Skelter" in earnest, by commanding high-ranking follower Charles "Tex" Watson (b.1945) to take Susan Atkins (1948–2009), Patricia Krenwinkel (b.1947), and Linda Kasabian (b.1949)

to 10050 Cielo Drive and murder whoever they found there. Upon entering the property, "Tex" shot and killed young Steven Parent (1951–1969), a friend of the caretaker, in his car on the driveway. Polanski was in Europe, set to start filming *The Day of the Dolphin* (1973), but eight-months pregnant Tate and her friends, Jay Sebring (1933–1969), Abigail Folger (1943–1969), and Wojciech Frykowski (1936–1969) were all brutally stabbed by Watson, Atkins, and Krenwinkel, while Kasabian stood guard outside. Tate's unborn child was choked *in utero*, its blood used to spell "PIG" on the front door—you guess it—to incriminate the Panthers.

13. On the late night of August 10, Manson took the four Cielo Drive murderers alongside Leslie Van Houten (b.1949) and Clem Grogan (b.1951) on a new killing spree. Manson, Watson, Krenwinkel, and Van Houten were dropped off at the house of Leno (1925–1969) and Rosemary LaBianca (1930–1969) at 3311 Waverly Drive in Los Feliz. After Manson and "Tex" had the couple tied up in separate rooms, Manson left, leaving Watson, Krenwinkel, and Van Houten to do the stabbing. Carving "WAR" into Leno's stomach, they used the blood to write messages like "Death to pigs" and "Rise" on the walls. After helping themselves to some food, they hitchhiked back to Spahn Ranch.

14. Meanwhile, Atkins, Kasabian, and Grogan were sent to murder a Palestinian actor, but Kasabian deliberately led them to the wrong Venice Beach address, so the plan was aborted.

Thus, the case would later become known as the "Tate-LaBianca Murders," though Manson and other followers would murder another man, Spahn ranch hand and former stuntman Donald "Shorty" Shea (1933–1969) days later. Kasabian quicky fled the Family and went back home to New Hampshire—later, she would turn herself in, and become the prosecution's chief witness.

15. For a while, law enforcement could find no connection between the Tate and LaBianca murders, which were investigated separately. Surprisingly, it would be the unrelated dune buggy scheme investigation that put pressure on Manson and the Family, even leading to brief arrests. That's when things started to unravel, as the cult's friend network and criminal associates began to crack and informed the LAPD about the involvement of Manson and his cronies in all the killings.

16. The ensuing December of 1969 LAPD arrest warrants would result in Manson's arrest, and a nationwide manhunt for the scattered Family members who took part in the Tate-LaBianca murders. The trial that began on July 15, 1970, would be a proverbial shitshow, with a buckskin-dressed Manson carving an "X" into his forehead (he would later fashion it into a swastika), and Atkins, Krenwinkel, and Van Houten doing the same afterwards. Still-loyal family members also carved Xs into their foreheads and did the best they could to disrupt the proceedings by harassing witnesses, loitering at the courthouse, threatening

to set themselves on fire, and even killing Van Houten's lawyer, but to no avail. By the time the trial was over, on January 25, 1971, Manson, Atkins, Krenwinkel, and Van Houten were all found guilty of the twenty-seven counts against them, and sentenced to death, as was "Tex" Watson, who had been tried separately.

17. In a strange twist of fate, Manson, Watson, Atkins, Krenwinkel, and Van Houten would all escape execution when the California Supreme Court *People v. Anderson* verdict caused all death sentences imposed in California prior to 1972 to become void. Manson would die as a consequence of colon cancer on November 19, 2017. Their every parole appeal overturned, Watson, Atkins, Krenwinkel, and Van Houten still sit behind bars, as do other criminal Family members like Bruce M. Davis (b.1942), and Bobby Beausoleil (b.1947).

18. While awaiting trial, Manson finally saw the release of his one and only album, LIE: *The Love and Terror Cult*. On top of that, he also made the cover of *Rolling Stone* magazine ("Charles Manson: The Incredible Story of the Most Dangerous Man Alive"), his music stardom dream coming true at last. The album sold poorly, but some of its songs have since been covered by other bands like Guns N' Roses. Featured in dozens of films and TV shows, Manson's dreadful legacy still permeates our world, including latter day follower James Mason (b.1952), a notorious American neo-Nazi terrorist and founder of the *Atomwaffen* Division, an organization responsible for at least eight deaths.

BONUS FACTS

If you thought Jethro Tull's magic flute gimmick was lame enough, brace yourself for "Wizard Rock," a product of *Harry Potter* mania going wrong since the early 2000s. "Potterheads" are also to blame for an abnormal increase in pet owl adoption . . . and quick abandonment the minute they realize these birds take a lot of work.

The "Spooklight," also called the Hornet Spooklight and Joplin Spook Light, is an unnerving ball of light seen wandering around at the "Devil's Promenade," on the Missouri-Oklahoma border.

The accelerated, overheated metabolism of bats allows them to carry around over 130 virus varieties, including Ebola, Nipah, and Coronavirus, without ever getting sick.

In 2021, sixty-five-year-old Austrian Walter Erhart got bitten in the genitals by a five-foot-long python snake which had sneaked into his toilet from a neighboring apartment.

In 2019, Frank Frazetta's cover illustration for *Eerie* magazine #23 sold for $5,400,000, surpassing the previous record for a Frazetta piece—$1,790,000 paid for his *Death Dealer* #6 in 1990.

THE POSTMAN ALWAYS SHOOTS TWICE

Not only women, children, and hippies—the evil trifecta—go berserk from time to time. Founded in 1775 during the Second Continental Congress, the United Stated Postal Service (USPS) currently employs around six hundred thousand over-stressed people, each one of them only a bad day away from potentially "going postal."

Perry B. Smith (b.1928): Three months after resigning from his twenty-five-year job as a career postman, and distraught over the suicide of his son, also a mailman, on August 19, 1983, Smith blasted his way back into his former Johnston, South Carolina, workplace with a twelve-gauge shotgun, chasing down and killing the local postmaster, and wounding two of his former colleagues as they fled the place, as well as a policeman who arrived at the scene. He was sentenced to life, plus an additional ten years.

Patrick Sherrill (1941–1986): The day after being berated by his Edmond, Oklahoma, USPS supervisors—having two bosses never leads to anything good—on August 10, 1986, Sherrill armed himself with three semi-automatic pistols, and headed to the office where, between 7:00 a.m. and 7:15 a.m., he methodically gunned down fourteen colleagues (including one unlucky supervisor), and injured six others, before blowing his own brains out. Turns out the man was a former Marine and National Guard pistol team member—something his supervisors should have taken into account. The "going postal" expression was coined after his killing spree.

John Merlin Taylor (1937–1989): Described as the "ideal postman," and an Escondido career mail carrier for twenty-seven years, Taylor shot his own wife in 1989, and then drove to the Orange Glen post office where he opened fire on his best buddies, killing two of them before turning the gun on himself. Presumably brain-dead, his relatives gave permission to unplug him from life support two days later.

Joseph M. Harris (1956–1996): Born in prison, and ultimately dying in prison too, this troubled man was let go from the Ridgewood, New Jersey, post office in April of 1990. In 1991, after losing a $10,000 investment with stockbroker Roy Edwards, Harris dressed himself in a black ninja costume and went to the Edwards' home, where he gunned him down after raping his wife and two daughters. Feeling empowered, the night of October 9, 1991, Harris sliced his former USPS supervisor to a pulp with a samurai sword, and then shot her boyfriend. Early the following morning he put on a gas mask and a bulletproof vest. Armed with two machine guns and three hand grenades, as well as his aforementioned *katana*, he "went postal" on two former colleagues as they arrived for work.

After a four-hour standoff with the police, he finally surrendered.

Thomas McIlvane (1960–1991): On November 19, 1991, the day after his appeal for reinstatement at the Royal Oak, Michigan, USPS had been rejected, this black belt martial artist with a history of aggressive behavior toward both colleagues and customers decided to act on his previous threats to "make Edmond look like Disneyland." Walking into the post office with a sawn-off semi-automatic rifle tucked under his raincoat, he singled out his supervisors and shot four dead, wounding another six people before shooting himself. He died the next day.

Bruce W. Clark (b.1937): After twenty-five years on the job, this postal clerk argued with his supervisor, James Whooper III (b.1945), punching him in the back of the head at the City of Industry, California, USPS processing center on July 10, 1995. Returning ten minutes later with a revolver tucked in a brown paper bag, he pulled it on Whooper, shooting him point-blank twice, before being restrained by two coworkers until the police showed up. He was sentenced to twenty-two years in prison for the crime.

Anthony Deculit (1960–1997): Reprimanded for sleeping at work, and then passed over for a promotion, during a December 19, 1997, overnight shift, this postal worker pulled a nine-millimeter handgun and lethally shot Joan Chitwood (b.1942), the supervisor he had feuded with. The following dozen shots he fired wounded two others, before he took his own life, in spite of other colleagues pleading with him not to do so.

After this incident, the USPS Workplace Environment Analysis program (implemented since 1993) started to bear fruit, with no new killings registered through 2005, when budget cuts gradually reduced supervision until its 2009 shutdown.

Jennifer San Marco (1961–2006): Believing herself to be the target of a postal conspiracy, San Marco, a former Santa Barbara Police Department dispatcher, and USPS clerk with a history of mental illness and paranoid racist outbursts which saw her removed from her post in 2003, shot and killed her neighbor, and then drove to the Goleta, California, mail processing plant where she shot and killed six employees before turning the gun—a legally purchased fifteen-round, nine millimeter Smith & Wesson model 915—on herself.

Grant Gallaher (b.1961): Upset about the added extra work to his delivery route, career mailman Gallaher got his Magnum revolver and drove to the Baker City, Oregon, post office on April 4, 2006, striking his supervisor, forty-nine-year-old Lori Hayes-Kotter, with his postal vehicle as she walked across the parking lot. Entering the office on foot but failing to find the postmaster anywhere, the upset carrier walked back to the parking lot where he executed the supervisor as she lay on the pavement. Gallaher was arrested and sentenced to life, or a minimum of thirty-five years in prison for the murder of the supervisor, and the failed attempt on the postmaster's life.

Julius Kevin Tartt (1967–2006): Yet another postman with a beef with his supervisor, this career carrier for the San Francisco Bayview USPS annex went to the home of Genevieve Paez, fifty-three at the time, and mother of four, and shot her in the back of the head as she left for work in the morning of November 28, 2006. Weeks later, the police would find Tartt dead from a self-inflicted gunshot wound.

DeShaune Stewart (b.1994): On December 23, 2017, this young USPS employee arrived naked at the Dublin, Ohio, post office,and proceeded to gun down his supervisor, fifty-two-year-old Lance Hererra-Dempsey, and then paid a visit to the postmaster, Ginger Ballad, fifty-three at the time, lethally smashing her head against the floor. In 2019 he was indicted of both crimes by reason of insanity.

Brandon Scott Hole (2002–2021): A young, pimple-faced, former FedEx employee who just happened to browse white supremacist websites a little too often, drove to the company's Indianapolis facility on April 15, 2021, and shot his way in from the parking lot, killing eight mainly Sikh employees before committing suicide. This was the latest of a string of attacks affecting private carriers since the 1990s. It has been assessed that with shipping systems being massively sped up by automation, the pressure workers face to adjust themselves to machines is taking its toll on their mental health. It may not be long before "going postal" is replaced by "going Amazon" also, as the online retail giant's callous workplace culture and robotic time-management system forces its people to over-perform for up to eighty-five hours a week ... while hiding out to cry as they pee inside bottles, according to news reports.

BONUS QUOTES

"I'm tired of pretending like I'm not bitching, a total rock star from Mars, and people can't figure me out; they can't process me. I don't expect them to. You can't process me with a normal brain."
—Charlie Sheen

"Happiness is having a large, loving, caring, close-knit family in another city."
—George Burns

"Any man who hates dogs and babies can't be all bad."
—W. C. Fields

"A woman is just a woman, but a good cigar is a smoke."
—Rudyard Kipling

INGLORIOUS BASTARD

Long viewed as the ultimate villain and mass-murderer, the twisted mind of Adolf Hitler (1889–1945) was vicariously probed by psychoanalyst Walter C. Langer (1899–1981) on assignment for the Office of Strategic Services (OSS). The resulting 1943 report, widely circulated among the Allies, would reveal just how fragile, sexually troubled, and self-destructive this foe was. After it was declassified in 1968, four years later Langer published the mass-market version, The Mind of Adolf Hitler: The Secret Wartime Report (Basic Books; 1972), to great acclaim. Long since in the public domain, some of its frightful conclusions are quoted below for the benefit of the present generation.

1. As He Believes Himself to Be:
"He feels that no one in German history was equipped as he is to bring the Germans to the position of supremacy which all German statesmen have felt they deserved but were unable to achieve. This attitude is not confined to himself as a statesman. He also believes himself to be the greatest war lord . . . "

"Then, too, he believes himself to be the greatest of all German architects and spends a great deal of his time in sketching new buildings and planning the remodeling of entire cities. In spite of the fact that he failed to pass the examinations for admission to the Art School, he believes himself to be the only competent judge in this field."

" . . . Hitler believes himself destined to become an Immortal Hitler, chosen by God to be the New Deliverer of Germany and the Founder of a new social order for the world. He firmly believes this and is certain that in spite of all the trials and tribulations through which he must pass he will finally attain that goal."

2. As the German People Know Him:
" . . . Professor Max von Gruber of the University of Munich, the most eminent eugenist in Germany stated: 'It was the first time I had seen Hitler close at hand. Face and head of inferior type, crossbreed; low receding forehead, ugly nose, broad cheekbones, little eyes, dark hair. Expression not of a man exercising authority in perfect self-command, but of raving excitement. At the end an expression of satisfied egotism.'"

"It was this Hitler that the German people knew at firsthand. Hitler, the fiery orator, who tirelessly rushed from one meeting to another, working himself to the point of exhaustion in their behalf. Hitler, whose heart and soul were in the Cause and who struggled endlessly against overwhelming odds and obstacles to open their eyes to the true state of affairs."

"As soon as Hitler came to power new weapons for self-aggrandizement were put into the hands of the propagandists and they made good use of them. Unemployment dropped off rapidly, roads that the Germans never dreamed of sprung up overnight, new and imposing buildings were erected with astounding rapidity. The face of Germany was being lifted at an incredible speed. Hitler was keeping his promises; he was accomplishing the impossible. Every success in diplomacy, every social reform was heralded as world-shaking in its importance. And for each success, Hitler modestly accepted all the credit."

3. As His Associates Know Him:
"His primary rules were: never allow the public to cool off; never admit a fault or wrong; never concede that there may be some good in your enemy; never leave room for alternatives; never accept blame; concentrate on one enemy at a time and blame him for everything that goes wrong; people will believe a big lie sooner than a little one; and if you repeat it frequently enough people will sooner or later believe it."

"Hitler also becomes nervous and tends to lose his composure when he has to meet newspapermen. Being a genius of propaganda, he realizes the power of the press in influencing public opinion and he always provides the press with choice seats at all ceremonies. When it comes to interviews, however, he feels himself on the defensive and insists that the questions be submitted in advance."

"One of Hitler's hobbies that is carefully hidden from the public is his love for pornography. He can scarcely wait for the next edition of *Der Stürmer* to appear, and when it reaches him he goes through it avidly. (. . .) In addition, Hitler has a large collection of nudes and, according to Hanfstaengl and others, he also enjoys viewing lewd movies in his private theater, some of which are prepared by Hoffmann for his benefit."

4. As He Knows Himself:
"There was general agreement among the collaborators that Hitler is probably a neurotic psychopath bordering on schizophrenia. This means that he is not insane in the commonly accepted sense of the term, but a neurotic who lacks adequate inhibitions. He has not lost complete contact with the world about him and is still striving to make some kind of psychological adjustment that will give him a feeling of security in his social group."

"From our experience with other neurotic psychopaths we are probably on firm ground when we suppose that Hitler's mind is like a battle royal most of the time with many conflicting and contradictory forces and impulses pulling him this way and that. Such a state of confusion is not easy to bear. A large part of his energies is usually wasted in wrestling with himself instead of being directed toward the external world."

"As one surveys Hitler's behavior patterns, as his close associates observe them, one gets the impression that this is not a single personality, but two that inhabit the same body and alternate back and forth. The one is a very soft, sentimental, and indecisive individual who has very little drive and wants nothing quite so much as to be amused, liked, and looked after. The other is just the opposite—hard, cruel, and decisive person with considerable energy—who seems to know what he wants and is ready to go after it and get it regardless of cost."

5. Psychological Analysis and Reconstruction:
"There is a possibility that Hitler has participated in a homosexual relationship at some time in his life. The evidence is such that we can only say there is a strong tendency in this direction that, in addition to the manifestations already enumerated, often finds expression in imagery about being attacked from behind or being stabbed in the back. His nightmares, which frequently deal with being attacked by a man and being suffocated, also suggest strong homosexual tendencies and a fear of them."

"Hitler's outstanding defense mechanism is one commonly called *projection*. It is a technique by which the ego of an individual defends itself against unpleasant impulses, tendencies, or characteristics by denying their existence in himself while he attributes them to others."

"From a scientific point of view, therefore, we are forced to consider Hitler, the Führer, not as a personal devil, wicked as his actions and philosophy may be, but as the expression of a state of mind existing in millions of people, not only in Germany, but to a smaller degree in all civilized countries.

To remove Hitler may be a necessary first step, but it would not be the cure."

6. His Probable Behavior in the Future:
" . . . we may be reasonably sure that as Germany suffers successive defeats Hitler will become more and more neurotic. Each defeat will shake his confidence still further and limit his opportunities for proving his own greatness to himself. In consequence he will feel himself more and more vulnerable to attack from his associates, and his rages will increase in frequency."

"It is not wholly improbable that in the end he might lock himself into this symbolic womb and defy the world to get him."

"Hitler might commit suicide. This is the most plausible outcome. Not only has he frequently threatened to commit suicide, but from what we know of his psychology it is the most likely possibility."

BONUS FACTS

Marie Antoinette's infamous "Let them eat cake" quote is likely an invention of Rousseau (1712-1778).

According to a 2006 BBC report, back in the day Pentagon scientists planned to create an army of remote-controlled cyborg insects.

ESCAPE FROM HIGH CASTLE

Continuing to command the morbid curiosity of many, the time has come to look at some of the fringe theories claiming Hitler somehow managed to escape his own insanity, and flew his defeated Reich, instead of eating a bullet down at the Führerbunker in 1945.

1. As predicted by Langer, upon hearing of Benito Mussolini's (1883–1945) partisan execution in Italy, and with the Red Army closing in on his position, Adolf Hitler (1889–1945) committed suicide alongside his recently wed mistress, Eva Braun (1912–1945), their bodies dropped into an explosion crater, doused in gasoline, and set on fire, presumably to avoid desecration. Their entourage would follow suit a couple of days later.

2. In order to boost the morale of the remaining Reich soldiers, the newly appointed head of state, navy commander Karl Dönitz (1891–1980), broadcast a message stating Hitler had heroically perished leading an assault on the Red Army. Dönitz should lead the short-lived Flensburg Government, until Germany's unconditional surrender on May 8, 1945.

3. Meanwhile in Berlin, among the chaos of the city's fall, the human remains that could be recovered at the Führerbunker surroundings were

haphazardly collected, and buried at an undisclosed location. Information is power, and paranoid Soviet authorities were not keen on sharing any of it. With the exception of Hitler's and Braun's dental bridges, which were duly shipped to Kremlin archives, during the following decades SMERSH, and then the KGB, would repeatedly exhume and rebury those remains beyond recognition.

4. On June 9, 1945, Stalin would tell the Allies Hitler was in Spain or Argentina, while former Nazi officials facing arrests and prosecution would all tell conflicting stories as to his supposed European whereabouts, but it would be British counter-intelligence agent Hugh Trevor-Roper (1914–2013) who put most rumors to rest when he found out what really had happened at Hitler's bunker.

5. The source of all modern escape hypothesis, Soviet misinformation continued undeterred, including the supposed discovery of a woman's skull fragments they claimed to be Hitler's, only to disavow those claims years later. In 2017, however, renowned French forensic pathologist Philippe Charlier (b.1977) was given access to the Soviet archives, and confirmed without the shadow of doubt those teeth did belong to Adolf.

6. Before 2017, however, the possibility of Hitler and Braun escaping to southern Argentina was lent a semblance of credibility many conspiracy

theorists still cling to, due to Operation Paperclip (which saw the Allies snatch German scientists from the Soviets' purview), and Otto Skorzeny's (1908–1975) own "rat line," which smuggled many former colleagues of his to South America via Switzerland and Italy, while Skorzeny himself remained safely tucked away in Spain.

7. During the early 1960s, just as Israeli Mossad agents were chasing down Nazi war criminals in Buenos Aires, a joint FBI and CIA operation investigated newly surfaced Hitler "sightings," in Colombia and Argentina, but no lead proved conclusive. Regardless, the lure of Hitler's iconic figure has been too hard to resist for alternative "researchers" who continue to peddle these rumors. In the sage words of Third Reich historian Richard J. Evans (b.1947), "Despite all the evidence to the contrary, more book-length arguments for the survival of Hitler in Argentina have appeared in the twenty-first century than in the whole of the 55 previous years." (*The Hitler Conspiracies: The Protocols - The Stab in the Back - The Reichstag Fire - Rudolf Hess - The Escape from the Bunker*; Oxford University Press; 2020).

8. Ultimately, Hitler's myth endures best in plain old science-fiction; like Philip K. Dick's Hugo award winner *The Man in the High Castle* (1962), with its syphilis-stricken Führer (a fate changed by the novel's 2015–2019 streaming series adaptation), or Norman Spinrad's *The Iron Dream* (1972), in which a young, struggling-artist Adolf

emigrates to America to become a pulp novelist. By contrast, Ira Levin's realistic sci-fi thriller *The Boys from Brazil* (1974) presents an evil Dr. Josef Mengele (1911–1979) conspiring to impregnate unsuspecting women with Hitler's clones. Finally, Timur Vermes's 2012 *Er ist wieder da* (Look Who's Back) presents a scathing satire of the modern world as seen through the eyes of a time-traveling Führer. Germany's need to come to grips with its Nazi past—as opposed to escaping or banning it—has come full-circle at last.

BONUS QUOTES

"Everybody talks about the weather but nobody does anything about it."
—Mark Twain

"Any idiot can face a crisis. It's this day-to-day living that wears you out."
—Anton Chekhov

"I am more of a sponge than an inventor. I absorb ideas from every source. My principal business is giving commercial value to the brilliant but misdirected ideas of others."
—Thomas Edison

"I don't recall your name, but your manners are familiar."
—Oliver Herford

BUTTERFLIES

As long as there are prisons in this world, there will be men doing their utmost to elude confinement. Some of the most daring, miraculous, and even ridiculous real-life escapes will be found below, as performed by saint and sinner alike, all connected through their mutual desire for freedom.

Saint Peter (1–68 AD): Imprisoned by King Herod Agrippa I (11–44 AD), according to Acts 12, in light of a previous escape, Peter the Apostle was chained and placed inside a cell with a guard on each side, while four squads of four soldiers each kept watch outside. On Passover night, however, right before his planned execution, a luminous angel struck him awake and asked Peter to follow him. Thinking it the product of a dream, Peter followed the angel outside, and suddenly found himself freed.

Saint Paul (4–67 AD): According to Acts 16: 16-34, Paul the Apostle and a disciple named Silas were imprisoned after the former exorcised an exploited girl, but their prayers brought about an earthquake which opened every cell door and loosened all prisoner chains. However, Paul and Silas refused to leave their cell, and instead used the event to convert their jailer, who was about to take his own life. The man brought them into his home that very night to nurse and feed them before their official release the next morning.

John Gerard (1564–1637): Operating secretly in Elizabethan England for eight years, this Jesuit priest survived horrifying torture at the Tower of London, and despite his injuries managed to climb a rope strung across the Tower moat on October 4, 1597, with the presumed aid of Nicholas Owen (c.1562–1606), who would end up being tortured to death at the Tower, later becoming the patron saint of escape artists when canonized in 1970. Gerard would continue his English ministry for another eight years, even helping his Tower jailer escape the country, before leaving for Rome, and writing his memoir, *The Autobiography of a Hunted Priest*.

Hugo de Groot (1853–1645): A Dutch polymath considered the intellectual father of the international society doctrine which ended the Thirty Years War (and would eventually bring about the United Nations in modern times), in 1618 de Groot received a life sentence over his involvement in a local civil-religious conflict, and was imprisoned in Loevestein Castle, from which he escaped three years later, hidden inside a book chest, fleeing to exile in Paris.

Jack Sheppard (1702–1724): Famous during his lifetime both on account of his four daring prison escapes, the first of which he managed in April 1724, only three hours after his arrest, by breaking through the jail's timber ceiling and lowering himself to the ground with a rope made from bed sheets . . . while still in irons! His second escape a month later would see him and his mistress,

Edgeworth Bess, lower themselves from their shared cell by similar means after filing off their manacles. With the aid of Bess, Sheppard would be smuggled out of prison a third time in August, dressed as a woman, escaping the death warrant now over his head. Turned into a cockney hero, he would avoid capture until September, when he unwisely returned to London. Imprisoned in isolation at Newgate Prison, yet again he managed to escape with his leg irons and chains still on. Not long after, however, he was recaptured and promptly hanged, but by then he had already been immortalized in the literature of the day by none other than the bestselling author of *Robinson Crusoe*, Daniel Defoe (c.1660–1731).

Giacomo Casanova (1725–1798): At age thirty, the world-famous Italian libertine, conman, and author was arrested on charges of lewd behavior and sentenced to five years of imprisonment at the Piombi, a minimum security prison for aristocrats and clergymen, through the roof of which he escaped with the aid of a renegade priest into a European exile which lasted twenty years.

Billy the Kid (1859–1881): Born Henry McCarty, the legendary outlaw was captured alongside Tom Pickett (1858–1934) and others by the equally legendary lawman Pat Garrett (1850–1908) at Stinking Springs. Taken in shackles to Fort Sumner, and then to Las Vegas, Nevada, he was eventually tried and sentenced to death by hanging in Mesilla, New Mexico. Undeterred, he asked to be taken to an outhouse behind the courthouse where he managed to kill two deputies and run away, still in his shackles. A bounty on his head, he was eventually found and shot dead by Pat Garrett three months later.

John Dillinger (1903–1934): Like Jack Sheppard and Billy the Kid before him, Dillinger was turned into a criminal celebrity by the press of his time and managed to escape from prison twice. The first time, he was broken out of the Allen County Jail in Lima, Ohio, by members of his first gang impersonating State Police officers. The second time, in 1934, he daringly used a fake carved pistol to threaten his way out of the Lake County Jail (a supposedly escape-proof facility where he was kept while facing murder charges) in Crown Point, Indiana, without—obviously—firing a single shot. Seven months, several shootouts, and one botched plastic surgery later, Dillinger was finally gunned down by FBI (then BOI) agents, upon exiting the Biograph Theater in Chicago.

Henri Charrière (1906–1973): Sentenced to life in prison and ten years of hard labor in the St-Laurent-du-Maroni penal colony in French Guiana, in 1933, for a crime he didn't commit, Charrière, a.k.a. *Papillon* ("Butterfly"), managed to escape months after his arrival, but after a series of misadventures in Colombia , he was recaptured and put in solitary confinement for two years. Subsequent escape attempts had him sent to the *Bagne de Cayenne* camp (better known as the Devil's Island for its unusually harsh conditions), which he escaped for good in 1941 with the aid of another prisoner, who drowned on the way to the shore. After further adventures throughout Colombia, he reached Venezuela and made a new life for himself, achieving celebrity status over there as well as in his homeland with the publication of his celebrated memoir, *Papillon*, in 1969.

Yoshie Shiratori (1907–1979): Considered a folk hero in his native Japan, where he escaped imprisonment four times thanks to his impressive ingenuity, he was first jailed in Aomori Prison in 1936, escaping months later by picking his cell lock using the metal wire from his bathing bucket. Caught while stealing supplies from a hospital weeks later, he was then given a life sentence and sent to Akita Prison in 1942. Escaping a second time by climbing up the ceiling beams to a skylight, he was recaptured at the house of one of the guards, and transferred to Abashiri Prison (Hokkaido), where he was kept in handcuffs, though he managed to corrode them with miso soup and escape again, taking advantage of a wartime blackout, but was caught soon after and sentenced to death. Despite being placed in a special cell at the Sapporo Prison, yet again he managed to dig a tunnel in the floor using miso soup bowls in 1947. Years later, he would turn himself in, seeing his death sentence commuted to fourteen more years in a Tokyo prison until finally released in 1961.

Roger J. Bushell (1910–1944): Born in South Africa, this RAF squad leader achieved long-lasting fame as the mastermind behind the 1944 "Great Escape" from the Stalag Luft III POW camp. Having attempted escapes from Stalag Luft I and, months later, while on transfer from POW camp Oflag X-C to Oflag VI-B, he jumped from the train and spent a year hiding in Prague until betrayed, arrested, and sent to Stalag Luft III. There, he put a plan in action that would see the building of three tunnels, one of which would allow seventy-six prisoners to escape. In the end, however, seventy-three were recaptured, and fifty of those were summarily executed, including squad leader Bushell.

Alfred Israel Wetzler (1918–1988) and Rudolf Vrba (1924–2006): At a time when reports of the atrocities going on at Nazi concentration camps were still met with disbelief, these men (Vrba only a teenager back then) achieved the impossible. On April 7, 1944, Wetzler and Vrba hid for four nights inside a hollowed-out place in a wood pile at the outer perimeter of Birkenau (Auschwitz II), before escaping dressed in stolen civilian clothes. Their "Vrba–Wetzler report," a thirty-three-page document detailing the camp's ground plan, gas chamber details, and even a Zyklon B canister label, was the first to reach the Allies and be regarded as credible. Its publication and distribution led to several targeted bombings in Budapest which wiped out the Nazi officials who handled deportations to camps, saving the lives of an estimated two hundred thousand Hungarian Jews.

Alfred G. Hinds (1917–1991): A British Army deserter and career criminal, "Houdini Hinds" broke out of three high-security prisons while serving a twelve-year sentence for a 1953 jewel robbery he appears not to have committed. First, in 1955 he snuck through the locked door of his cell and climbed over and out of the Nottingham Prison wall using two wooden doors he had built at the workshop. Recaptured by Scotland Yard many months later, he escaped a court hearing by padlocking the two officers escorting him into a toilet cubicle. Caught five hours later at the airport, he was sent to Chelmsford Prison, which he also escaped by duplicating a set of keys he stole from a guard. Captured again twenty-two months later while in Dublin, Ireland, he was flown back to England and served the remainder of his sentence at the maximum-security Parkhurst Prison in the Isle of Wight. A celebrity upon his release, he became a member of Mensa, and a speaker of some note.

Frank Lee Morris (1926–?): Alcatraz inmate number AZ1441 had a long history of crime, a successful prison escape (from Louisiana State Penitentiary), and a high IQ (133), when he was sent to Alcatraz on January 20, 1960. Alcatraz inmates AZ1476 and AZ1485, John William Anglin (1930–?) and his brother Clarence (1931–?), were bank robbers with a history of Atlanta Penitentiary escapes, when transferred to Alcatraz in 1960–61. Inmate AZ1335, Allen West (1929–1978) had been in Alcatraz since 1957, after an unsuccessful escape attempt from the Florida State Prison. Morris, West, and the Anglin brothers had all previously met at the Atlanta Penitentiary, and were a match made in hell. Digging holes beneath their sinks, by June 11, 1962, Morris and the Anglins managed to sneak through the ventilation system, and paddle their way to freedom aboard a makeshift raft wearing life preservers, all taken straight off the pages of *Popular Mechanics*, while leaving papier-mâché dummies "sleeping" behind in their cell bunks. Unfortunately, West didn't manage to get out of his cell on time and was left behind. Their story is consigned to legend and popular culture—including a superb 1979 film adaptation, *Escape from Alcatraz*, starring Clint Eastwood (b.1930)—ever since. Morris and the Anglin brothers were never seen again, and the case remains open.

Ronald "Ronnie" Biggs (1929–2013): A member of The Great Train Robbery gang (which managed to steal 2.6 million pounds from a Royal Mail train heading from Glasgow to London in 1963), he was the only one of its members to successfully escape imprisonment at Wandsworth Prison in 1965 (using a rope ladder to climb out and drop onto a waiting van). Fleeing first to Paris, France, where he got plastic surgery and reunited with his family, and then to Australia, he was forced to leave alone for Brazil in 1969, where he lived as a local celebrity until returning to Britain to finally turn himself in to the authorities, back in 2001.

William "Billy" Hayes (b.1947): An American student originally sentenced to four years and two months in a Turkish prison for smuggling *hashish* (Asian marijuana), Billy soon got caught up in a diplomatic row, which put him on a never-ending journey through Turkey's grueling prison system until finally escaping Imrali Prison with the help of a bribed guard on October 2, 1975, and rowing a boat to Greece. On his return to America, he pursued a career as an author, taking a cue from Henri Charrière's *Papillon* with his own bestselling *Midnight Express* (1977), which was adapted to film by Oliver Stone (b.1946) and Alan Parker (1944–2020) in 1978.

Joaquín Archivaldo Guzmán Loera (b.1957): Better known as "El Chapo," this Mexican drug lord and former leader of the Sinaloa Cartel was known for pioneering the digging of smuggling tunnels across the US-Mexico border when first captured in 1993. In 2001 he made his first escape from a federal maximum-security prison hidden in a laundry cart by bribed guards. He stayed on the run for fourteen years until finally recaptured in 2015. Making use of his "career capital" as a tunnel builder, it took him only seventeen months to build a *Top Secret!* (1984)-style tunnel (equipped with artificial light and air ducts!) to freedom. Arduously caught again in 2016, in 2017 he was finally extradited to the United States, where he's currently serving a life sentence at ADX Florence (Colorado).

Irish Republican Army: Not all escapes are an individual affair. On July 27, 1922, the IRA placed an explosive device on the wall of the Dundalk Gaol (Prison) in Ireland, and after their imprisoned members sent a signal, the bomb was detonated, making a huge hole in the wall through which 106 prisoners escaped. These same prisoners would return a few months later, and take over the whole prison by force, freeing remaining IRA members from the *gaol*. Fifty years later, the IRA would organize yet another daring escape when they broke out Chief of Staff Seamus Twomey (1919–1989) and two other members by landing a hijacked helicopter in the training yard of Dublin's Mountjoy Prison. In 1983, thirty-eight IRA members would yet again conduct a successful prison escape from Northern Ireland's HM Prison Maze, a.k.a. "The Maze," at the time considered inexpugnable.

Formerly notable mass escapes of extremists from prisons like the 1971 Punta Carretas Prison (Uruguay) tunnel escape of over one hundred *Tupamaro* militants, or the 1990 Santiago Public Prison (Chile) escape of 49 leftist radicals, have been overshadowed in modern times by the 2011 Sarposa Prison (Kandahar, Afghanistan) escape of 475 Taliban members, and the 2021 Owerri Custodial Centre (Imo, Nigeria) break-out by the Indigenous People of Biafra separatist movement, which freed a staggering 1,844 prisoners.

KEYSER SÖZE

A rare feat, the highest degree of escape artistry possible in this life, whether voluntary, forced, or fateful, involves vanishing (or being disappeared) without trace—at least to the degree acquaintances, government, or the public at large would be concerned with.

Owain Glyndŵr (1359–?): The last native Prince of Wales, this prince revolted against English rule as the Middle Ages waned, but while initially successful, he was finally defeated by the better equipped armies of natural strategist Henry of Monmouth, who would later become King Henry V (1386–1422). While driven from his strongholds, Glyndŵr was never captured, nor betrayed by his fellow Welsh people, going into hiding until 1415, when he presumably passed away.

Henry Every (1659–?): The famed English "arch-pirate" who terrorized both the Atlantic and Indian oceans during the late seventeenth century, "Long Ben" managed to bolt and elude capture at age thirty-seven with all his loot, after what has been called the most profitable act of piracy in history, the September 7, 1695, Grand Mughal raid, which netted him and his associates 600,000 pounds worth in gold and jewels treasure (around 126,600,000 modern-day dollars!).

Benjamin Bathurst (1784–?): An unlikely hero of modern-day fantasy, this eighteenth- century

British diplomat—as in *spy*—traversing Prussia under an assumed identity during the turbulent Napoleonic Wars disappeared alongside his servant around November 25, 1809. An extensive search instigated by Bathurst's wife, Phillida, was conducted by local authorities, but only the man's fur coat and trousers turned up, giving substance to the possibility of foul play. Be that as it may, since 1939 Bathurst has been repeatedly portrayed as a space-time traveler by popular writers of science fiction.

Matías Pérez (c.1800–?): While ascending in his hot-air balloon from Havana's *Campo de Marte* ("Mars Field") park in 1856, this pioneering Portuguese-Cuban aeronaut forever vanished among the clouds only to be ingrained as a popular adage, *"voló como Matías Pérez"* ("flew away like Matías Pérez"), applied by Cubans to someone who disappears into thin air.

Solomon Northup (1807–?): This famed African American violinist and author of the bestselling memoir *Twelve Years a Slave* (1853), left on that book's promotion tour never to return home. Some claim he was snatched again, while others say he never quite reconnected with his old family after twelve years away from them, but his trail had gone cold by 1857.

Ludwig Leichhardt (1813–?): A German naturalist of some repute, Leichhardt participated in two Australian land exploration journeys, under the auspices of the Paris Geographical Society and the Royal Geographical Society, both of which invested him with their highest awards. On his third expedition to the Australian hinterland in 1848, Leichhardt, along with his entire party (five men, seven horses, twenty mules, and fifty oxen), forever faded into the desert sands, and only a tiny brass name tag belonging to the explorer has been found since.

Ambrose Bierce (1842–?): "It beats old age, disease, or falling down the cellar stairs. To be a gringo in Mexico—ah, that is euthanasia." So wrote Bierce, one of the greatest—and most feared—American writers and literary critics of all time, as he rode into Revolutionary Mexico back in late 1913. Reports had him joining Pancho Villa's army at Ciudad Juárez, accompanying it all the way to Chihuahua, and then into oblivion, as stated in his last letter to his dear friend—and presumed lover—Blanche Partington (1866–1951).

William J. Sharkey (1847–?): A very bad apple falling far from its well-to-do family tree, this minor Democratic Party politician murdered another man in cold blood over a gambling debt. Found guilty of manslaughter and imprisoned at "The Tombs," the Manhattan municipal jail, Sharkey escaped solitary confinement with the aid of his lover, a Maggie Jourdan—*no connection, I swear*—who smuggled him women's clothing. Fleeing to Cuba in 1873, he was never seen or heard from again, although it has been speculated that he moved to Spain afterwards.

Marvin Clark (1852–?): The oldest, still-active missing person case in the United States, Clark was a retired Oregon marshal who vanished while en route from Tigard to visit his daughter in Portland, during the Halloween weekend of 1926. His wife received a postcard from Bellingham, Washington, featuring a seemingly jumbled message in her husband's handwriting, which lent credence to the theory of a sudden strike of dementia, but Clark himself was never seen again.

Colonel Percy Fawcett (1865–?): Coming across a likely forged, 1753 document labeled "Manuscript 512," about an alleged ancient city in the Brazilian *sertão* (caatinga), this British "Indiana Jones" became obsessed with finding what he called the "Lost City of Z." After five unsuccessful expeditions between 1906 and 1920, the persistent surveyor attempted a seventh 1925 outing which would see him and his son Jack (as well as a friend of Jack's) swallowed by the Amazon jungle, never to return.

Robert LeRoy Parker (1866–?) and Harry Alonzo Longabaugh (1867–?): Better known as the world-famous outlaws Butch Cassidy and the Sundance Kid, respectively, these members of Wyoming's "Wild Bunch" gang fled the United States in 1901 alongside Sundance's girlfriend Etta Place (1878–?). With the Pinkerton Detective Agency hot in pursuit, the trio would buy a ranch in southern Argentina, and attempt a number of botched train robberies to supplement their income, which would see Butch and Sundance flee again to the north.

While, according to legend, they eventually met their death under a Bolivian army bullet shower—surprisingly good at wasting *bandidos*, if "Che" Guevara (1928–1967) is any indication—but their death was never officially confirmed, and their final resting place is still a mystery. Etta Place, however, supposedly returned to America, successfully avoiding capture, and disappearing from all records around 1908.

Lieutenant Alejandro Bello Silva (1887–?): Disappearing during his March 1914 qualifying flight for certification as a military pilot—which he obviously failed to pass—on the way back to Santiago from the coastal Chilean town of Cartagena, Bello never landed anywhere, and subsequent expeditions going well into the twenty-first century have failed to locate any crash remains from his biplane. Much like Matías Pérez in Cuba, Bello also made it into the local lingo, the phrase *"más perdido que el teniente Bello"* applied to someone who has lost his way, literally as well as metaphorically.

Joseph Force Carter (1889–?): Gone missing on August 6, 1930, after leaving the Billy Haas's Chophouse on 332 West 45th Street, New York, and taking a taxicab, the sensational search (which included a grand jury inquiry, and a $10,000 reward offered by the producers of the 1933 film *Bureau of Missing Persons*) for this corrupt New York State Supreme Court Justice yielded no results. His missing persons file was officially closed in 1979, and "pulling a Judge Carter" became part of the culture until a certain "Jimmy Hoffa" came along.

Amelia Earhart (1897–?): The first female pilot to make a solo, nonstop transatlantic flight in 1932, aboard her cherry-red Lockheed Vega 5B, the record-breaking "Queen of the Air" disappeared alongside her navigator, Fred Noonan (1893–?), while attempting to circumnavigate the globe aboard a twin-engine Lockheed 10 Electra, halfway between Australia and Hawaii, back in 1937. A celebrity in her lifetime, Earhart's vanishing still commands much public interest.

Jim Thomson (1906–?): The son of a wealthy textile manufacturer, James Harrison Wilson Thomson was born in Greenville, Delaware, and joined the OSS (Office of Strategic Services, a precursor of the CIA) during World War II, conducting operations in Africa and Southeast Asia, before working as military attaché at the United States legation in post-war Thailand. Turning to commercial pursuits, he would cofound the enormously successful Thai Silk Company Ltd. in the late 1940s. On March 26, 1967, while on vacation in Malaysia, Thomson went for an after-lunch stroll and never returned. The massive 1448-day search delivered no findings either.

Michael Rockefeller (1938–?): Committed to the study of the New Guinea Asmat tribe, this adventurous ethnographer (who also happened to be a fourth-generation Rockefeller family heir, and the son of then-governor Nelson Rockefeller; 1908–1979) was never seen again after he attempted to swim to shore from a capsized canoe. The following handsomely funded investigation could not discern whether he had been the victim of drowning, a shark attack, local cannibalism, or all of the above, as no remains were ever found.

Elizabeth Eaton "Connie" Converse (1924–?): Never quite "making it" in the late 1950s New York music scene, by 1963 this talented yet extremely introspective folk singer–songwriter moved to Michigan where she worked as the Managing Editor of an academic journal (*Journal of Conflict Resolution*). A decade later, and in spite of her friends' and family's best efforts to lift her spirits, a burnt out and depressed Connie filled her Volkswagen Beetle with all of her belongings and left Michigan, destination unknown. Her music, at least, would eventually be rescued from oblivion by her one-time friend, cartoonist Gene Deitch (1924–2020), via the home tape-recordings he had preserved. Collected in the 2009 album *How Sad, How Lovely*, it allowed Connie to reach a fresh new worldwide audience she never would have thought possible in her own time.

Jimmy Hoffa (1913–?): The fittingly named James Riddle Hoffa was a powerful trade unionist tightly linked to organized crime. While serving as president of the Teamsters Union, in 1967 he was given thirteen years in prison on counts of jury tampering, attempted bribery, conspiracy, and mail fraud, a sentence commuted by then-president Richard Nixon (1913–1994) in 1971, on the condition he resign from the International Brotherhood of Teamsters (IBT). Four years later, Hoffa would go missing on his way to meet with two unfriendly Mafia capi. Presumably murdered and declared dead in 1982, his true fate remains, yes, a riddle to this day, while his reputation has stayed as controversial as ever.

BONUS FACTS

South Carolina's "uninhabited" Morgan Island is home to 3,500 rhesus macaques since 1979, imported and maintained there by the FDA for lab experiments.

In seventeenth-century Britain, ill-mannered women were forced to wear a metal muzzle, known as a "scold's bridle," locked around their head.

Nine hundred and twenty-eight nuclear tests were conducted just sixty miles away from Las Vegas, at the Nevada Test Site between 1951 and 1992.

Among their many unique traits, octopuses are natural-born boxers, known to "punch" pesky fish, and occasionally humans too.

DEE-BEE COOP, WHERE ARE YOU?

On the evening of November 24, 1971, D. B. Cooper jumped out of a passenger aircraft and into legend. Conjecture upon conjecture, the truth remains as elusive as the man himself, an unsolvable puzzle for both law enforcement and those private investigators who turned Cooper into their very own "Moby Dick."

1. A black suit, white shirt, and black tie–wearing gentleman, carrying a black leather briefcase (as nondescript as a middle-aged man could get in early 1970s) headed toward the now-defunct Northwest Orient Airlines counter at the Portland International Airport, and bought the $18.52 one-way ticket to Seattle aboard Flight 305 as "Dan Cooper."

2. Boarding the plane last, with no security checks to worry about, Cooper walked back to his last row, middle seat—18E—and requested two bourbon-and-soda highballs from flight attendant Florence Schaffner (b.1948).

3. Carrying only thirty-six out of its eighty-nine passenger capacity, which was unusual for that rainy Thanksgiving eve, the Boeing 727-100 aircraft got ready to take off at 2:50 p.m. Dominating all the surrounding unoccupied rows but for twenty-year-old undergrad Bill Mitchell sitting right across the aisle, our mystery man half-rose from his seat and, excusing himself, handed Schaffner (sitting in one of the jump seats attached to the rear door right behind him) an envelope, which she tucked into her pocket, thinking it a clumsy flirtation attempt.

4. Upon Cooper's insistence, the flight attendant finally opened the envelope and took the message out. Written in uniform felt-tip pen capitals it read:

> **I HAVE A BOMB IN MY BRIEFCASE.**
> **I WILL USE IT IF NECESSARY.**
> **YOU ARE BEING <u>HIJACKED</u>.**

5. As the plane accelerated and lifted off the runway at 2:58 p.m., Schaffner passed the note to flight attendant Tina Mucklow (b.1949), who had just arrived to join her at the back, before sitting next to the hijacker. Opening the briefcase on his lap, Cooper showed her what appeared to be a bomb, and stated his demands:
>   - Two hundred thousand dollars in "negotiable American currency"
>   - Four manually operated parachutes (two primaries, and two reserves)
>   - A fuel truck at the airport, ready to refuel the plane upon arrival

6. As Schaffner went to the cockpit with the list, Mucklow used the intercom to emergency-signal the pilots and stayed in the back with Cooper. In her own words "I was there for the hijacker to kind of keep him feeling safe, reassured, comfortable and not detonating that bomb." (*Rolling Stone*; January 12, 2021).

7. When it became clear Schaffner would not return from the cockpit, Cooper asked Mucklow to sit next to him and relay messages on the *interphone*, a term passengers wouldn't normally use. He also sent her to get his original note back (as well as the envelope Schaffner had written his demands on). When she returned, he was wearing his signature horn-rimmed sunglasses.

8. Chain-smoking Raleigh cigarettes throughout the flight, Cooper was careful not to leave his "Earn a High-School Diploma!" matchbook behind. His conversations with Mucklow, however, revealed familiarity with the plane itself (such as knowing the overhead compartments carried oxygen bottles), and the area both on and above the ground. The criminal also stood out due to his collected, polite, and articulated demeanor. In her words: "He seemed rather nice. He was never cruel or nasty. He was thoughtful and calm all the time." (*New York*; October 18, 2007).

9. Flight 305 was kept circling 6,000 feet above Puget Sound (to prevent debris and body parts from hitting a populated Seattle area, should the bomb go off) while authorities rushed to meet Cooper's demands. Told to be patient and keep their seatbelts fastened due to "minor difficulties" requiring the burning of fuel before landing, the passengers didn't suspect a thing—including young Bill Mitchell, who wondered why the blonde

stewardess seemed so interested in an old guy wearing *long thermal underwear* over his socks.

10. Informed that his demands had finally been met, Cooper instructed the *airstairs* (another technical term for the truck carrying the passenger staircase), the fuel truck, and the vehicle carrying the money and parachutes be lined at "ten o'clock" from the plane, fifty yards away on the runway. The aircraft finally touched down at 5:39 p.m. on track 16R, and the hijacker ordered all of the cabin window shades to be shut, to discourage any snipers.

11. Once Mucklow had retrieved the money ($10,000, previously micro-filmed unmarked twenties from the L 1963A or 1969 series), Cooper allowed for the still-unsuspecting passengers to leave the aircraft, though the bills had come in an untied heavy canvas bank bag instead of the knapsack he instructed. After they were on their way, and as Tina started bringing in the parachutes (Cooper expertly examined all and noted a lack of "D" rings), the other attendants (Schaffner, and first-class stewardess Alice Hancock) approached Cooper to request they be released too. He agreed but requested Mucklow stay aboard.

12. Unbeknownst to both the authorities and Cooper, one of the chutes was a dummy (sewn shut and marked with an "X") which had been picked in haste alongside the others, but that wasn't the one he would choose to cut the nylon suspension ropes from with his pocketknife, in order to wrap the money bag. Then he tied the end of a six-foot-long nylon cord to the bag, and the other end around his waist, before easily cinching an old-but-working, military-issue chute on (it would later be revealed he took "X" as his reserve). Mucklow relayed his instructions for a flight bound for Mexico City, at 10,000 feet altitude, the landing gear down, and the flaps lowered at *precisely fifteen degrees.*

13. After the gas had been pumped, and agreeing on a Reno, Nevada, stopover for another refuel necessary to reach Mexico, at 7:36 p.m. the 727 took off from SEA-TAC with its flight crew in the cockpit, Mucklow still by Cooper's side in the cabin, and two McChord Air Force Base F-106s in tow at a safe distance. Taking the standard Victor 23 low-altitude course, the aircraft cruised south toward the Columbia River and the Willamette Valley across it.

14. Cooper ordered Mucklow to head for the cockpit, close the curtain leading to the first-class section of the plane behind her, and turn off the cabin lights. He also assured her he would bring the bomb attaché with him and disarm it. Around 8:04 p.m., a panel light flashed in the cockpit indicating to the crew that the hijacker had managed to open the aft stairwell. Wanting to check if he was still on board, Tina buzzed him on the interphone, and above the noise they heard him say "Everything is fine now." Nine minutes later, a change in air pressure followed by an upward tail jerk indicated Cooper had made his jump.

15. At 10:15 p.m., the 727 landed at Reno, and was thoroughly searched. The criminal, the money, and two parachutes were gone, as was the plastic sign explaining how to operate the aft stairwell (it would be found by a deer hunter in 1978). Aboard, the FBI found his black tie, tie-clip, eight Raleigh cigarette butts (eventually lost), a primary chute, and a reserve one cut to shreds. The ensuing forty-five-year-long whatever-it-takes manhunt, code-named NORJAK (Northwest Hijacking), would only deliver ever-growing frustration.

16. The fact that news wire services rechristened the hijacker "D. B. Cooper" after a ruled-out suspect (out of eight hundred!) didn't help either, nor did the 1980 explosion of Mount St. Helens, which would have blown to bits any physical remains, provided DBC had landed farther to the east. Then in 1980, and against all odds, a breakthrough.

17. On the cool but sunny Sunday of February 10, 1980, the Ingram family, recently moved to Vancouver from Oklahoma, went along the banks of the Columbia River for a picnic. As eight-year-old Brian Ingram raked the sand with his forearm to make a campfire, a bulge in the sand caught his eye. It belonged to one of three packets of round-edge-worn, semi-waterlogged twenty-dollar bills (two containing $100 bills each, the other only ninety), their rubber bands disintegrating as the Ingrams examined them. As the FBI would later confirm, these belonged to part of the Cooper ransom loot—but then again, the investigation came to an impasse, as conflicting hypotheses on how the money got there, or where it had been, reached no consensus, other than that the money probably hadn't been buried at that spot very long, and had possibly been washed ashore when the river had risen.

18. Six years later, the recovered "treasure" was split between the Ingram boy (who had been rewarded $750 for his original find) and the airline insurance company, while the FBI kept fourteen bills for further research. As of the publication of this book, the remaining 9,710 bills haven't been found. No longer a child, Brian Ingram sold fifteen Cooper bills for $37,000 at a Dallas, Texas, auction in 2009. Seven years later, the FBI officially closed the NORJACK investigation for good.

BONUS FACT

It has been well established that the death of Princess Diana of Wales (1961–1997) triggered the transatlantic Beanie Baby frenzy which caused young mothers to trample each other over the royal purple Princess Ty Beanie Baby Bear. The boom—as is usual with all market bubbles—would be followed by a swift bust a short two years later.

INTERNATIONAL MAN OF MYSTERY

Women want to be with him, men want to be him, but who exactly was the man they are after? Blurred by his immense legend, D. B. Cooper has nonetheless been extensively profiled, a sharply defined snapshot which ruled out every suspect back in its day—as well as any other Cooper copycat or publicity-seeking wannabe coming to the fore since—as amusing as they may be.

Appearance: Carefully dressed like a dull salesman, some characteristics did stand out for the two flight attendants who saw him up close. He was five foot, ten inches tall, 180 pounds, mid-forties, olive skinned, brown-eyed, with good manners, and an education.

Location: Several of his comments to Mucklow revealed knowledge of the area, both on and above ground. Particularly, knowing the McChord Air Force Base (where he presumed his demanded parachutes would be picked) was only twenty minutes away from SEA-TAC was something half of the city residence wouldn't know. He also recognized Tacoma from above Puget Sound and was eager to jump from the aircraft relatively quickly as it approached the southern Seattle suburbs. It all points to a man who either was a Pacific Northwest resident, or a regular commuter. Possibly even an Air Force veteran.

Experience: Cooper knew his way around old military parachutes, how they worked, and how to use them. This speaks volumes, as most forty-five-year-old men of the period would have received paratrooper training (commandos, Green Berets), possibly World War II, but most likely for the Korean War. Assuming the bomb he carried was real, or even a prop made to look real, its set up was familiar to bomb experts as the type of portable demolition explosive often taken by paratroopers behind enemy lines.

Expertise: Cooper was all too familiar with the Boeing 727-100. He knew facts never disclosed to civilian flight crews or even airlines, such as the precise speed-reducing flap setting of 15 degrees unique to the aircraft, its stable low-flight capability, and the aft stairwell external activation by a single rear cabin switch, as well as the possibility of deploying it during flight, which made it ideal for bail-out, as proven by the CIA during its Vietnam War clandestine operations. Furthermore, modern findings of rare metal and mineral fragments (such as bismuth, aluminum titanium, cerium, strontium, etc.) in his tie, confirm he had to be involved with Boeing's research and development.

Motive: In his Norjak: *The Investigation of D. B. Cooper* (1986) book, the FBI agent in charge of the operation, Ralph Himmelsbach (1925–2019), stated that criminals who attempt daring, high-stakes robberies almost always do so out of equally steep, urgent need ... perhaps the kind of need created by the sudden loss of your job, as Boeing implemented massive layoffs in the years immediately preceding the hijack?

Origin: *Dan Cooper* is a Franco-Belgian series of graphic novels created by Albert Weinberg (1922–2011) published since 1957. Though unknown in the United States, its title character, a Canadian ace pilot and parachutist, would have been well known to Canadian boys and men at the time. Having no noticeable accent, Cooper's request for "negotiable American currency" stands out. Would it be possible, after all this time, that the famed hijacker who beat the system and got away with it was Canadian all along?

BONUS QUOTES

"Idiot: A member of a large and powerful tribe whose influence in human affairs has always been dominant and controlling."
—Ambrose Bierce

"She was chaste, very chaste. Of course, sometimes they caught her, too."
—Norm Crosby

"God gave us a penis and a brain, but only enough blood to run one at a time."
—Robin Williams

NORTHWESTERN EXPOSURE

The "Jack McGee" to D. B. Cooper's "Hulk," reporter Bruce A. Smith continues his dogged pursuit of the elusive DBC, while attending to his duties as editor of the online news website The Mountain News of Mount Rainier, Washington. Self-publishing his findings in the massive DB Cooper and the FBI: A Case Study of America's Only Unsolved Skyjacking volume, now in its third printing, Mr. Smith kindly answered the following questionnaire.

Who are you, and what do you do?
I am an investigative journalist, along with being a professional storyteller.

Why did you make D. B. Cooper your object of study?
As I wrote in my book, I became reacquainted with D. B. Cooper as a beat reporter for the *Eatonville Dispatch* in 2006 when local authors wrote a book about their friend, Barb Dayton, and her confession to being D. B. Cooper. It is a compelling story.

What sets the D. B. Cooper skyjacking apart from other high-stakes heists?
It has never been solved. As such, it was the first of its kind.

What sets D. B. Cooper himself apart from other criminals?

He was older than most when he committed his crime, and he didn't get caught, or even identified!

In which ways did the FBI botch the investigation?
Lost evidence: they gave DBC a forty-hour head start on the ground search. They didn't interview the ATC who handled the flight when Cooper jumped. Poor supervision and management of documents and field reports: they refused to share information with other agents, field offices, and journalists; and were reluctant to pursue leads developed by the Citizen Sleuths.

Such as?
Tom Kaye and the Citizen Sleuths have uncovered a treasure trove of evidence. First, they found titanium and special machined bits of metal on the tie in 2009. Then they found rare earth minerals in 2016. Last year they found springtime-only diatoms on the bills. That is revolutionary evidence, and the FBI has not followed up on any of it. In addition, Eric Ulis has located the ATC who handled the flight when Cooper jumped, and his commentary adds more weight to the Western Flight Path (WFP) that Eric and Robert Nicholson have been developing over the past few years. Eric also discovered vital information buried in FBI documents on a second piece of the aircraft that was discovered in the Cinebar, WA, region, adding additional weight to the thinking that the FBI's flight path is incorrect. Eric has also located hundreds of acres of wildlife refuge areas under the WFP that have had virtually no human footprints

in the past fifty years; they're possible LZs where Cooper could have landed, buried his chute, and then walked to T-Bar to bury the money.

Did D. B. Cooper jump from the plane or hide in plain sight?
Although no one saw D. B. Cooper jump, it is the most plausible explanation for his absence in Reno when the FBI boarded the plane.

Could he have survived a jump in those conditions?
Yes, and many skydivers and commandos survive daily in comparable circumstances.

Was he a "lone wolf," as presented by the media, or did he have accomplices?
It's possible he had accomplices, although there is no overt evidence that he did. I believe he may have.

Of all the D. B. Cooper alleged suspects, who do you think presents the strongest case?
None of them.

Do you have suspects of your own?
I have none. However, I strongly believe that DBC was a commando or some kind of special ops kind of guy. So do guys in Special Forces.

How did D. B. Cooper achieve cult status in American culture?
America loves a folk hero who "Beat the Man." DBC

is now becoming a mythical figure in American life, comparable to Geronimo, and Chief Joseph.

Do you have any favorite books on the case?
Skyjack, by Gray, and D. B. Cooper: The Real McCoy by Calame and Rhodes.

What sets your book, D. B. Cooper and the FBI: A Case Study of America's Only Unsolved Skyjacking, apart from the pack?
My book is the only case study written on D. B. Cooper, and it is one of the few to take a close look at the FBI and how they handled the case. I spoke to over a dozen FBI agents, three crew members, five passengers, and copycat Robb Heady. They all were helpful—in varying degrees—in my understanding of the facts of this case.

The book is available at Amazon and can also be ordered in any bookstore. If anyone would like an autographed copy, they can mail me a check for thirty bucks, and I'll send them a copy.

Why does D. B. Cooper matter in this day and age?
D. B. Cooper shows us some of the underpinnings of what it means to be an American. Nine hundred confessions, 1,100 suspects—most of whom were thrown under the bus by jilted lovers—the limitations of law enforcement, the desire of so many men to solve this case and, in some small way, make our world a safer place.

V

MYSTIFYING MYSTERIES

"I look up toward the night sky, visible through two high arches above my office windows. Almost all the way to the top of the arches the clouds glow with Manhattan's light. At the pinnacle there is darkness, and it draws me. I'm not only scared and upset, frankly I'm also curious. I want to know what's going on out there. As I watch, the night sky grows a little darker."
—Whitley Strieber

A SKELETON IN EVERY CLOSET

Long a magnet for madness and crime, the Cecil Hotel in downtown Los Angeles, California, conjures dread among criminal and paranormal investigators alike.

1. Built in 1923 as a fashionable hotspot for business travelers and tourists, the Cecil saw its fortune shift dramatically with the advent of the Great Depression in 1929. A magnificent ruin in a neighborhood, the infamous "Skid Row," increasingly populated by homeless drifters, junkies, and criminals throughout most of the twentieth century.

2. Its first suicide on record happened on January 2, 1927, when fifty-two-year-old Percy Ormond Cook blew his own head off after failing to reconcile with his wife and child. Four years later another man, W. K. Norton (forty-six), registered under a false name, also killed himself, by ingesting poison pills. The following year, 1932, a Benjamin Dodich (twenty-five) shot himself, while in 1934 Army Medical Corps Sgt. Louis D. Borden (fifty-three) slit his own throat. A Grace E. Magro (age unknown) fell to her death from the ninth floor in 1937. Marine Corps fireman Roy Thompson (thirty-five) would also fall from the building in 1938. A year later, a Navy officer by the name Erwin C. Neblett (thirty-nine) committed suicide, as would teacher Dorothy Seger (forty-five) in 1940.

3. In 1944, Dorothy Jean Purcell (nineteen) would drop her newborn baby boy off the building, a tragic event that was followed by yet another series of jumpers, including Robert Smith (thirty-five) in 1947, and Helen Gurnee (fifty-five) in 1954. The year 1962 was marred by the suicides of Julia Frances Moore (fifty), and Pauline Otton (twenty-seven), who tragically fell on a man, George Gianinni (sixty-five), who was just passing by (as revealed by his squished corpse with hands still tucked in his pockets). At this point, the hotel had well-earned the nickname it became known by, "The Suicide."

4. But not all deaths at the Cecil were self-inflicted. Retired telephone operator "Pigeon" Goldie Osgood was found stabbed and raped in her room on June 4, 1964. Her murder remains unsolved to this day. No more deaths were registered at the hotel until 1975, when an unidentified twenty-something woman going by the name "Alison Lowell" jumped off from her room on the twelfth floor. Then in the 1980s, the Devil moved in.

5. Paying fourteen dollars a night, serial killer, rapist, kidnapper, pedophile, burglar, and all-around psycho Richard "Night Stalker" Ramirez (1960–2013) made the Cecil his home during the mid-1980s, engaging in part of his killing spree from its premises, where his blood-soaked clothes didn't raise any eyebrows. After Ramirez's capture and conviction of nineteen death sentences (all of which he cheated on by dying from cancer in 2013), allegedly "reformed" serial killer Johann "Jack"

Unterweger (1950–1994) moved into the hotel, where he was suspected of strangling three sex workers with their bras, his M-O while in Europe.

6. Going through several renovations in an effort to distance itself from its bloody past, in 2013 the Cecil, now re-branded "Stay on Main," witnessed another strange death, when the body of Canadian Elisa Lam (twenty-one) was found in one of the roof's water tanks, as a security video later surfaced showing Ms. Lam behaving erratically in the hotel elevator. Suicide or foul play, her death remains unsolved, as does the fall from the building of an unnamed twenty-eight-year-old man two years later. By then, the hotel had already been immortalized on countless films, TV shows, and music videos.

7. Perhaps the most iconic death ever to be connected to the Cecil, that of the "Black Dahlia," was definitely not suicide. Found chopped in two at Leimert Park, seven miles away from the hotel in 1947, it later surfaced the victim, aspiring actress Elizabeth Short (1924–1947), had been seen at the hotel bar with a friend and two sailors. However, the police maintained she was last seen alive at the Millennium Biltmore Hotel, not the Cecil, on January 9, and was not seen again until found dead on January 15. Her murder, too, remains unsolved.

THE NINTH GATE

Wanton death abounds not only in hotels. Sometimes beautiful historic landmarks mysteriously attract the desperate and the downtrodden too, as historically proved by San Francisco's own Golden Gate Bridge, America's number one suicide spot.

1. Largely considered one of the Wonders of the Modern World, this beautiful, one-mile-wide, *orange vermilion* suspension bridge began to be built in 1933, and by the time of its opening in 1937 it had claimed the lives of eleven men.

2. Soon after the bridge's official opening Harold B. Wobber, a forty-seven-year-old lighterman with PTSD (he was a World War I veteran) became the first suicide victim in the bridge's history, despite a bystander's efforts to prevent him from jumping. He would soon be followed by an estimated two thousand people (official count having ended at 997, in 1995, to prevent instances of "record breaker" jumpers).

3. With the Pacific side closed to pedestrians, the bay-facing deck registers the most jumps. It has been calculated that the 245 feet, four-second-long, seventy-five-miles-per-hour fall is met by hard-hitting ice-cold water which kills most people on impact. The 5 percent who briefly survive die either from drowning or hypothermia, a quick and mostly painless release which still attracts many, though the steel mesh, safety net installation currently underway might thwart their efforts as early as 2021, with 2020 already reporting a steep decline in the number of deaths.

4. The most dramatic Golden Gate suicide deaths include:
- Five-year-old Marilyn DeMont and her father, foreman August DeMont (thirty-seven) in 1945.
- Charles S. Gallagher Sr., who jumped off the bridge in 1954 while facing an unfavorable company audit, only to be followed into the icy waters by a depressed Charles S. Gallagher Jr. a few days later.
- Marc Salinger (twenty-eight), a former golf caddy of John F. Kennedy (1917–1963) who, never having fully recovered from the trauma of JFK's assassination, also took his own life at the bridge in 1977.
- Three-year-old Kellie Page, thrown off the bridge by her father, Steven Page, shortly after he shot and killed her mother, before jumping himself.
- Victoria's Secret founder Roy L. Raymond (1947–1993).
- Activist Paul Aladdin Alarab (1958–2003), who barely survived another fall from the bridge in 1988 and returned to protest there again in 2003, but didn't live to tell the tale.

5. Filming at the Golden Gate day and night for ten thousand hours during 2004, the crew of documentary film *The Bridge* managed to capture twenty-three of that year's twenty-four death toll.

The film also caught many people being saved from jumping, and interviewed J. Kevin Hines (b.1981), a man who changed his mind halfway through falling, survived the hit, and was kept afloat by a sea lion until rescued. This act of God saw him turn his life around and become a nationally famous suicide prevention speaker.

6. Other than the Golden Gate, and listed by their death toll, the world's most infamous suicide locations include the Yangtze River Bridge (Nanjing, China) with two thousand casualties, the Prince Edward Viaduct (Toronto, Canada) with 492 suicides, and finally the Aokigahara forest (Mt. Fuji, Japan) with 105 suicides per year. Of course, they all pale when compared to Switzerland, a country where legal assisted suicide has taken the lives of 3,248 people as of 2020.

BONUS FACTS

Despite having no soccer skills whatsoever, for a whole decade Brazilian con-man Carlos Kaiser (born Carlos Henrique Raposo; 1963) managed to swindle many professional teams, and live the life of a soccer star without playing any matches.

On July 11, 2021, sixteen people were instantly burned to a crisp while taking selfies atop of a watchtower in Jaipur, India, during a thunderstorm.

HOLIDAY ROAD

Crazy architecture, oversized-object sculptures, and other roadside enigmas caught American travelers' eyes—and pockets—until the old roads system came to be superseded by the modern Interstate Highway System in the mid-1950s, which sent many out of business. Yet, as a silent testament to a bygone era, some continue to thrive ...

Lucy the Elephant: Standing in Margate City, New Jersey, since 1881, the oldest surviving "novelty architecture" attraction in America is a sixty-five-foot-high wood and tin echo of its now defunct seventy-eight-foot plaster Parisian cousin, the Elephant of the Bastille. Its design was patented by Irish inventor James V. Lafferty (1856–1898), who came to prominence by building similar elephant structures all over the country, and still holds well despite a brief mid-century period of disrepair. Declared a National Historic Landmark in 1976, these days it even offers overnight stays at an Airbnb.

The Brown Derby: Nothing says "Hollywood" like this restaurant shaped like a giant derby hat built at 3427 Wilshire Boulevard, Los Angeles, by playwright and manager Wilson Mizner (1876–1933) in 1926. So popular it spawned a franchise, with non-hat-shaped "Brown Derbies" opening in Hollywood, Beverly Hills, Los Feliz, and other locations; the original place was demolished, and rebuilt again as an even larger hat in 1936, at 3377 Wilshire Boulevard. While forever immortalized in movies and cartoons, the restaurant closed for good in the 1980s, but its remnant structure lives on in the same location, sitting atop the Brown Derby Plaza shopping mall.

Cabazon Dinosaurs: Forever roaming Riverside Country, California, Dinny the Dinosaur and Mr. Rex are concrete dinosaurs (a brontosaurus and t-rex respectively) originally created by Claude K. Bell (1897–1988) out of salvaged construction material to attract customers to his Wheel Inn Café, which opened in 1958. Dinny's construction began in 1964 and took eleven years to complete. Rex was made in 1981, but plans for a mammoth and a prehistoric garden were scrapped after Mr. Bell's passing in 1981. Somewhat appropriately, Dinny's belly currently holds a *creationist* museum, and gift shop.

Jolly Green Giant: Originally designed for the Minnesota Valley Canning Company by Leo Burnett (1891–1971) in 1935, the character was, and still is, a mascot for the Green Giant canned beans brand, currently owned by B&G Foods. Since 1979, its fifty-five-foot fiberglass statue proudly towers over the city of Blue Earth, Minnesota, where it attracts an estimated ten thousand visitors a year.

Longaberger Building: Formerly the headquarters of the now-defunct Longaberger Company, an American manufacturer and distributor of handcrafted maple wood baskets, this 180,000-square-foot building—rightfully shaped as a basket—opened its doors in 1997 and closed them for good almost twenty years later. Heritage, Ohio, is currently fighting for its preservation and addition to the National Register of Historic Places.

Enchanted Highway: Extending north from Regent to the Gladstone exit on Interstate 94, east of Dickinson, North Dakota, this large collection of scrap metal sculptures (which include the giant Tin Family, a Covey of Pheasants, and the World's Largest Grasshopper) draws around six thousand cars to Regent every year, and is the work of one man, local sculptor Gary Greff (b.1949), who also runs a gift shop, and turned the former town high school into a medieval theme hotel, the Enchanted Castle.

Cadillac Ranch: Heading west out of Amarillo, Texas, on old Route 66, this 1974 art installation, a line of ten buried-by-the-nose Cadillacs, has been immortalized in plenty of music video-clips and movies (including Disney-Pixar's *Cars*). Created by Chip Lord (b.1944) and Hudson Marquez (b.1947), and originally intending to depict the evolution of Cadillacs from 1949 to 1963, the cars are periodically repainted as part of publicity stunts, only to be haphazardly spray-painted—or set on fire—by visitors.

Hole N" The Rock: Utah's most famous roadside attraction, this 5,000-square-foot home that was carved into a huge rock by US Highway 191, in Canyonlands Country, by the Christensen family (they began to live on the premises in 1952, while visitors were allowed in as soon as 1957) is advertised with huge twenty-foot-tall white letters on the side of the cliff. In addition to seven-dollar house tours the site now includes three gift shops, the largest collection of local artist Lyle Nichols's metal sculptures, and a popular petting zoo as well.

The Thing? Museum: Hailed by more than 240 signs along Interstate 10, between El Paso, Texas, and Tucson, Arizona, lies this one-of-a-kind hall of the weird that, since 1965, treats visitors to dinosaurs, aliens, tortured souls, Hitler's Rolls-Royce, and a Conestoga wagon from the *Oklahoma!* musical, all leading to The Thing itself. What is The Thing? You'll have to see it to believe it!

Balls of twine: There are several gigantic balls of sisal twine in America, the largest of which can be found in Cawker City, Kansas.

A community effort (apparently the people of Cawker hate to be out-twined by other towns), as of 2018 this ball weighed over ten tons.

The world's second-largest ball of twine was rolled by a single man, a Francis A. Johnson, and can be found in Darwin, Minnesota, weighing almost nine tons.

The third-biggest twine ball in size is actually the second heaviest at 9.6 tons, rolled by a James Frank Kotera in his own yard at Lake Nebagamon,

Wisconsin. A fourth ball weighing six tons may be found at the *Ripley's Believe It or Not!* Museum of Branson, Missouri, but lost all respect when found to be made of *nylon* twine.

Milk bottles: No other product in the world is as wholesome as dairy, and there are enough giant milk bottles everywhere to attest to it.

Built in 1933 as an ice-cream parlor, abandoned, and then restored and placed in front of Boston Children's Museum since 1977, the forty-feet-tall **Hood Milk Bottle** would hold 58,620 gallons if it were a real bottle.

The **Benewah Milk Bottles**, on the other hand, are two milk bottle-shaped landmarks in Spokane, Washington, built in 1934 and 1935 respectively, to sell Benewah Creamery Company dairy products. The one on Garland Avenue currently houses Mary Lou's Milk Bottle diner, while the one on the Cedar Street strip-mall is part of the Stepping Stones Pediatric Therapy center.

The **Milk Bottle Grocery** (2426 N. Classen Boulevard, Oklahoma City, Oklahoma) added a large metal Braum's milk bottle to the roof of the already unusual triangular brick building in 1948, which currently stands empty, while the bottle itself is in dire need of restoration despite being included in the National Register of Historic Places.

Coffee Pots: Needing something stronger than milk? A historic stop along the Lincoln Highway (Pennsylvania), the eighteen-foot-tall silver-painted building known plainly as **The Coffee Pot**

was built in 1927 as a white and red lunch stand next to a service station, but has since been restored and moved on its own across the street to the Bedford Fairgrounds.

Another 1927 gem still serving coffee after all these years, the twenty-five-foot-tall **Bob's Java Jive** was built in solid concrete as the Coffee Pot Restaurant by a Tacoma, Washington, veterinarian, Dr. Otis G. Button, and currently retains its original white and red color scheme.

But perhaps the oldest surviving coffee pot in America is the **Old Salem Coffee Pot** in Winston-Salem, North Carolina. A seven-foot-tall tin coffee pot (which could hold up to 740 gallons of coffee), made to promote a tin shop owned by brothers Julius and Samuel Mickey all the way back to 1858, is America's oldest roadside attraction.

Paul Bunyans: A staple of American and Canadian folklore, the legendary Paul Bunyan has been immortalized by many statues as tall as the lumberjack himself.

The first one was built in Bemidji, Minnesota, in 1937, and followed by several others in that state—including an amusement park located in the town of Brainerd!

Another thirty-foot-tall Bunyan statue was built with concrete in 1959, to commemorate the centennial of Oregon's statehood.

A third, truly gigantic monument featuring a towering forty-nine-foot-tall Bunyan and a forty-five-foot-tall Babe was erected in the 1960s at the Trees of Mystery park near Klamath, California.

Perhaps the most famous of all, however, has been terrorizing the children of Bangor, Maine, since 1959. A fairly realistic fiberglass depiction of the mythical axe-wielding hero standing thirty-one-feet-tall at Bass Park, it was prominently featured in Stephen King's IT (1986) novel, and the 2019 It *Chapter Two* movie adaptation.

Big Things: Even as low-cost flights are coming to replace its traditional continent-wide road trips, Australia's answer to America's roadside attractions, "big things" continue to be built to this day, with classics like Coffs Harbour's Big Banana, Bowen's Big Mango, Woombye's Big Pineapple, Goulburn's Big Merino, and Glenrowan's Big Ned Kelly—it doesn't get more Australian than that!—recently joined by Adelaide's Big Pigeon from 2020, and Calen's Big *Thongs* (meaning "flip-flops") displayed as late as 2021.

BONUS QUOTES

"War hath no fury like a noncombatant."
—Charles Edward Montague

"Actors with political views are a dime a dozen."
—Tom Hanks

"Fart for freedom, fart for liberty—and fart proudly."
—Benjamin Franklin

GRAVITY FALLS

An important fixture in the roadside attractions circle, gravity hills are places where the surrounding land obstructs the horizon in a way that their downhill slope seems to be going uphill, which makes people, things, and vehicles look as if defying gravity. Places resting on such slopes or built cleverly tilted on level ground also take advantage of such an illusion, often marketing it as the product of either quantum forces or supernatural activity.

Richfield Gravity Hill: The plain-looking Richfield Road in Rowan County, North Carolina, hides a secret. There's a graffiti-scribbled road section lying about thirty minutes outside Salisbury, where cars in neutral supposedly roll uphill ... when sprinkled with baby powder. According to one local legend, a mother and her child were hit and killed by a speeding truck as the woman tried to push her own car uphill, her spirit reliving the ordeal since.

Prosser Gravity Hill: A run-of-the-mill gravity hill found in a stretch of North Crosby Road about 10–15 miles north of Prosser, a "START" line painted on the pavement marks the spot where your vehicle will be pulled up by an old, reputedly haunted grain elevator.

Spook Hill: Another supposedly haunted gravity hill, this time in Lake Wales, Florida, local lore pins the phenomenon on the ghost of a Native American chief who battled an alligator in the area, which delights in playful ghost imagery to the point Casper the Friendly Ghost has become the elementary school mascot.

Blaine Christian Church: Located on the southwest corner of the intersection at Joyfield and Putney, in Blaine Township, Michigan, since 1895 this church has been pulling sinners back up Putney Road as soon as their vehicles reach a slight dip at the bottom of a gentle, seemingly downhill grade.

Laurel Caverns: The largest cave in Pennsylvania is a privately owned tourist attraction—including a gift shop and a mini–golf course—near Farmington where, other than its wondrous geological formations, some of its many steeply inclined passageways are used to delight families with gravity-defying balls which seem to roll upward.

Oregon Vortex and House of Mystery: Opened to the public in 1930 by Scotsman John Litster (1886–1959), a paranormal investigator who purchased the property after a friend invited him to America to assess a nearly collapsed turn-of-the-century former Old Grey Eagle Mining Company outpost office. Litster concluded the cabin rested in a 165-foot radius magnetic spot which bends light, defies gravity, and alters mass, and did what any sane person would do: turn it into a tourist attraction.

Mystery Spot: The owner of a welding shop and auto repair garage in Santa Cruz, California,

George Parther (1891–1946) purchased three acres of hillside redwood forest on October 21, 1940, coming—as is usual in every "vortex" story since—upon a 150 feet in diameter area which defied every instrument but his portable radio. Against conventional wisdom, George built a single wall, two-bedroom redwood shack on level, which he then lowered to this strange spot where it's been attracting 1,400 tourists a day on average, for the last eighty years.

Cosmos Mystery Area: Seventeen miles south of Rapid City, South Dakota, lies yet another tourist trap offering all the usual tropes of similar "vortices"—including standing at odd angles, chairs balancing on two legs, and water flowing backwards—spread over two hillside cabins, the first of which was supposedly discovered by two enterprising college students in 1952 while looking for a place to spend the summer in the Black Hills.

Montana Vortex and House of Mystery: A fun stop on the way to Glacier National Park (two miles east of Columbia Falls, on Highway 2), this quaint Montana attraction takes gravity hill tilt illusions to the next level, through a cleverly designed skewed cabin supposedly sitting amid three interlinked "quantum or gravitational anomalies" that make trees bend, and people shrink. The nifty gift shop is also well worth a look, though nothing supernatural occurs there.

Hudson Bay: The one place in the world where gravity really is weaker than in the rest of the planet is located in Canada but has no "spots" to speak of. The phenomenon baffled scientists for nearly forty years before they figured out the reason gravity is at its weakest there. Put simply, gravity being proportional to mass, when the mass of an area is made smaller, its gravity gets reduced, which is exactly what happened to the Hudson Bay when compacted by the weight of the massive Laurentide Ice Sheet during the latest ice age. Scientists also calculate it may take another five thousand years for Earth's mantle to rebound there, restoring gravity to normal levels.

BONUS FACTS

On March 8, 2021, former *Wonder Woman* comic artist José Delbo (b.1933) earned $1,850,000 selling non-fungible tokens, a.k.a. "bitcoin for nerds," featuring the DC/Warner-owned hero, leading both DC and Marvel comics to issue edicts forbidding such non-sanctioned trade-offs using their properties.

Allegedly transmitting a short, monotonous, buzzing tone since the 1970s, a Russian shortwave station UVB-76, known as "The Buzzer," continues to broadcast this strange signal twenty-four hours a day.

IN ANCIENT TIMES . . .

The original roadside attraction if ever there was one, the megalithic ruin we call Stonehenge remains a genuine historical mystery, but after decades of study science and archaeology have managed to uncover a few secrets surrounding its original construction and purpose.

1. Set on England's Salisbury Plain, Wiltshire, amid a dense complex of Neolithic and Bronze Age monuments (including several hundred burial mounds), Stonehenge consists of two rings of standing stones, an outer ring made of sandstone blocks called *Sarcens*, and an inner ring made of *bluestones* (volcanic basalt) which surrounds five *trilithons* (arches made of two bulkier Sarcens and a smaller lintel stone) arranged like a horseshoe with its open end facing northeast, which in turn surround yet another circle of bluestones.

2. The whole thing didn't plant itself, but rather took many generations of Britons, from the Neolithic to the Bronze Age, to build and rebuild it over a period of 1,500 years. It all started with a cemetery (in those days, basically holes filled with cremated remains), surrounded by a circular ditch built over five thousand years ago. At some point five hundred years later, builders decided to replace wooden posts with stone boulders imported from as far as Wales, which caused the construction to drag quite a bit.

3. It is entirely possible that what began as a cemetery and crematory ended up becoming something else, as the culture around the place surely changed over millennia, but nobody knows what the final construction was meant for, since it was produced by people who left no written records, other than 115 axe carvings on the stones themselves.

4. It is generally accepted, however, that the trilithons are aligned to the sunset of the winter solstice, and the opposing sunrise of the summer solstice, which suggests rituals were conducted at the site. Modern research also revealed Stonehenge to be part of a much larger complex, which includes the Stonehenge *Cursus*, a five-thousand-year-old two-mile-long trench running parallel to it.

5. People continued to be buried in those grounds well into the Anglo-Saxon period, but the earliest surviving description of the site dates back to 1130 AD, when historian Henry of Huntingdon (c.1088–1157) came up with the name *Stanenges* ("stone doorways") to describe it.

6. Knowing little, of course, doesn't prevent theories from running wild. In Huntingdon's time, some attributed Stonehenge's construction to none other than the wizard Merlin, while modern-day fans pin it on either druids or UFOs, depending on which way the cultural wind blows.

7. During our era, Stonehenge began to be excavated as early as 1620, and its first burial pits were found in the early 1800s. After its first restoration in 1901, a first aerial photograph was taken from a balloon in 1906. Fallen stones also had to be raised again and reset in 1797, 1900, and 1958.

8. Stonehenge's last private owner, Baronet Cecil Chubb (1876–1934), purchased the land for 6,600 pounds at an auction in 1915, and donated it to the Crown three years later, on the condition that the monument's preservation be assured.

9. Unfortunately, in 1905 the place had already seen its first drunken festival when seven hundred so-called "neo-druids" in wizard garments carried out a reclaiming ceremony. Despite a second restoration in 1963, man-made erosion of the monument became so severe that in 1977 mounting the trilithons (sigh) had to be forbidden, and the entire place roped off to keep visitors at a distance, but festivals continued to be held until 1985, when their prohibition led to the infamous "Battle of the Beanfield" between formerly peaceful New Age travelers and local police.

10. Fortunately, by 2013 renewed conservation and visitor management efforts had borne fruit, with one of the two roads leading to the site being re-routed underground, and a new center built (manned by 154 volunteers) which, as of 2016, received five hundred thousand schoolchildren a year. Visits inside the monument had by then also been allowed to limited numbers of people.

SPINAL TAP

Like a druid's fever dream, dozens of replicas of the original prehistoric monument, ranging from the astronomically accurate to the plain ridiculous, can be found in the world today.

Maryhill Stonehenge (1925): An accurate concrete recreation of the original Stonehenge, not its modern ruin, it was built just off Highway 97, in Maryhill, Washington. Commissioned by businessman Samuel Hill (1857–1931) as a memorial to the Klickitat County soldiers fallen during World War I—the first of its type in America. It currently belongs to the Maryhill Museum of Art, and admission remains free.

Carhenge (1987): Dedicated at the June 1987 summer solstice by its creator, artist Jim Reinders (b.1928) and his family, this automobile homage to the original Stonehenge as it stands today (all thirty-eight of its major stones are present and accurately placed, though not astronomically aligned) was conceived by Reinders as a memorial to his father who had passed in 1982, and inspired by both a recent trip to England and the Cadillac Ranch installation. Built on Highway 87, three miles north of Alliance, Nebraska, it was considered mainly an eyesore by the locals who, nonetheless, went to its site en masse to witness the 2017 solar eclipse.

Stonehenge II (1989): This "90 percent as wide and 60 percent as high" plastered steel-mesh homage to the original Stonehenge doesn't even pretend to be accurate, but rather a work of art. As such, it also takes the license to include similarly made Easter Island *moai* replicas guarding it on each side. It was originally commissioned by retired Dallas hotel owner Al Sheppard to his neighbor, artist Doug Hill, in 1989, five years before the former's passing, and relocated to the Ingram, Texas, Hill Country Arts Foundation campus in 2011 after the property it stood on had been sold to new owners. As chance would have it, its new location lies directly under the path of an upcoming 2024 total solar eclipse!

Gunma Astronomical Observatory Stonehenge (1999): Not unlike the Maryhill Stonehenge, this solstice-aligned concrete recreation of the original Stonehenge found in Gunma, Japan, sits on the premises alongside a replica of eighteenth-century Indian astronomical park Jantar Mantar. Japan's very modern Gunma Astronomical Observatory was designed for both astronomical research and public use and remains the most visited in the whole country.

Permian Basin Stonehenge (2004): Built with donated quarry stones on the edge of the University of Texas, at the Permian Basin Campus (UTPB) in Odessa, this version of Stonehenge has the same diameter and solstice alignment as its British counterpart, but only 70 percent of its height. Also, to save money and allow a faster assembly, Sarcens were made from two stones stacked on top of each other, rather than a single one.

Foamhenge (2004) and Bamahenge (2012): Made from Styrofoam and fiberglass respectively, they are the work of Virginia artist-sculptor Mark Cline (b.1961), who first came to prominence with his life-sized dinosaurs, and built Foamhenge as a roadside attraction (which had to be restored and relocated to Centreville, Virginia, in 2017). Years later, while repairing a bunch of hurricane-damaged dinosaurs he had made for Alabama billionaire George W. Barber (b.1940), the latter commissioned Cline with a "henge" of his own, and the stormproof Bamahenge was the result. While fairly accurate in terms of the "stones" general dimensions and alignment, neither replica contains as many megaliths as the British original.

Stonehenge Aotearoa (2005): A modernist wood-and-concrete remake of the original, this New Zealand "henge" is a ninety-eight-foot-diameter circle of twenty-four pillars capped by lintels, with a sixteen-foot-tall sundial obelisk at its center. Made as a working astronomical park, it is aligned with the southern hemisphere's solstices and equinoxes.

Mystical Horizons (2005): While technically not a replica, nor a straight-up homage, this modernist "twenty-first-century Stonehenge" was the vision of aerospace engineer "Jack" Olson (1922–2001), who wanted to build an astronomical site complete with six granite walls with slots that act as a solar calendar, a large sundial, and a sighting tube fixed on Polaris.

After his passing, the people of Bottineau, North Dakota (famous for another roadside attraction, the thirty-foot-tall "Tommy Turtle"), banded together to make the man's design come true along Highway 43.

Esperance Stonehenge (2011): Privately built from 137 locally quarried Australasian Granite stones of up to fifty-five tons, this full-sized solstice-aligned replica of the original Stonehenge is a profitable tourist attraction in Esperance, Australia.

Henges galore: It would take a whole book to list every "henge" in the world, especially those not even making the barest attempt at resemblance seriously, like South Carolina's "Phonehenge," Topeka's "Truckhenge," or the many non-perennial "strawhenges" and "snowhenges" made with straw bales and ice respectively. While interesting in its conception, New York's "Manhattanhenge," which sees sunsets and sunrises align with the east–west streets of the city, also doesn't qualify, though one cannot help but think the sun triggered a similar sense of wonder in ancient Britons.

BONUS QUOTE

"I did not come here to guide lambs, I came to wake lions."
—Javier Milei

BIO-DOME

An unwitting "Stonehenge" of modern times, future generations may soon forget the original meaning and purpose behind the creation of the ambitious-yet-misguided Biosphere 2 facility.

1. A closed ecological system built between 1987 and 1991 in the outskirts of Oracle, Arizona, Biosphere 2 was a new kind of global ecology lab intending to study the interactions between life systems, and our own relationship with said systems via farming technology. Ultimately, the project sought to gain understanding that would aid future space colonization.

2. Its 3.14-acre greenhouse structure was comprised of seven sun- and gas-powered *biome* areas: a 20,000-square-foot rainforest; a 9,100-square-foot ocean with a coral reef; a 4,800-square-foot mangrove; a 14,000-square-foot savannah; a 15,000-square-foot desert; a 27,000-square-foot agricultural system; and finally a fully equipped human habitat.

3. The first highly publicized "mission," from September 26, 1991, to September 26, 1993, was undertaken by a group of eight *biospherians* led by Dr. Roy Lee Walford (1924–2004), who talked the team into following the calorie restriction diet he had tried on mice, after it became apparent they could only grow about 83 percent of the food they needed.

4. While constantly hungry, the equally never-ending pressure of corporate and media attention meant failure was not an option.

5. Over time, the desert area came to be covered in shrubs due to greenhouse water condensation, rainforest and savannah trees became weak due to the lack of wind, ocean corals over-reproduced, becoming a pain to maintain, and most of the insect and vertebrate animal species simply died. Unsurprisingly, cockroaches and invading "crazy ants" did very well, practically colonizing the entire facility.

6. Trapped in an oxygen-deprived, man-size ant farm, the inevitable internal rift brought over by accusations of secret food caches, smuggled supplies, and data-tampering split the hungry and pest-ridden biospherians into two opposing camps that threatened to turn the entire endeavor into an airtight "Lord of the Flies" reenactment. Eventually, and to their credit, professional cooperation was strictly maintained in the face of mounting obstacles, but by the time they finally emerged from the place many lifelong friendships among the participants had been destroyed along the way.

7. As media caught on to the fact they were covering what was basically an overblown $150 million-dollar eco-friendly reality show, by the time an improved-yet-ill-fated second mission was undertaken by a new team of biospherians on

March 6, 1994, the company which owned and ran the project, Space Biospheres Ventures, was in serious financial and administrative trouble. Run aground by Steve Bannon (b.1953), who in all fairness had been brought over to manage its decline, SBV was finally dissolved on June 1, 1994, and Mission 2 cut a short three months later.

8. From 1996 to 2007 Biosphere 2 was taken over by Columbia University, which continued to make use of the facility for research, until the lease was transferred to the University of Arizona, which ended up fully purchasing the place in 2011. The UA currently runs several small research projects in it, its campus open to visitors looking to have a glimpse at a future that could have been.

BONUS QUOTES

"I'm not glad Stan Lee is dead;
I'm sad you're alive."
—Bill Maher

"You use the word 'amazing' to describe a goddamn sandwich at Wendy's. What's going to happen on your wedding day, or when your first child is born? How will you describe it? You already wasted 'amazing' on a sandwich."
—Louis C. K.

"Politics is show business for ugly people."
—Roger Stone

ON SWIFT WINGS

In order to protect that which is treasured or sacred, throughout history prized possessions have been subjected to curses cast toward eventual thieves or looters. At times explicitly inscribed, but often just inferred by folklore, the following cursed objects have captured the imagination of people for centuries.

The Tomb of Tutankhamen: Famed for their curse inscriptions on markers protecting temples, tombs, and property, Egyptians did not place any curse on King Tut's resting place, nor its treasures. A couple of weeks after the death of the expedition's financial backer, George Edward Stanhope, Earl of Carnavon (1866–1923), from an infected cut, bestselling Victorian esoteric novelist Marie Corelli (born Mary Mackay; 1855–1924) claimed in a letter to the *New York World* that she had warned the Earl of the "dire punishment" falling upon anybody intruding into the ancient tomb, and the yellow journalism of the day just took it from there. Knowing that of the fifty-eight people present for the 1922 opening of the tomb, only eight died within a dozen years, the famed and very poetic inscription supposedly found in the antechamber, "Death shall come on swift wings to whoever disturbs the peace of the pharaoh," has long since been proven a hoax, rather than a hex.

The Ring of Silvianus: Found in Hampshire, England, in 1785, this fourth-century AD British-

Roman solid gold ring formerly owned by a man named Silvianus (whose name is inscribed along the band) was stolen by a Senicianus, upon whom Silvianus placed a *defixio* (lead curse tablet) discovered decades later at the site of a Nodens temple in Gloucestershire. It read: "For the god Nodens. Silvianus has lost a ring and has donated one half [its worth] to Nodens. Among those named Senicianus permit no good health until it is returned to the temple of Nodens." Said to have inspired J. R. R. Tolkien's *Lord of the Rings* (1954), nobody knows for sure if the curse worked, but with both the original owner and the thief long dead, the ring is currently on exhibition at The Vyne museum in Hampshire.

Muramasa Swords: Forged by semi-legendary fifteenth-century swordsmith Sengo Muramasa, with their wavy edge (*hamon*) and fish-belly tang (*nakago*), these *katana* (samurai swords) favored by the *shōguns* and warriors of the Tokugawa era (1603–1868) began to be depicted as cursed and blood-lust-inducing, in popular anti-Tokugawa *kabuki* dramas as the shogunate began its decline in early nineteenth-century Japan.

The Basano Vase: A fifteenth-century Neapolitan urban legend about a four-pound silver vase gifted to a young bride the night before her wedding. After she was found dead the next morning for no apparent reason, the vase was then given to a family member who also suffered an unexplained death, and everyone coming to own the thing allegedly died shortly afterwards over the next five hundred years. While supposedly surfacing in auction in the late 1980s—as is usually the case with such myths, names and places are always obscured—the legend gained momentum and detail (such as fake photos or illustrations, dire warnings, a lid which releases evil when uncapped, etc.) for a while in the press, before fading again.

The Hope Diamond: Perhaps the most famous—or infamous—of India's Golconda Diamonds, this 45.52-carat boron-rich (which explains its blue hue) stone was purchased in 1666 by French gem merchant Jean-Baptiste Tavernier (1605–1689) and sold to King Louis XIV (1638–1715) in 1668, becoming known as *Le Bijou du Roi* ("the King's Jewel"). Stolen after the French Revolution, it resurfaced at London's Hope & Co. private museum in the nineteenth century, eventually being sold to wealthy Americans by the Cartier London branch, exchanging hands until finally bequeathed to the National Museum of Natural History in 1958. A Victorian legend surrounding its "curse" (likely to boost its sale) purported the gem to be stolen from the eye of a statue of Indian goddess Sita, hence bringing misfortune to all who purchase it.

The Dead Man's Chair: Considered one of the most haunted items in the world, "Busby's Stoop Chair," as it is also known, is an inn chair where a convicted murderer and counterfeiter by the name of Thomas Busby supposedly sat while awaiting his 1702 execution at the nearby Sandhutton crossroads (New Yorkshire, England), where his body was dipped in tar and hung to rot. Since all local criminal records were lost in a fire years later, stories pertaining to the reason for the man's conviction have been largely made up, but patrons sitting in the chair soon began dropping like flies, or so the legend goes. Kept at the renamed Busby Stoop Inn for 376 years, at the behest of a vicar the new owner finally donated it to the Thirsk Museum in 1978, on the condition it was hanged from the ceiling so no one would sit on it again, which hasn't stopped the chair from attracting film crews from all over the world.

Washington's Teeth: Gradually losing his teeth since he was twenty-four years old, founding father George Washington (1732–1799) is known to have purchased hundreds of teeth from slaves in order to attempt transplantation, and possibly furnish some of his four known sets of bulky, painful-on-the-gums dentures some people today believe to be, or should be, cursed. By the time of his first presidential inauguration on April 30, 1789, Washington had only a single molar left, and wore a completely artificial set made of brass, ivory, and gold.

Black Aggie: A knock-off of the 1891 "Nirvana" sculpture by Augustus Saint-Gaudens (1848–1907), "Black Aggie," as it is popularly called, was illegally commissioned to sculptor Edward Pausch (1856–1931) by an unscrupulous Connecticut granite salesman, who then sold it to General Felix Agnus

(1839–1925) as a Saint-Gaudens original for Agnus's cemetery memorial; the ensuing lawsuit almost cost Pausch his career. Repeatedly visited and vandalized by strangers over rumors that its eyes glow red at night, and no grass would grow under its shade, the bootleg statue was donated by the Agnus family to the Smithsonian in 1967, and currently sits behind the Dolley Madison House on Lafayette Square, Washington, DC.

Robert the Doll: On exhibit at Key West's Martello Gallery—Key West Art and Historical Museum—this spooky 1904 German-made doll owned by eccentric artist Robert Eugene Otto (1900–1974) as a child (and currently wearing one of his sailor outfits) is said to have been banished to the home attic after the mischievous Otto kid blamed it for a bunch of strange happenings (overturned furniture, stuffed animals slashed open, etc.). Claimed to be heard dragging its feet in the attic for a while, Otto would bring it down as an adult to scare children off his property. These days Martello Gallery staff claim to have found it posing differently every morning, but fortunately for everyone this real-life "Chucky" doll is kept trapped inside a glass case.

Annabelle: Yet another allegedly possessed toy, this Raggedy Ann doll currently sits in a glass cage at the Occult Museum in Monroe, Connecticut, founded by paranormal investigators Ed (1926–2006) and Lorraine Warren (1927–2019) in 1952. The Warrens acquired "Annabelle" from a very frightened nurse in 1970, but while most critics have dismissed the doll and every other item in their museum—as well as the Warrens themselves—as Halloween hokum, that didn't stop New Line Cinema from building an entire multi-million-dollar film franchise (dubbed "The Conjuring Universe") around it all, where the fictional Annabelle looks far scarier than its real-life counterpart—not to mention using Raggedy Ann would have required paying a hefty licensing fee.

BONUS FACTS

In 1994, sixty schoolchildren in Ruwa, Zimbabwe, claimed to have seen a UFO and bug-eyed aliens near their school playground. Similar reports occurred in other parts of Zimbabwe, as well as in Zambia and South Africa.

A large scale American psychological warfare deployed during the Vietnam War, Operation Wandering Soul broadcast "ghostly" voices of supposed Viet Cong dead calling their brothers in arms to surrender.

In 2021, California nurse Leah Lokan (1956-2021) was dragged from her tent and mauled to death by a grizzly bear while fellow campers tried to *spray* the bear away to avoid harming it!

CANCEL CULTURE

Is the pen indeed mightier than the sword? Can words smite, injure, kill … curse? If the following list of books claimed to damage or pollute their readership proves anything, it's that the power of language may potentially cause a real effect on the world at large, if only in the form of a backlash against their publication.

Picatrix (eleventh century AD): Though it sounds like the name of Pikachu's BDSM-loving sister, this is the Latin title given to Arabian anthology *Ghāyat al-Hakīm* (*The Goal of the Wise*), which collected a series of ninth-century texts on various eastern philosophies, astrology, alchemy, and sorcery. A pseudo epigraphical volume, meaning it was ascribed to a noted person to gain a semblance of authority, in this case mathematician Maslama al-Majriti (950–1007), it was translated to Spanish in the thirteenth century, becoming a major influence in all subsequent western European esoteric (modern-day "New Age") philosophy.

Codex Gigas (thirteenth century AD): Measuring thirty-six inches tall, by twenty inches wide, this hefty 165-pound, nine-inch-thick (310 pages) Romanesque illuminated manuscript is the largest of its kind preserved since the Middle Ages, hence its name which means "Giant Book" in Latin. Legend has it the "Devil's Bible," as it is also called, was made by a renegade monk in one night to escape his death sentence but ended up damning his soul by striking a co-authorship deal with the devil to fulfill the task. Quaint myths aside, the manuscript was completed after thirty years of hard-yet-loving labor by a large group of Bohemian (modern day Czech Republic) Benedictine monks. It is also an anthology, containing the entire Christian Bible alongside essays by Flavius Josephus (37–100 AD), the encyclopedia of St. Isidore of Seville (c.560–636), the *Chronica Boemorum* written by Cosmas of Prague (c.1045–1125), a number of medical texts, and much more. Looted by the Swedish in 1648, it now sits in the National Library of Stockholm, proudly displaying its famous double-spread illustration of the New Jerusalem and a fearsome, very eastern-looking Satan.

The Voynich Manuscript (c.1420): An undecipherable, six-hundred-year-old puzzle from Renaissance Italy, this manuscript with its made-up language ("Voynichese"), its fictional organisms, star constellations, and naked women, among other illustrations of varying quality, was purchased in 1912 by Polish antiquarian bookseller Wilfrid Voynich (c.1865–1930) at the Villa Mondragone in Italy. Analyzed by dozens of expert and amateur cryptographers since, its code, if there is one, remains unbroken, but artistically it has inspired some very modern offspring, like the 1981 *Codex Seraphinianus* by Luigi Serafini (b.1949), and *After Man: A Zoology of the Future* (1981) by Dougal Dixon (b.1947).

The Book of Abramelin (c.1608): Attributed to Talmudist Rabbi Yaakov Moelin (1365–1427), *The Book of the Sacred Magic of Abramelin the Mage* is likely the product of early seventeenth-century German esoterica. Possibly ripped off earlier manuscripts like the *Liber incantationum, exorcismorum et fascinationum variarum*, and even the *Book of Soyga*, it was circulated in manuscript form—as all good forbidden books do—its twelve earliest extant copies found scattered all throughout Europe (a first printed version would be published in the early eighteenth century). An epistolary novel—like *Dracula!*—about a man named Abraham of Worms passing his secrets (the Cabalistic magic to conjure angels and demons he learned from Egyptian-Jewish mage "Abramelin") to his son. Translated to English in 1897 by British occultist Samuel L. MacGregor Mathers (1854–1918), the book served as inspiration for Mathers's Hermetic Order of the Golden Dawn, and also to his frenemy Aleister Crowley (1875–1947), founder of the Thelema cult—in short, nothing good ever came of it.

Historia del huérfano (1621–2017): A picaresque, pseudo-autobiographical novel detailing the adventures—in life, and in love—of a young man named Andrés de León (the secret pen name of Archbishop Martín de León y Cárdenas; 1584–1655) who travels through the Spanish Empire (Lima, Potosí, Puerto Rico, and Cádiz) in the late sixteenth century before finding God and becoming a friar.

Its publication originally arranged for 1621, it has been well documented that every single person who ever undertook *The Orphan's Story* typesetting died tragically before completing the work. Eventually, the original manuscript was wisely locked up in a chest until rediscovered in 1965 at the Hispanic Society of America archives. Fifty-two years later, and now certain its curse had been lifted, it was finally published by the *Fundación José Antonio de Castro* in 2017.

Grand Grimoire, a.k.a. *The Red Dragon* (c.1750): Not unlike *The Book of Abramelin* which preceded, and likely inspired it, this bundle of pseudo epigraphical hocus-pocus is part of a larger eighteenth-century publishing trend which includes several other grimoires that pinned the blame—surprise, surprise—on the Jews. Supposedly written by Cabalistic mage "Antonio Venitiana del Rabina" in the sixteenth century and based on original writings by King Solomon (c.990–931 BC), it was picked as true, and incorporated into the devil-summoning rituals of that lovable French loon, Éliphas Lévi (1810–1875), already mentioned in a previous chapter.

***Narrative of the Life of James Allen, alias Jonas Pierce, alias James H. York, alias Burley Grove, the Highwayman, Being His Death-bed Confession to the Warden of the Massachusetts State Prison* (1837):** Transcribed by the prison warden, one printed copy of this confessional memoir by illiterate highwayman James Allen (1809–1837) was bound in its author's own skin and gifted to the only man who ever resisted him, a John A. Fenno, as per Allen's wishes. The Fenno family kept the curious keepsake until 1905 when they donated it to the Boston Athenaeum (a scanned version is currently available at their website).

Oera Linda (c.1850): A fake manuscript from a time rife with fake manuscripts (e.g., *The Book of Mormon*; 1830), the *Oera Linda* pretended to have been written in 1256 AD in "Old Frisian" (or rather, a bespoke version of it), and cover the myths and history of the Frisian people (ancient Germans) from 2194 BC to 803 AD. Nevertheless, what sets this forgery apart is the fact it was later adopted by some Nazis (including the nefarious Heinrich Himmler; 1900–1945) as their very own "Nordic Bible," which inspired the foundation of the *Ahnenerbe* ("ancestral heritage") association, a Nazi think-tank devoted to spreading their racial doctrine. Surviving the demise of the Third Reich, the *Oera Linda* reemerged—where else?—in late 1970s Atlantis-themed books by a Robert J. Scrutton, which were subsequently picked up by fringe, thinly-veiled supremacist New Age and Neopagan authors (for more on the whole Atlantis delusion and its links to Nazism, read *The Astonishing Bathroom Reader*; 2020).

Excalibur (**Unpublished**): Loving a good, cursed book legend (and possibly the myth surrounding "Gloomy Sunday," a.k.a. the "Hungarian Suicide Song") pulp author and future Church of

Scientology founder L. Ron Hubbard (1911–1986) circulated his own rumor about a manuscript he supposedly had written after a near-death experience during the war, which contained the sum of all knowledge. He claimed reading it had driven some people to suicide, while others just lost their marbles altogether. Hubbard asserted this manuscript, alternatively titled *Dark Sword* or *The One Command*, formed the basis for his bestselling *Dianetics: The Modern Science of Mental Health* (1950). In the 2012 movie *The Master*, a fictionalized Hubbard named Lancaster Dodd (Philip Seymour Hoffman; 1967–2014) digs the buried *Excalibur* manuscript out of the desert, and finally publishes it as *The Split Saber*, to the dismay of some of his followers.

Hitler = SS (1987): Originally serialized in French underground magazine *Hara-Kiri*, this scandalous 1987 graphic novel by cartoonist Philippe Vuillemin (b.1958) depicts the Auschwitz misadventures of a Jew, a flamboyant gay man, and a Communist who would individually prefer that the other two suffer the most. Despite being printed in a very limited edition by a small-press publisher, when it reached the wrong hands, namely French Interior Minister Charles Pasqua (1927–2015), it unsurprisingly caused an uproar. Subjected to a number of lawsuits preventing it from ever being reprinted in France and Spain, the book succeeded in raising questions about freedom of speech in western Europe.

CORNHOLED

If writing is considered the undisputed sign of intelligent life, crop circles are either its dimwitted son, or super-intelligent extraterrestrial pictographic messages humans are not smart enough to decipher.

1. Odd patterns of flattened or scythed crops were a rare but not-unheard-of occurrence as far back as the high Middle Ages, and possibly even farther back. Often, these were blamed on supernatural phenomena, such as Satan suddenly having an urge to mess around with the work of poor, illiterate farmers.

2. By the early 1960s "corn circles," as they became known (though they could be inflicted upon any grain crop, reeds, cane, grass, snow, or sand), began to be imputed on UFOs when artistically creative "saucer nests" began to appear in the United Kingdom, Australia, and Canada, suspiciously within easy access roads.

3. When the UFO craze reached the quaint English town of Warminster, in Wiltshire (near Stonehenge), becoming the spot for UFO watchers in Britain during the mid-1970s, two local friends named Doug Bower and Dave Chorley decided to run along with it and create their own "saucer nests," using a wood plank "stomper" attached to two hand-held ropes, and a baseball cap fitted with a loop of wire to help them walk in straight or

circular paths. What these unwitting "folk artists" didn't expect was for their little prank to catch on as it did.

4. In 1991, the elderly Bower and Chorley finally laid claim to around two hundred patterns made between 1978 and 1991, but thousands more have appeared all over the world, often stomped by teams of people under the cover of night, like the "Circlemakers" art collective does for advertising firms in the UK. As a Smithsonian magazine rightly put it: "Since Bower and Chorley's circles appeared, the geometric designs have escalated in scale and complexity, as each year teams of anonymous circle-makers lay honey traps for New Age tourists." (Rob Irving and Peter Brookesmith; 2009)

5. These days even devoted "croppies" (the crop circle fandom) admit 80 percent of such patterns, however creative, to be man-made—anonymity enhancing their enchantment—but what about the remaining 20 percent? It is generally accepted that a fraction may be the product of a natural vortex (whirlwind, ball lightning, etc.), but the lack of serious scientific studies makes it hard to separate the wheat from the chaff—*ahem!*

6. One such study by noted-if-inconsistent astronomer Gerald Hawkins (1928–2003), author of *Stonehenge Decoded* (1965), examined twenty-five patterns registered between 1978 and 1988, and concluded that all formations, from simple "tryout/rehearsal circles to complex fractals, were

built using semi-hidden construction lines" used at the design stage. Turns out those wire lines are indeed noticeable if you know where to look.

7. Further studies on the unexplained 20 percent have also shown an incidence of super-heated electromagnetic radiation bending the stalks. Either current circle artists are radically modernizing away from "stompers" or something else is at play. Be that as it may, patterns vanishing under harvesting blades doesn't help research, and neither does the long-term damage to crops help agriculture in any way.

8. Be them immortalized on low-quality cable TV shows, fictional films like *Signs* (2002) and *Chicken Little* (2005), or advocated by true believers like Pat Delgado (1922–2012), or David Icke—him again?—who used to claim they were a manifestation of the "spirit of the earth," crop circles clearly aren't going anywhere, at least until the public at large decides it's had enough.

BONUS FACT

During the 1930s, several Nazi summer camps opened in the United States, including Long Island's Camp Siegfried, Wisconsin's Camp Hindenberg, New Jersey's Camp Nordland, and the Deutschhorst Country Club in Sellersville, Pennsylvania.

APOCALYPSE WOW!

Not every expression of extraterrestrial intelligence is as plain as a pictogram. While astronomical bodies with shifting magnetic fields can certainly produce radio waves, not all signals present the markers of a natural phenomenon, however "lost in translation" they become during their interstellar journey.

LGM1: The first radio pulsar (a compact, highly magnetized star) ever discovered, PSR B1919+21 was detected and nicknamed (after "little green men") by then-student Jocelyn Bell Burnell (b.1943) at the Mullard Radio Astronomy Observatory in Cambridge, United Kingdom, on November 28, 1967. Hailing from the Vulpecula constellation it was originally considered to be the product of an alien civilization, until other pulsars sprung up elsewhere in the universe.

Wow! Signal: Arriving from a star ("2MASS 19281982-2640123") identical to our Sun in the Sagittarius constellation, on August 15, 1977, "6EQUJ5" was a strong, seventy-two-second narrowband radio signal caught by the Ohio State University Radio Observatory, a.k.a. "Big Ear." Identified days later by astronomer Jerry R. Ehman (b.1939), who scribbled the famed "Wow!" next to it, it was never detected again, despite many attempts, and remains an unexplained mystery. Searching for extraterrestrial intelligence since 1963, "Big Ear" was tellingly demolished by terrestrial stupidity in 1998, to make way for a golf course. In 2012, as part of a *Chasing UFOs* TV show publicity stunt, three replies to the Wow! Signal were transmitted toward the Sagittarius constellation.

FRB121102: First discovered in 2007, ephemeral yet very powerful radio pulses of unknown origin called Fast Radio Bursts (also known as Lorimer Bursts, after Duncan Lorimer; b.1969) have been the source of much speculation, and this one—shot out from the vicinity of a black hole within the Auriga constellation (three billion light-years from us)—even more so, as it seems to be emitting a rather continual sequence of bursts since 2012.

H164595b: Detected only once by the Russian Academy of Science's RATAN-600 radio telescope in Zelenchukskaya, Russia, on May 15, 2015, the signal originating from planet H164595b (which orbits a similarly named star 92.2 light-years away) was kept secret until coming under the scrutiny of SETI researchers a year later. If indeed artificial, it was speculated to be some sort of space beacon powered by the energy of the entire star.

Tabby's Star: One thousand, four hundred, and seventy light-years away from us, in the constellation Cygnus lies this star, officially designated as KIC 8462852, but informally named after the astronomer who announced it to the world in 2015, Tabetha S. Boyajian (b.1980). In some circles it is also jokingly called the "WTF" star on account of its mysterious luminosity fluctuations, which some have speculated to be the result of being surrounded by a Dyson-type mega-structure of some sort, causing quite the media uproar back in the day.

Oumuamua: Not every sign of intelligent alien life is radio or corn based. This flat, reddish, 3,000-foot-long shard of deep space debris, labeled "1I/2017 U1," passed through our Solar System in 2017, but not before conjecture matched its tumbling speed. According to Harvard astronomer Avi Loeb (b.1962), *Oumuamua* (meaning "scout" in Hawaiian) may well be an alien artifact of some sort. Be that as it may, we're unlikely to find out as the accelerating object continues its sojourn far from our reach.

FRB 20180916B: Yet another unusual FRB with a broadcast pattern, this one has reached us from a spiral galaxy 500 million light-years away. According to CNN: "Between September 16, 2018, and October 30, 2019, researchers with the Canadian Hydrogen Intensity Mapping Experiment/Fast Radio Burst Project collaboration detected a pattern in bursts occurring every 16.35 days. Over the course of four days, the signal would release a burst or two each hour. Then, it would go silent for another 12 days." (Ashley Strickland; February 12, 2020)

Tau Bootes Signal: As published in the journal *Astronomy and Astrophysics* on December 16,

2020, using the Low Frequency Array (LOFAR) radio telescope in the Netherlands, researchers from Cornell University (United States) managed to track a weak radio signal coming from an exoplanet in the Tau Bootes binary star system, fifty-one light-years away from us. It remains to be seen if it is a natural or artificial phenomenon.

BLC1: Made official on December 18, 2020, this was a "Wow!" type of narrowband signal coming from the Proxima Centauri red-dwarf star system. It was detected by the Breakthrough Listen Project after thirty hours of observations conducted between April and May of 2019 at Parkes Observatory in Australia, but much like its "6EQUJ5" cousin, it has failed to replicate.

Skyquakes: Often blamed on everything from supersonic jets to meteor bursts, "mistpouffers" have been compared to cannon blasts or distant thunder. These still-unexplained "sonic-booms" sending shockwaves through the skies have been noticed by vast swaths of the world population since ancient times, but most often by those living near large bodies of water—*for more on what that means, read on!*

BONUS QUOTE

"Old age is no place for sissies."
—Bette Davis

A CASE OF CONSCIENCE

Eight years after the famed Public Policy Polling survey disclosed that 28 percent of Americans believed extraterrestrials to exist, a 2021 Pew Research Center poll has revealed their number has grown to encompass two-thirds of the population.

1. **Sixty-five percent** of college-educated adult Americans believe intelligent life exists on other planets, a number which rises to **76 percent** in the under-thirty adult demographic.

2. **Eighty-seven percent** of Americans believe UFOs are not a threat to national security; only **10 percent** believe they pose a major threat.

3. **Eighty-seven percent** had heard or read little or nothing at all about the government releasing information about UFO sightings, while only **12 percent** heard or read a lot about it. Unsurprisingly, **80 percent** of the latter believe UFOs to be evidently extraterrestrial.

4. **Forty-seven percent** believe military-reported UFOs are not evidence of intelligent life outside of Earth, against an **11 percent** of Americans who take those reports as credible.

5. **Seventy-four percent** of Americans deem UFOs neutral, while **17 percent** say they are friendly, and a minority of **7 percent** think them unfriendly.

6. Forty-nine percent of the American people believe the government is doing a bad job when it comes to releasing UFO evidence, while **45 percent** think exactly the opposite.

Ironically, one of the smallest and most conservative theocracies in the world, the Vatican, has been speculating about—and some would say *preparing for*—the implications of the existence of extraterrestrial life since 1891. Long past the misguided Renaissance trials of Giordano Bruno (1548–1600) and Galileo Galilei (1564–1632), scientist-priests from the Vatican Observatory, including the Vatican Advanced Technology Telescope (VATT) in Arizona, are currently at the forefront of serious astrobiology research and discussion about the possibility of sentient life in other worlds.

BONUS FACTS

Skipper, an Australian shepherd-collie mix born with six legs and two tails in 2021 has reportedly become the first to survive such rare deformity.

Treadmills were originally introduced to British prisons in 1818 by Sir William Cubitt (1785–1861) as a form of inmate punishment.

Cemeteries have been illegal in San Francisco since 1901, when all graveyards were moved to the neighboring town of Colma.

IN MY WORLD IT MEANS HOPE

In his 1970 book, Invisible Residents, Fortean writer Ivan T. Sanderson (1911–1973) made an interesting observation. Considering that most of the world's oceans remain vastly unexplored, that water is the best alternative to break the fall of spacecraft, and that most UFO sightings have taken place above or near large bodies of water; wouldn't it make sense to replace the flying "F" in UFO with the "S" of submersible? Couldn't we also indulge the possibility that some USOs may have made our oceans their home for long stretches of time? Let's look at the most compelling cases lending credence to his claim.

The Exercise Mainbrace Interruption: "Exercise Mainbrace" was a peacetime naval demonstration conducted during the fall of 1952 by nine NATO navies (United States Navy, the British Royal Navy, French Navy, Royal Canadian Navy, Royal Danish Navy, Royal Norwegian Navy, Portuguese Navy, Royal Netherlands Navy, and Belgian Naval Force) from the Norwegian Sea to the Barents Sea and including the North Sea and the Baltic Sea. What nobody expected was UFOs—or shall we say USOs?—crashing the operation, as it happened when a RAF Meteor jet was tailed by a silver "saucer" above the North Sea. Then triangular-shaped UFOs were spotted on September 13, flying through the night sky at an estimated 900 miles per hour. Finally on September 20, a silver sphere also tailed the NATO fleet from a distance. This prompted a serious British intelligence inquiry, which concluded that while it would be unfeasible to continually monitor all skies all the time, they could indeed filter any RAF UFO sighting reports internally before ever reaching the press.

The Kinross Incident: Scrambled from the Kinross Air Force Base, after an unidentified object was radar-spotted above restricted air space over Lake Superior, First Lieutenant Felix "Gene" Moncla Jr. (1926–?) and Second Lieutenant Robert L. Wilson (1931–?) caught up with the bogie aboard their F-89C Scorpion jet before it disappeared from the ground control radar's scope, never to be seen or found since that stormy night of November 23, 1953. The Air Force's shoddy attempts at a cover-up only managed to increase public interest in this case.

The Golfo Nuevo Hunt: In 1958, Argentina initiated our world's first interplanetary war against an unidentified USO appearing at the *Golfo Nuevo* ("New Gulf") down in the province of Chubut (Argentinian Patagonia) in the south Atlantic Ocean. It all began on October 19, when Argentinian navy freighter *Heroína* ("Heroine") zeroed in on a glowing cigar-shaped object they deemed a "Soviet submarine." Despite the USSR's denial of any operations in the area, the resulting twenty-five-day massive sub hunt in Argentina's territorial waters, including the deployment of depth charges, yielded no results; yet the mysterious object, or others just like it, have been spotted off-and-on again in or above the water during the following months and years.

The Antarctica Sighting: A Brazilian meteorologist working for the US Navy during "Operation Deep Freeze II" in Antarctica, on March 16, 1961, Rubens Junqueira Villela (b.1930) and two other crew members saw a silver object break through the thirty-seven-foot-thick ice shelf at high speed, and disappear into the clouds above, leaving a boiling, steaming ice hole in its wake. Interested in the UFO phenomenon since, Doctor Villela would take part in eleven further Antarctica expeditions, nine of those under the *Programa Antártico Brasileiro* (PROANTAR).

The Shag Harbor Crash: Nicknamed the "Canadian Roswell," it refers to the reported October 4, 1967, nightly sighting and water splash—some say crash—of a brightly-lit sixty-foot-diameter USO off the coast of Shag Harbor, a small fishing town in Nova Scotia. Two days later, similar objects were seen hovering over Sambro, Mahone Bay, and Halifax. A Canadian navy operation was quickly launched to recover the Shag Harbor USO but found no trace of it and the search was finally abandoned on October 9, and the place has become a staple of UFO lore since.

The Ra Encounter: Seeking to demonstrate that long-distance ocean voyages were possible using ancient boat designs, in 1970 legendary explorer and experimental archaeologist Thor Heyerdahl (1914–2002) successfully sailed his papyrus Ra II boat across the Atlantic from Morocco to Barbados. Just before reaching the latter, the Ra II and its occupants came across what Heyerdahl described as " . . . a round, pale disc; a ghostly, aluminum-colored, gigantic moon which stood in the Northwest and appeared to come toward us." The US Navy would later chalk it down to falling Poseidon rocket debris, but as is usual with government rationalizations, UFO aficionados smelled yet another cover-up.

The USS *Trepang* Photos: As reported by the Black Vault conspiracy website in 2017, and widely relayed by more mainstream media outlets since, leaked photos of USOs allegedly taken from aboard the USS *Trepang*—a fast-attack nuclear submarine—on its 1971 maiden voyage back from the Arctic polar ice cap, were published in fringe French magazine *Top Secret*, before the Vault got hold of some original scans. Let's just say they have to be seen to be believed, but even the Vault recognizes that at least one of the photographed objects looks suspiciously like a balloon carrier.

The Valentich Disappearance: On October 21, 1978, while en route with his Cessna above Australia's Bass Strait, pilot-in-training and UFO aficionado Frederick Valentich (b.1958–?) promptly informed air traffic control that he was being tailed by a large, illuminated aircraft "orbiting" 1,000 feet above him. Minutes later, in his last communication to Melbourne, he claimed it wasn't an aircraft after all, before being interrupted by screeching sounds. Valentich never landed at his King's Island destination, and his fate remains a mystery to this day.

The Lake Baikal Diving Encounter: One of the freakiest alien encounters on record happened in Siberia, in 1982. Declassified by Russian military in 2009, confidential documents attest that Lake Baikal, the world's oldest (thirty million years), and deepest (5,387 feet) lake witnessed the regrettable death by decompression of three diving trainees after going in pursuit, and then fleeing from what was later described as humanoid creatures dressed in tight metallic diving suits and helmets—*Aquaman eat your heart out!* Also in 2009, International Space Station astronauts photographed what appeared to be a flying saucer emerging from the frozen lake surface, but it was later revealed to be a ring of warmer water produced by methane emissions.

The Persian Gulf Lightwheels: Reported by mariners since ancient times, these rotating rimless wheels of pulsating light, dubbed "crop circles of the sea," have been seen on, under, and even above the surface of warm seas, and though attributed to plankton bioluminescence, their perfect geometry, and the fact they seem to willfully converge around ships, makes some theorists think otherwise. Recent sightings include a double 2007 encounter by the USNS *Concord*, and the 2009 USS *Milius* incident.

The Malibu Underwater Anomaly: Spotted in 2014 on Google Earth about six miles off the coast of Point Dume in Malibu, California, a three-mile-wide supposedly oval-shaped "columned" structure sitting 2,000 feet below the surface stirred quite the media interest in its day, which carelessly deemed it an "underwater alien base." Upon closer examination from other angles "Sycamore Knoll," as it is now called, was revealed to be a perfectly natural outcropping of the continental shelf, its "columns" only jagged ridges.

The Baltic Sea Anomaly: In June 2011, while sonar-mapping the ocean floor of the northern Baltic Sea, at the center of the Gulf of Bothnia, Swedish undersea salvage operations firm Ocean X, specialized in the recovery of rare liquors, was startled by what appeared to be the remains of a two-hundred-foot-diameter "Millennium Falcon-style spaceship." Scientists quickly dismissed the find as a natural basalt formation, and the "discovery" as a publicity stunt.

The Bahamas Shipwreck: While scouting the wreck of English ships related to Sir Francis Drake (c.1540–1596) in 2018, using maps made by none other than NASA astronaut Gordon "Gordo" Cooper (1927–2004), treasure hunter Darrell Miklos (b.1963) came across a different sort of Caribbean ship: a mysterious otherworldly structure covered in coral, which he claimed could be the remains of an ancient spaceship. Despite the publicity generated, the exact nature of Miklos's findings remains inconclusive.

The 2021 Pentagon Report: Long after three videos of fast-maneuvering USOs made by the US Navy in 2004 and 2015 were leaked to the press in 2007 and 2017, public uproar gave the Department of Defense no choice but to release them officially in 2020. Prompted by Congress, on June 25, 2021, the Pentagon finally released a serious-enough report on 144 cases of what they called "unexplained aerial phenomena," admitting that, excluding the one deflating weather balloon, the remaining 143 sightings between 2004 and 2021 remain, well, unexplained. While they blamed their scant results on "the limited amount of high-quality reporting," they did acknowledge these are physical objects of various shapes (defined as "tic-tac," "sphere," "acorn," "pyramid" and "metallic blimp"), and the presence of propulsion systems in at least eighteen of them.

BONUS QUOTES

"I always wanted to be somebody, but now I realize I should have been more specific."
—Lily Tomlin

"I'm not a dictator. It's just that I have a grumpy face."
—Augusto Pinochet

"The only way to be punk rock in LA is to be Republican."
—Trey Parker

INVISIBLE RESIDENTS

Fiction—where else?—has dealt with the possibility of alien visitors living among us for quite some time. The most outstanding—if not utterly conspicuous—are listed below.

Clark Kent: Created by Jerry Siegel (1914–1996) and Joe Shuster (1914–1992), and subsequently turned into the ultimate American corporate mascot, appearing in all media imaginable since 1938, Kent is the plainclothes identity of Kal-El, the last son of doomed planet Krypton (more about it in the *Astonishing Bathroom Reader*; 2020) living among us as a mere human, "an act of discreet martyrdom," only to reveal his true nature as "Superman" when tragedy strikes.

As the great Jules Feiffer (b.1929) put it: "The particular brilliance of Superman lay not only in the fact that he was the first of the superheroes, but in the concept of his alter ego. What made Superman different from the legion of imitators to follow was not that when he took off his clothes he could beat up everybody—they all did that. What made Superman extraordinary was his point of origin: Clark Kent. Remember, Kent was not Superman's true identity as Bruce Wayne was the Batman's or (on radio) Lamont Cranston the Shadow's. Just the opposite. Clark Kent was the fiction." (*The Great Comic Book Heroes*; Bonanza Books; 1965). If this quote rings a bell, it's because you probably heard it paraphrased in Quentin Tarantino's *Kill Bill: Volume 2* (2004).

Carpenter: In *The Day the Earth Stood Still* (1951) nigh-human alien Klaatu and his robot bodyguard Gort arrive to Washington, DC, aboard a flying saucer with a peaceful interstellar offer for the President of the United States. Mistakenly shot by a fearful soldier, Klaatu assumes the human guise of "Carpenter," and does what any sensible alien with a limited budget would do: blend in, and find lodgings at a boarding house, where he connects with a boy, Bobby, and his widowed mother, Helen. Betrayed and shot dead, he is revived by the fearsome Gort aboard their spaceship upon hearing the *Klaatu barada nikto* ("I die, repair me, do not retaliate") command from Helen.

Played by Michael Rennie (1909–1971) in the original, the role was reprised by Keanu Reeves (b.1964) in the, dare we say, inferior 2008 remake, if only because Klaatu, much like every character ever played by Mr. Reeves, never makes the slightest attempt at seeming human.

The Body Snatchers: Quiet invaders from outer space, spores raining on a California field grow into seed pods capable of producing perfect copies of anyone coming into contact with them, only without any of those pesky emotions, generating mass instances of Capgras delusion (believing your loved ones have been substituted by impostors). A creation of ground-breaking writer Jack Finney (1911–1995) for his 1954 novel *The Body Snatchers*, it found its way naturally into several film adaptations, creating an archetypical science fiction scenario often imitated both in print and on the screen, with results varying from the lame (e.g., *The Host*; 2008) to the absolutely-frickin'-great (e.g., *The Faculty*; 1998).

J'onn J'onzz: Capitalizing on the 1950s UFO craze sweeping America, professional biochemist and part-time pulp science fiction writer Joseph Samachson (1906–1980) created "The Manhunter from Mars" for *Detective Comics* #225 (1955). Ripped from his family and home-world—yes, Mars!—by an experimental teleportation beam, J'onzz would use his telepathic abilities to appear in our mind as John Jones, a police detective who had been killed in action. A derivative, green-skinned Superman and The Shadow pastiche, the character would become a favorite among the most abstruse comic-book aficionados during the following decades, but as the superhero craze still sweeps mainstream television and film, for the past twenty years DC Comics and Warner Brothers have seen fit to shove "The Martian Manhunter" in the general public's face as well.

Martin O'Hara: Putting the "Martian" into TV sitcom's *My Favorite Martian* (1963–1966), Uncle Martin (played by the immense Ray Walston; 1914–2001) is a 450-year-old anthropologist from Mars named Exigius 12¼, who literally crashes into reporter Tim O'Hara's (Bill Bixby; 1934–1993) life and home; his hidden antennas, powers, and inventions conveniently providing whatever the scripts needed for its starring duo's zany exploits. The original series had a short-lived 1973 animated spin-off, *My Favorite Martians*, and an ill-conceived 1999 film remake where Uncle Martin is played by the no-less-great Christopher Lloyd (b.1938). More importantly, the show's premise directly provided the template for quality sitcoms like *Mork and Mindy* (1978–1982), and *3rd Rock from the Sun* (1996–2001), not to mention the *Saturday Night Live* 1977 skit "The Coneheads," which was made into a 1993 movie.

Thomas Jerome Newton: Introduced in the 1963 novel by Walter Tevis (1928–1984), *The Man Who Fell to Earth*, Newton is a decadent Anthean extraterrestrial, coming to save his dying species from a terrible drought brought about by nuclear war, yet ultimately succumbing to his own alcoholism and government entrapment instead. Too good for the run-of-the-mill science fiction enthusiast, *The Man* was adapted into a slick 1976 cult-film starring—who else?—David Bowie (more on him below), and a best forgotten 1987 TV pilot starring Lewis Smith (b.1956). There is also a rumored Showtime series adaptation still in the works.

Ziggy Stardust: A fictional persona of a fictional persona, Ziggy was created by the innovative musician-performer "David Bowie" (born David Robert Jones; 1947–2016) for his conceptual glam rock albums *The Rise and Fall of Ziggy Stardust and the Spiders from Mars* (1972), and *Aladdin Sane* (1973), which tell the story of an alien rock star coming to Earth to deliver a message of hope before a coming apocalypse. Turned into a messiah by the adoring crowd, Ziggy eventually reaches American soil where he falls prey to the over-the-top rock 'n' roll lifestyle, leaving behind a glittery streak that endures to this day.

Ford Prefect: Posing as an unemployed actor from Guildford (Surrey, England), alien reporter Ix is a contributor to the fictional *Hitchhiker's Guide to the Galaxy*. A Douglas Adams (1952–2001) creation for the real-life 1978 BBC radio comedy *The Hitchhiker's Guide to the Galaxy*, and its following prose and screen adaptations. Upon arrival to Earth from his Betelgeuse Five homework, Ix mistook cars for the dominant life-form, hence taking a very British car model name as his own alias. Originally portrayed by Geoffrey McGivern (b.1952), the character was played by David Dixon (b.1947) in the 1981 BBC TV adaptation, and Mos Def (b.1973) in the 2005 Disney feature film.

Mork from Ork: Introduced in the "My Favorite Orkan" back-door pilot episode of sitcom *Happy Days* (1974–1984), where he attempts to abduct Richie Cunningham (Ron Howard; b. 1954), Mork (played by Robin Williams; 1951–2014) is an offbeat alien from the humorless planet Ork. Arriving to Boulder, Colorado, in the late 1970s aboard an egg-shaped UFO, and on a mission to study the human race (though one may well suspect his superiors just wanted to get rid of him), Mork befriends—and eventually marries—the lovely Mindy (Pam Dawber; b. 1951). A victim of its own initial success, which brought in much network meddling, *Mork & Mindy* declined in viewership and ended after four seasons, generating an animated Hanna-Barbera spin-off, and even a single-season Brazilian remake in its wake.

Scott Hayden: Not to be confused with the DC Comics character, nor the Ziggy Stardust song, the touching 1984 sci-fi romance film *Starman* introduces us to an unnamed energy being from another planet who falls for the falsely advertised peace message of the Voyager 2 probe, only for his spaceship to be blown to bits by the American government. Scrambling to adapt to Earth's environment, the alien clones the body of a recently deceased man named Scott Hayden (Jeff Bridges; b. 1949), and takes the latter's shocked widow, Jenny Hayden (Karen Allen; b. 1951), hostage on a cross-country sojourn to the Barringer Crater in Arizona, where he hopes to be picked up by his people before his temporary "meat-suit" dies for good. Needless to say, Jenny and "Scott" fall in love, and as things get steamy, he ends up impregnating her. His dire circumstance forcing him to abandon his new human family, supposedly for good, he ultimately returned to reacquaint with his son thanks to the power of television, and a new identity, Paul Forrester (Robert Hays; 1947), in the short-lived but highly enjoyable *Starman* series (1986–1987).

Jesse: Convicted of insurrection and sent to a backward planet—ours—as punishment, with a floating, sardonic watchful eye drone (named Control) in tow, a gruff, powerful alien war veteran played by character actor Martin "Cobra Kai" Kove (b.1946), takes the name "Jesse" (like Klaatu, from the clothes he finds) in CBS's 1989 filler show, *Hard Time on Planet Earth*. A thirteen-episode, *Fugitive*-style show, *Hard Time* follows the misadventures of Jesse as he tries to do some good while crisscrossing the country and adapting to human culture the best he can. Universally panned by overzealous critics, its admittedly small audience still remembers the show, and Jesse, with a nostalgic smile.

The Solomons: Dick (John Lithgow; b.1945), Sally (Kristen Johnson; b.1967), Harry (French Stewart; b.1964), and Tommy Solomon (Joseph Gordon-Levitt; b.1981), are a research party from another galaxy pretending to be a family. Their Commander, Dick, gets a job as a physics professor at a state college, while Sally and Harry basically slack around from one menial job to the next, and Tommy goes to high school (though he's actually the oldest of the group, he got trapped in a teenage body). Taking the best *Mork & Mindy* tropes to the next level, *3rd Rock from the Sun* was a popular syndicated show during its 1996–2001 heyday, and remains so on streaming, its misfit Solomon family beloved by all, no matter which part of the universe it came from.

Dr. Harry Vanderspeigle: Shot down over the American Southwest, Captain Hah Re uses his superior technology to blend in among the human population. Assuming the identity of retired doctor Harry Vanderspeigle, he discreetly secludes himself in a lake cabin near the northwestern town of Patience. Such is the premise of the *Resident Alien* comic-book series published by Dark Horse comics since 2012. But while the comic's Vanderspeigle is a quiet and articulated humanoid from a refined alien civilization coming to study us, his TV series counterpart (played to perfection by Alan Tudyk; b.1971) is an out-of-this-world, eight-foot-tall, evil octopus bent on the extinction of mankind. Tudyk's Vanderspeigle (and he truly makes the character his own "Mork from hell") is also brought out of seclusion far too early into its adaptation to remotely human behavior, which makes his involvement as the town's new doctor-detective all the more awkward, for him as well as everybody around him—and wanting to murder and possibly eat a child who can see his true form doesn't help one bit!

BONUS QUOTES

"The sole cause of man's unhappiness is that he does not know how to stay quietly in his room."
—Blaise Pascal

"You're in pretty good shape for the shape you're in."
—Dr. Seuss

CHALLENGER OF THE UNKNOWN

Coming face-to-face with the extraterrestrial and the supernatural, mild-mannered accountant Preston Dennett dons his Mutual UFO Network investigator badge to prod the dark recesses of reality as we know it.

Who are you and what do you do?
My name is Preston Dennett. I come from a large family and have five brothers and sisters. I live in Reseda, California, where I work part-time as a bookkeeper. I have researched UFOs and the paranormal since 1986.

Why did you make UFOs the object of your study and writing?
I grew up very skeptical of UFOs. I just did not believe they were real. If anybody told me they thought they saw a UFO, I just laughed at them and shook my head. All that changed on November 17, 1986, when I heard a report on the news about a famous UFO sighting over Alaska by Japanese Airline Pilot, Kenju Terauchi. I was amazed to hear such a credible person reveal his sighting. I thought he was either lying or *misperceiving*, but it interested me enough to start asking my family, friends, and coworkers what they thought about UFOs. I got an incredible shock when I discovered that many of them have had incredible UFO

encounters. My brother and his two friends saw a metallic saucer with colored lights and chased it in their car. My sister-in-law and two of her friends saw a UFO hovering over Van Nuys Airport. She later had a face-to-face encounter with gray aliens. My other sister-in-law described a series of encounters with little, blue-skinned beings who visited her repeatedly when she was a small child. A friend (a private pilot and flight instructor) shared her sighting of an egg-shaped object which flew over her home. Another friend told me about his encounter involving an object which hovered and swooped down toward he and his friend, scaring them badly. They may have had missing time. I mentioned UFOs at the office where I work and was surprised to hear one coworker tell me about her family's encounter with a star-like object that darted overhead for several hours. Her daughter told me about her fully conscious abduction by gray aliens. Another coworker told me how she, her friend, and her mother were followed home by a UFO. They all had missing time. When I found out that many people I knew and trusted had all these encounters, I was shocked and scandalized. I could barely believe it, but I knew they weren't lying. Before long, I started reading UFO books, joining UFO organizations, and formally interviewing people. I wanted to find out for myself if UFOs were real.

When and how did you become a MUFON field investigator?
I joined MUFON in 1987 and began attending the

local meetings here in Southern California. I became a field investigator in 1988. I took the field investigator test, which was much more difficult than I expected. There were lots of questions about the history of UFO encounters. But there were also lots of questions about astronomy, meteorology, photography, and other scientific subjects. I had to study hard, but I only got two or three questions wrong. I was very excited to start investigating UFOs officially. I was delighted and happy to meet other investigators and people interested in UFOs and made many friends there.

What general process do you follow when going after a lead?
Investigating a UFO incident depends on the type of the encounter. The first thing I do is conduct an informal interview with the main witness to see if an investigation should be made. Then I do a formal recorded interview and make sure their story hasn't changed. I then look for any other witnesses to the event and interview them. I ask for references to make sure that the witness is reliable and not suffering from any mental problems. I ask for any physical evidence that might confirm their encounter. I check the time and date of the sighting to see if there were any reports from other people in the area. I study the location to make sure the sighting cannot be explained by any type of astronomical phenomena, conventional aircraft, weather phenomena, or any other prosaic explanation. If it's a complicated case involving multiple encounters or an abduction, I will do a

third or fourth interview (or more) to make certain I have all the information regarding the UFO incident. Some investigations are short, but others can last weeks, months, or even years.

How many credible witnesses or contacts have you interviewed regarding the UFO phenomenon?
I don't have the exact number, but I'd estimate that I've interviewed several hundred people. Not all of them are credible. One witness turned out to be taking hallucinogenic drugs. In another case, a witness described an object with white, red, and green lights. After interviewing them and researching the area, I discovered they were seeing planes coming in for a landing at the local airport. Other times, people who are not familiar with astronomical phenomena such as shooting stars have believed mistakenly that they were seeing UFOs.

Which accounts struck you the most?
There are many cases which I find particularly incredible. One involved a Navy medic who had an encounter with fifteen-foot-tall praying-mantis-type beings. Probably my best and most complicated case involved a wave of UFO encounters over the Santa Monica Mountains in California from 1992 to 1994. This case involved dozens of witnesses and included sightings, landings, abductions, and more. I even contacted the local police station and they referred new witnesses to me. I ended up writing an entire book about the incident: *UFOs over Topanga Canyon*.

It remains one of my favorite cases and I'm still getting new information about it.

Have you had any close encounters with UFOs yourself?

Yes, I have seen UFOs on several occasions. I never saw one until I started investigating them. But after I found out they were real, I started actively searching for them. I wanted to see them myself and eventually I did. Once I went to a UFO meeting in Santa Monica, California, and a man spoke about his own contacts. After the meeting, he said he'd call down a UFO. Sure enough, we saw a strange star-like object come down exactly when and where he said it would. It looked like a shooting star, but the amazing thing was that he predicted its appearance. On another occasion, I was driving late at night near my home when a small orb of light the size of a golf ball dropped down out of the sky and hovered in front of my car windshield before suddenly darting away. On another occasion, I met a UFO contactee, and she was able to call down a UFO: a giant sphere covered with golden lights. It was the size of a house and hovered right next to us for a few moments and then took off at high speed. On yet another occasion, I was leading a CSETI meeting and saw a huge anomalous light hovering overhead. I've had other sightings, but those are probably the best.

What is your position regarding USOs? Are you familiar with Ivan T. Sanderson's work?

Yes, I have read Sanderson's book, *Invisible*

Residents, which was one of the first books to investigate USOs. I began getting USO reports very early on in my investigations. As I began to get more and more cases, I finally started investigating them more deeply and eventually wrote a book about them. I am absolutely convinced that they do exist. I suspect that our oceans, lakes, and rivers have many USOs hiding in them, especially in the oceans. These objects can move very quickly underwater. They can also move in and out of the water with ease. Some USOs like to target boats and hover underneath them. My favorite USO case occurred in 1971 on the east coast of the United States. I interviewed a Navy Officer on the USS *Clamagore*, a navy submarine that was carrying nuclear missiles. A USO showed up and paced the submarine for 15 minutes. It's one of many amazing USO cases I have investigated.

Do you believe extraterrestrials may be living among us on dry land as well? Are there any reasons for concern?
Yes, I am convinced that there are ETs on Earth. Some ETs look just like human beings, so it's entirely possible that many of them are walking among us. I also know that gray ETs and other types of ETs have the ability to disguise their appearance. There are reports of people who have seen ETs in very public places such as gas stations, subways, cafes, casinos, train stations, buses, convenience stores, schoolyards, and other locations that you would never suspect. There may also be alien bases at various locations on Earth,

such as Mount Shasta, California. There are also many people who have reported ETs working along with humans in such locations as Area 51 in Nevada, or Edwards Air Force Base in California. I wrote about several cases of this type in my book, Not from Here: Volume 1. For the most part, I do not think we need to be concerned or afraid about this. ETs are very advanced. If they wanted to take over our planet, they could easily do so. They have been around a very long time, and they still have not taken over.

What can you tell us about alien healings? How do they work? Who do they benefit?
Many people have been healed as the result of a UFO encounter. I've documented more than 300 cases of this kind in my book, The Healing Power of UFOs. The cases date back more than 100 years and are still occurring today. They have occurred all across the world. All kinds of people are being healed. The cases are evenly divided between men and women. Elderly people have been healed, as have very young children, including babies. People have been healed of all kinds of conditions, including injuries, burns, broken bones, cuts, animal bites, infections, stomach aches, colds and flues, back-aches, stomach aches, eye problems and more. People have been healed of serious diseases such as heart disease, liver disease, kidney stones, jaundice, tumors and cysts, diphtheria, diabetes, arthritis, blood clots, epilepsy, Chagas disease, Crohn's disease, eczema, high blood pressure, multiple sclerosis, muscular dystrophy, ulcers,

cerebral aneurysms, rheumatism, AIDs, and many other serious and chronic conditions. There are more than thirty cases of people who have been healed of cancer. Some people are visited in their bedrooms and healed. Others are struck by a beam of light which heals them. Many are taken onboard a craft and given an operation. Often the healing is done using lights and strange instruments. Some people are given medicine. Some are healed by mind power or hands-on healing. In about 10 percent of the cases, people are visited in their hospital room and healed in a hospital. While I was able to locate more than 300 cases, I suspect there are many more that we never hear about, simply because many people do not report what happened to them. It's difficult to say why the ETs heal some people and not others. Many people who are healed have a long history of UFO contact. Another reason some people are healed appears to be because they are doing good work for humanity in some way. There are many cases involving doctors, social workers, environmentalists, human and animal rights activists, inventors, teachers, police officers—anyone whose job or profession is providing a service to the progress of humanity. I am convinced that healing humanity is one of the primary alien agendas.

What general writing process do you follow when compiling and laying out your information?
The hardest part of writing a book is really the research, which can take anywhere from six months to several years. It takes a lot of time and effort

to locate and research the information. Once this part is done, then I organize the information in a way that makes it easy to understand and categorize. The cases might be organized chronologically by date, or perhaps by locations, or by the type of UFO incident. The shortest time I've ever written a book is six months. Some projects, however, have taken five or ten years or even more. My books on UFO healings and on USOs both took many years to research and compile. It can be a very long, difficult, and arduous process. Thankfully, it's also very interesting and inspiring. Once the book is completed, it needs to be proofread and checked for errors and accuracy. You have to make sure whether or not the witnesses want to remain anonymous or allow their real names to be used. Then you have to find a publisher who is willing to publish your book. It doesn't stop there. Then you have to work hard to publicize the book by going on radio and television or speaking at UFO groups or UFO conventions. It's definitely hard work, but I love doing it, and I am inspired when people tell me that they enjoyed the book, or that it helped them to understand their own experiences.

How many UFO books have you published? Do you have any favorites?
So far, I have written twenty-seven books and more than 100 articles for magazines, journals, newspapers, and websites. I have several other books I'm currently working on, and plan to write many more. It's very difficult to pick my favorites.

I love all my books. But if I was forced to make a choice, I do have a few favorites. I think some of my best ones are *Inside UFOs* and *Onboard UFO Encounters*, because they are about people who have experienced extensive contact, people who have had face-to-face encounters or have been taken onboard a craft. I also love *The Healing Power of UFOs* which is my biggest book so far; that one took an enormous amount of research and shows a positive side to the UFO phenomenon that is often overlooked. Some other favorites include *Undersea UFO Base*, *UFOs over Topanga Canyon*, *Not from Here: Volumes 1-3*, and definitely *Schoolyard UFO Encounters*. But again, I have many other books I would like to write, and I'm sure I will soon have more favorite ones to add to this list.

Who illustrates the beautiful covers of your independently published ones?
Sometimes the publisher hires their own artist, but most of my book covers have been illustrated by my sister-in-law, Christine Kesara Dennett. I have worked with her from the very beginning. She started by illustrating my articles and working with the witnesses to accurately draw the UFOs and ETs they have seen. She has now done covers for many other UFO researchers. All my favorite book covers have been done by her. Probably my favorite one is the cover she made for *Inside UFOs*.

What is your latest volume about, and where can people find it?
My two latest books are *UFOs at the Drive-In:*

100 True Cases. This covers more than 100 cases of people who have encountered UFOs while at a drive-in theater. The other is called *Onboard UFO Encounters*, which presents fifteen true, original, firsthand cases of people who have been taken onboard UFOs and met ETs face to face. I also have another book about to be released. It's called *Wondrous: 25 True UFO Encounters* and is also about people who have had a wide variety of UFO experiences, including USOs, UFOs, landings, face-to-face contact, onboard UFO encounters, and even some government whistleblower accounts. All my books are available on Amazon and other online bookstores, or at bookstores. I have a website where I show all my books and have excerpts so that people can preview the books and see what they are about.

BONUS FACTS

In 1771, the inventor of the automobile, Nicolas-Joseph Cugnot (1725–1804) crashed his second prototype vehicle against a brick wall, the world's first car accident, and was subsequently arrested on the world's first DUI charges.

Originally without a distinctive name, scientists adopted a term, "thagomizer," coined by cartoonist Gary Larson (b.1950) in his *The Far Side* comic, to name the four spikes at the tip of a stegosaurus' tail.

THE FOURTH SMARTEST MAN IN THE WORLD

A charming character and voice actor with an IMDb page as long as a World Almanac, Derek McGrath (b.1951) earned a special place in the comic-book aficionado's heart with his portrayal of Dr. Benjamin Jeffcoate, "The Fourth Smartest Man in the World," in the 1980s superhero show My Secret Identity, among several other iconic characters

What geared you toward acting as a young man?
I think I was as young as 5 years old when I decided I'd like to be an actor. Some ill-informed fool told me you could sleep in late and meet girls. He was completely wrong about that; you can't sleep in late . . . this idea was reiterated during a backyard baseball game—I got hit in the head by the batter and knocked unconscious; the moment I opened my eyes I said to myself, "I want to be an actor."

What was your professional beginning in Canada like, and how did you transition into American film and television? Or was it the other way around?
I went professional in Canada at the age of eighteen when I won the role of Linus in *You're a Good Man Charlie Brown*. I think I got 230 dollars a week.
   The first thing I bought was a pair of shoes and a

chocolate milkshake. It was a big moment for me because I was making more than my father who worked in the mines and always insisted that I'd never make a dime as an actor. He was a good man but he lived a hard life and wanted to prepare me for disappointment. Like any actor I had my ups and downs but I managed to support myself over the next several years in Canada until an opportunity came to work in the states. I was performing at *Second City* when I got a call one day from a fellow named Al Rogers who told me he'd been up to Canada three times over the period of a year on a scouting mission for a pilot he was producing for ABC television; the show was called *Toast of Manhattan* and he wanted to know if I'd like to come down to write and perform for the show. Well, I was over the moon; it had been my dream to work stateside since I was a child; literally, I had dreams about it. So I said, "Well, when would you need me there?" To which he responded, "Well, I would have liked you here today but if you can make it by tomorrow that would be okay." I told him, I'd need a little more time than that because I had to give my notice at *Second City*. And that's where it could have totally unraveled because my contract required a two-week notice to vacate, God bless Andrew Alexandre; when I appealed to him to let me out early, he said, "Well, when Hollywood calls, you gotta go." And so I did. *Toast of Manhattan* never aired but it brought me to Hollywood.

How does voice acting differ from live-action acting? What skills do you bring from the latter into the former, and vice-versa?

So much of what happens on camera radiates from the face. A line can be read exactly the same way 15 times and whatever emotions or thoughts are playing out on your face can give fifteen different meanings to that line. Is the character lying, is he intimidated, is he harboring a deep-seated hatred, is he secretly in love etc. etc.? You don't have that luxury in voice acting. All you have is your voice, so in most instances you need to push the colors of your read to express whatever emotions you wish to convey. Still, good acting is good acting and most of the rules apply to both cases. Oh, and on camera pays more.

What was working for DIC Ent. like? Which of their animated productions and characters did you enjoy voicing the most? Why?

Working for DIC was enormous fun, until it wasn't. When we were recording *The Catillac Cats*, we had the entire cast assembled in the studio all at the same time. Which meant that we could play off each other, always my preference especially with comedy which requires timing and better the actor's timing than the editor's timing. Unfortunately, we were having a little too much fun and breaking each other up and causing retakes too often to the point where the director and the producers decided they had to break us up and bring us in separately. In that case, they bring you in individually and you only read your lines. Not nearly as much fun and I don't think you get the same spontaneity and quality of performance. In my experience, this is the way animated shows are normally done. Too bad.

Generally speaking, what was the main difference between working in Canadian and American television during the early 1980s?

Of course, acting is acting no matter which side of the border you're on but back in the eighties when I first arrived in Hollywood it was pretty exciting to be working on big big shows like *Cheers* and *Dallas* with big budgets and big stars and big name directors and Hollywood pizzazz. Show business with a capital S.

Much of the difference was ego. At least in Canada, you get a lot more respect when you say you're working in LA. After all, that's where all the big stars work and play. "Now you're working with the big boys" type of thing. And in the eighties Canada was still laboring under a big inferiority complex which I'm very happy to say has dwindled down to almost nothing in the present day.

What series of events brought you to *My Secret Identity*? What was the casting process like?

My Secret Identity was shot in Toronto but I was actually living in LA when I was cast to play Dr. Jeffcoate. They had auditioned practically every actor in Toronto but they still weren't satisfied that they'd found their guy. Karen Hazard, bless her heart, suggested me for the role even though I wasn't around to audition. I did a self tape which was very rare at the time but much more common nowadays. I booked a studio and hired a camera operator and taped my audition and sent it to Toronto. Didn't have smart phones back then.

When they offered the role I was very hesitant to

accept because I wasn't sure I'd enjoy working with a teenager for possibly the next five years. All depended on what that teenager was like, what if he was obnoxious and undisciplined? I actually turned it down three times for various reasons but finally acquiesced. I was still concerned about what Jerry O'Connell would be like until I met him. It was instant chemistry and we became fast friends from the moment we met . . . and the rest is history.

What unique point of view, sensibility, and performance traits did you bring into the role of Dr. Jeffcoate?
I think what they saw in me was a sincerity I bring to a performance; that and an apparent knack for characters of high intellect. Doctors. Lawyers. Professors. And dare I say, I have some comedic skills to bring to the fore. Don't mean to blow my own horn but you did ask.

What was working with young Jerry O'Connell like?
Jerry and I had a blast working together; we both share a sense of humor and we laughed a lot; plus we had great chemistry together. I was kind of like an alternate dad to him. His real dad is a great guy and we became good friends as well; he was always on the set acting as dad and manager for Jerry.

On average, how many hours of work (including makeup, actual filming and re-shoots, etc.) did you go through each day? How long did production and post production of each episode take?

Of course it varied but there were days when we worked really 18 hours or more; the longest day we shot, if I remember correctly, was twenty-two hours. We had to finish because it was the last day of that episode and we had to deliver it.

Which would you say is your favorite episode? Why?

I don't remember what number it was or what year we did it in or what it was called but it was a send-up of a *Dick Tracy* show. I played the bad guy and I channeled Al Pacino in a very over-the-top, pull out all the stops performance. My favorite episode because I love playing bad guys, especially when I call just let er rip and have as much fun with the character as I can muster.

What would you say sets this show apart from other shows of the era? What brought it to an end? Was it abrupt or foretold?

Aside from the obvious appeal of a young boy with super powers fighting crime, I think what set this show apart was the young boy's friendship with an older man who was not only his partner in fighting crime but a strong father figure, not only super intelligent but also very caring; the kind of father that a lot of young teenagers would love to have. The show also had a lovely balance of action and humor.

I think there were a couple of elements that killed the show. Firstly, in the first year, Jerry came up to my shoulders in height; by the third year I was up to his shoulders in height; he was no longer a kid who was into comic books but a rapidly maturing teenager who was more into cars and girls.

I think the major mistake the producers made was to change the relationship between Andrew and Dr. Jeffcoate. They said to themselves, "Why is this hip young teenager hanging around with this old scientist?" So, in season 3, they gave Jerry a young teenage best friend and they really cut back on the father-son relationship that I think was so appealing about the show. I guess they hadn't seen *Back to the Future*. The result was, the third season was the final season. "If it ain't broke, don't fix it."

What did you learn from this experience, and what did you bring from it, moving forward in your, already extensive, acting career?
Years ago, don't remember which show it was but I worked with a wonderful actor named Eugene Roche, who played the feckless captain in *Slaughterhouse 5*. Not sure what lead to the conversation but he said to me, "Never try to save the scene." I think I got to practice that notion on *My Secret Identity*. I learned to give what I've got and never push. Real is always better than fake and when you push, it's fake. Also, it was my first series and I had the wonderful gift of practicing my craft on a weekly basis, three or four days out of every week for three seasons; that's a wonderful opportunity to sharpen your skills. But certainly the most important thing I learned was "Never work with teenage boys," . . . kidding!

In your view, what changed most in television between the 1980s and the 2000s? Say, which would you say are the main differences between starring in a show like *My Secret Identity*, and beloved show *Little Mosque in the Prairie* some years ago?

Well, to truly answer that would take an entire book; you'd have to talk about cultural changes, technological advancements, changes in taste, changes in what is acceptable and what isn't and so on and so on and so on. Let me just say that for me it's still about showing up prepared, lines down and ready to go. The experience of being on the set really hasn't changed in essence; you still show up, report to whatever A.D. you can find, load your stuff intro your trailer, go to hair and makeup, get into your wardrobe, block whatever scene you're about to shoot. Go back to your trailer until they light the scene, review your lines, go back to the set when they're ready for you, shoot the scene. That part really hasn't changed at all and that is basically what the job entails. The only other differences are the technological ones; because of much improved light, you barely need any makeup anymore. (They used to put it on with a trowel when I started out years ago); plus you can view what you just shot instantly and the little scenes they have now on set; whereas that may be true, I rarely do watch the scene after I've shot it. I leave it up to the director to guide me in terms of what's working and what isn't. For me it's still about telling a story with sincerity and humor. Oh, and of course you always hope the catering service is a good one.

What's next in your career? Any new or upcoming projects you're looking forward to?
Haven't a clue. That too has remained the same.

BONUS QUOTES

"How do I stay so healthy and boyishly handsome? It's simple. I drink the blood of young runaways."
—William Shatner

"Those who make objectivity a religion are liars. They are scared of human pain. They don't want to be objective, it's a lie: they want to be objects, so as not to suffer."
—Eduardo Galeano

"Silence is the only answer you should give to the fools. Where ignorance speaks, intelligence should not give advice."
—Benito Mussolini

"Never stand begging for what you have the power to earn."
—Miguel de Cervantes

"Reading furnishes the mind only with materials of knowledge; it is thinking that makes what we read ours."
—John Locke

HOLLYWOOD GOLD

From humble beginnings as a journalist and writer of exploitation B movies, Stan Berkowitz made a name for himself in Hollywood as a "Jack of all trades," equally capable of producing police dramas as he is writing Saturday morning superhero cartoons.

What made you want to become a writer?
As a kid, 12, 13, 14, I made home movies with my friends. Crime stories, science fiction, monster movies, that sort of thing. When I got to UCLA, I eventually decided to major in film production. I wrote and directed some short films, but by the time I was ready for grad school, I'd run out of savings, so I couldn't afford to make any more movies. I had to switch over to screenwriting, which only required a pen and some paper.

What were your major writing influences as a young man, and what are your main ones now?
I like old film noir movies, so my early film school scripts showed that influence. More recently, I work mostly in genres, so what's contemporary in those genres is what has to influence me. I've also been influenced a bit by the writing styles of some of my friends.

What series of events brought you onboard *Supervixens* and then writing *Acapulco Gold*?

I was assigned by *Film Comment* magazine to interview Russ Meyer back in 1972. As we were chatting afterward, he told me he needed some people for the crew for his next film, and I volunteered. My work on the script of *Acapulco Gold* came about through a friend; he and I wanted to do a script about modern day piracy, and when we finished it, he sent it to a friend of his who was working at a film production company. They rewrote our script, then produced it (in Hawaii, so our title didn't make a lot of sense).

How did you make the transition from movies to television?
After *Acapulco Gold* came out, nothing much happened for me, but I kept writing spec feature scripts, and in circulating them, I eventually met a couple of guys who were doing TV series, and that's how I got started in TV. While I was a journalist, I was always writing spec feature scripts, and showing them to everyone I knew (and their friends). A couple of those friends of friends were producers, and they liked my writing samples, so when they were in a position to hire writers for shows, they gave me a chance.

What was television like in the 1980s?
It was much the same as it is now, except everyone shot on 35mm film, and only a few TV series were serialized; most did stand-alone episodes.

What is the usual time frame when writing television shows of either kind?

A week to write the outline for the episode, a week to wait for notes, then a week to write the script. Those are minimums for live action and animation; sometimes you're given more time — the deadlines aren't as crucial in animation.

What are the main duties of a television "story editor"?
In animation, the story editor supervises the other writers and rewrites their scripts when necessary. In live action, that duty is usually in the hands of an executive producer, and the story editor is little more than a staff writer, writing his own scripts, and often editing other writers' scripts when called upon to do so.

How and when did you get the T.J. Hooker job? What was the selection process like?
My agent happened to be representing one of the producers. This agent arranged a meeting for me with the producer, and soon after, I was brought aboard as a staff writer.

What was your first day like? Did you work from home or at the studio?
I had an office at the studio. The first day was devoted to reading scripts and outlines that had either been written for the preceding season, or were being considered for the upcoming season.

Was there any reviewing and rewriting involved? How much input did you get from producers, directors, actors, or studio executives in general?

The entire job was essentially reviewing, giving notes on scripts, and doing an occasional rewrite. Most of the notes that came in from the studio and network executives were filtered through the producers.

What did you enjoy the most about working on T.J. Hooker in that capacity?
That was early in my career, so the best part of the job was learning about production and seeing how a writing staff was organized.

What would be the typical television writing day schedule be like?
If you work on a staff in a production office, you'll come to work at a normal hour, and leave at dinner time, if you're lucky. If you're not lucky, you can end up working past midnight. As a freelancer, I wake up and start writing immediately. Then I'll have lunch and a brief siesta, then get back to work until dinner time. After dinner, I'll write until about 11 or so.

How did you go from being a story editor on T.J. Hooker to co-producing and writing Houston Knights?
Those two shows were produced at the same studio, so the executives knew me, and going from one show to the next was a fairly ordinary career trajectory.

What was it like to work with the show's creator, the legendary Michael Butler?

I never met Michael Butler, but I worked fairly closely with the show's other creator, Jay Bernstein. Jay was mercurial and subject to mood swings, but he always treated me with kindness and consideration. I'm the only writer whose name is on every episode; all the others were fired at least once, and some were rehired.

Other than writing, what were your co-producing duties on *Houston Knights*?
Casting, locations, sets, production rewrites, post-production notes.

How long did the production (including pre and post) of a single *Houston Knights* episode take?
You need a minimum of a month to write, prepare, shoot and edit an hour-long episode. Most take somewhat longer.

Are there any fun production anecdotes you would like to share?
Not really. On that show, I only had two emotions: fear and relief.

Was cancellation abrupt or foretold? Were there any reasons for it?
Looking at the ratings, you can pretty much tell whether a show will be renewed or not. The ratings make it obvious—except in the recent case of *Roseanne*, of course.

What unique point of view, sensibility, and storytelling did you bring into the *Superboy* show?

I didn't start on that show until they'd already produced fifty episodes; for the second fifty, they wanted a more adult, more serious approach, and that's what I tried to do, both in terms of my own writing and with the staff and freelance writers I brought in.

How did you transition back from live-action into writing for animated shows? What did you bring to the stories from your experience in live-action shows?
A friend from *Superboy* told me that an animated version of *Spider-Man* needed writers, so I applied. I suppose I brought a slightly more adult sensibility to my scripts for that show.

The main difference between animation and live-action is that in animation the writer has to be much more specific in terms of describing physical action; he can't rely on the actors to improvise (obviously). Also, there has to be more action; the writer can't allow animated characters to sit and talk to each other for two or three pages. The audience will become bored.

What specific set of traits makes a superhero story good or interesting?
A lot of freelancers who try to write superhero stories offer little more than a big fight; an interesting story will have the fight, but it should be about something more — issues, values stakes — and the hero shouldn't win just because he's stronger. There needs to be more to it — does the villain have a flaw that does him in?

Does the hero need to sacrifice something he values in order to win? Is the hero smart enough to use the villain's strength against him? That sort of thing. It's the hardest part of creating a superhero story.

What would you say changed the most in television between the late 1980s and the late 1990s?
Serialization. When I started, most episodic shows presented stand-alone episodes so that new viewers could drop in any time during the run of the series and not be at a loss. By the late 90s, serialized series were beginning to dominate, and now, in a time of binge-watching, the domination is complete.

⭐ BONUS FACTS

A rare engraved 22 carat gold egg from "The Cadbury's Creme Egg Mystery," a scavenger hunt-inspired advertising campaign organized by the confectionery company in the mid-1980s, went for a high bid of $42,600 in an early 2021 auction.

Victor "Lil Poison" De Leon (b.1998) became the youngest professional video game player in the world at age seven.

A mysterious low-frequency sound known as "The Hum" affects around 2 percent of the Northern Hemisphere population, since the early 1970s.

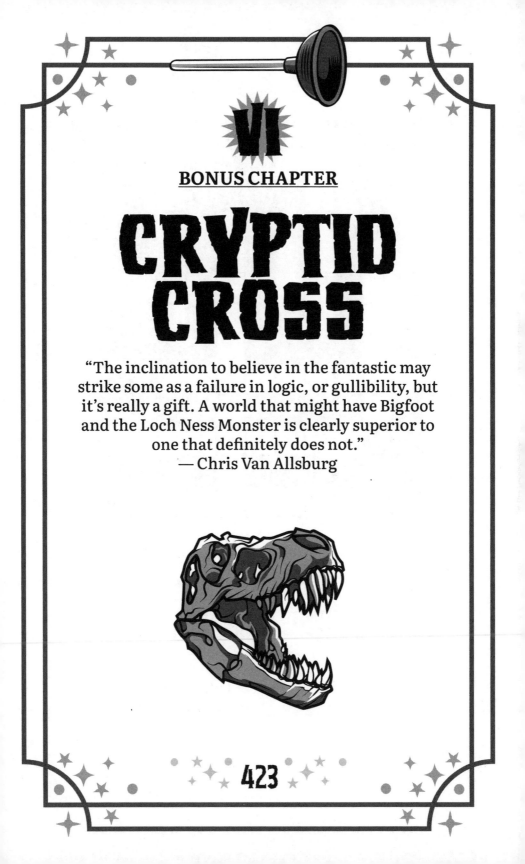

VI

BONUS CHAPTER

CRYPTID CROSS

"The inclination to believe in the fantastic may strike some as a failure in logic, or gullibility, but it's really a gift. A world that might have Bigfoot and the Loch Ness Monster is clearly superior to one that definitely does not."
— Chris Van Allsburg

ACROSS

4. Named after Lake Champlain
7. — Monster
9. Spotted in central Alabama in the 1930s (2 w.)
10. It means "goat-sucker" in Spanish
11. Also known as Bigfoot

DOWN

1. Humanoid aliens seen in Fresno, CA
2. — Giant
3. Twenty-nine percent of Americans think it is real
5. Georgia "Nessie"
6. Lake Tahoe "Nessie"
8. Florida Bigfoot (2 w.)

ACROSS

3. Large hare with antlers
7. —knockers
8. — Heeled Jack
10. Half-human, half-feline creature (2 w.)

DOWN

1. They sabotage aircraft
2. Arkansas Bigfoot (2 w.)
4. Steals apples
5. Psychopath in rabbit costume (2 w.)
6. Stone — Devil
9. Found in the San Pedro Mountains

ACROSS
1. — Monster
5. — Devil
6. "Weredog"
7. Giant supernatural bird
9. — Howler

DOWN
1. Said to be a harbinger of doom
2. Body of an orca, head of a wolf
3. Lee County, SC, swamp creature (2 w.)
4. Legendary race of little people
8. Head of a frog, stumpy legs, and a spiky tail

ACROSS

2. — eyed People
4. Pope — Monster
5. The Beast of —
6. Chesapeake Bay "Nessie"
9. Prowling aliens (2 w.)
10. New Jersey Bigfoot (3 w.)

DOWN

1. Missouri sky serpent
2. — Lizard
3. Cannibal spirit
7. — Moose
8. Hudson River sea serpent

ACROSS

3. — Dragon
6. Demon —
7. It stalks the town of Valle Crucis, NC
10. — Gliders

DOWN

1. Emily Isabella Burt
2. — Skull
3. Stunted albino dwarves (2 w.)
4. Missouri Monster abbr.
5. Lives under the USC tunnels (3 w.)
8. — Dinosaur
9. Lake Geneva's "Nessie"

ACROSS

2. — Kangaroo
4. Lizard with tusks
6. Wisconsin Satyr
8. — Penguins
9. Head of a beaver, body of a shark

DOWN

1. Monstrous wild hog
2. New England troll
3. Also known as the Gullah (2 w.)
5. — Stag
7. Lake Murray "Nessie"

ACROSS
1. Forest-dwelling hominid of Singapore (2 w.)
5. Australian chimera
6. Indonesian meat-eating bat
7. North African "bush dog"
9. Celtic "seal people"

DOWN
2. Scottish shape-shifting water spirit
3. Monster octopus of Japan
4. "Water hound" of Irish folklore (2 w.)
6. "Water hound" of Aztec mythology
8. — Dragon

ACROSS

1. Lake — Monster
3. British black fur predator
8. — Metal Man
9. It means "elephant killer" (2 w.)
10. Sea monster of Cyprus
11. Lake Windmere (UK) "Nessie"

DOWN

2. Two-headed turtle
4. — Black Panther
5. West Virginia Bigfoot (2 w.)
6. Vietnamese Bigfoot
7. Beast of —

ACROSS

2. — Monster
4. Also known as basilisk
7. Gloucester Sea —
8. Hairy South American cyclops
9. Giant snake with an elephant's head
10. Australian Bigfoot

DOWN

1. Amphibious creature of Goose Creek Lagoon, FL (3 w.)
3. Woolly-haired, goat-headed humanoid
5. Lake Okanagan, BC, water serpent
6. It means "red dwarf" in French (2 w.)

ACROSS

1. — Boomer
3. — Cats
5. Megalodon shark of New Zealand
7. Afghan Bigfoot
8. Bear — Monster
9. Hopkinsville —
10. White — Monster

DOWN

1. African brontosaurus (2 w.)
2. Vermont griffin (2 w.)
4. — Death Worms
6. — Watchers

ACROSS

1. Pacific Coast sea serpent
6. American northwest giant (2 w.)
7. Lake Memphremagog serpent creature
10. Giant reptilian bird

DOWN

2. West African jungle walrus

3. Also known as the "Chinese Wildman"
4. Mt. Saint Helens Bigfoot
5. Lake Erie "Nessie"
7. Giant striped feline from Tanzania
8. Willoughby Lake's "Nessie"
9. Welsh lake monster

ACROSS
1. — Blob
3. Seen in Hanging Hills, CT (2 w.)
7. Slavic six-legged, horned monster
8. Antarctic marine humanoid
9. — Beaver Eater

DOWN
2. Also known as "Old Tessie"
3. Subterranean troll
4. Nocturnal luminescent bird
5. Slide — Bolter
6. — Worm

ACROSS

3. — Cat
4. — Island Monster
5. Monster owl of the Alps
6. Northfield —
8. It means "The Screamer" in Slavic
9. Otter shape-shifters
10. Malevolent Scottish fairies

DOWN

1. Australian carnivorous creature
2. Cannibal humanoids of unknown origin (2 w.)
7. Glastonbury —

436

ACROSS

2. Indonesian sea monster (2 w.)
5. It means "The Leather" in Spanish (2 w.)
7. Also known as the Papua Devil Pig
9. Demonic canine
10. — Bushbaby

DOWN

1. Demonic camel from Arizona (3 w.)
3. Fiji —
4. — frog
6. Lake — Monster
8. Indonesian "wild men" (2 w.)

ACROSS

2. Also known as the Smiling Man (2 w.)
4. Japanese Bigfoot
6. South Dakota Bigfoot (2 w.)
8. Indonesian ghoul
9. Seen in Lake Worth Lagoon, FL (2 w.)
10. Sea-dwelling sheep-calf chimera

DOWN

1. — Monster
3. — Screamer
5. — Wildman
7. It means "recoiled eel" in Icelandic

ACROSS

2. It means "river child" in Japanese
6. Giant bird with a gorilla face (2 w.)
7. Mercy Brown turned into one
8. It means "The Owl" in Spanish (2 w.)

DOWN

1. Utah chimera (2 w.)
2. Congolese dinosaur
3. Black-eyed —
4. New Guinea dinosaur
5. Tennessee —
6. Seen in Ireland, and the South Dakota Badlands

ACROSS

3. German bird with antlers
5. Mongolian mountain deity
7. African giant spider (2 w.)
9. The Butler —
10. Indonesian corpse-eating reptile

DOWN

1. African soul-eating owl
2. Norwegian sea serpent
4. Russian Yeti
6. Swiss ghoul (2 w.)
8. — of Bodmin Moor

ACROSS

2. Raystown Lake "Nessie"
4. Nahuel Huapi Lake (Argentina) "Nessie"
6. South African monster fish
7. — Warak'in
8. Giant earthworm
9. — Tree

DOWN

1. Man-eating — of Nubia
3. African pterosaur
5. Lac — Screecher
6. Giant Congolese crocodile

ACROSS
1. Evil Native American spirit
4. — Monster
6. Lake Manitoba's serpent
7. — Ridge Vampire
8. Lanky, gray-haired monster from New Hampshire (2 w.)

DOWN
1. Maori sea serpent
2. New Mexico thunderbirds
3. Delaware prankster dwarves
5. — Lake Monster
6. — Man

ACROSS
4. Means "Devil Whale" in Spanish (2 w.)
5. Japanese turtle with a seaweed tail
7. — River Monster
8. — Shore Monster
9. New Guinea dinosaur

DOWN
1. — Bear
2. North African chimera
3. Monster sturgeon (2 w.)
5. — Monster
6. Extinct flightless bird of New Zealand

ACROSS
1. Charles Mill Lake Reservoir Bigfoot (2 w.)
3. British Mothman
5. Giant Congolese lizard (2 w.)
7. — Lake Monster
8. Missouri River monster

DOWN
2. Ohio —
4. Evil spirit from Tanzania
6. Lake Norman's "Nessie"
9. Indian cobra deity

ACROSS
3. — of Chiang Rai
5. British rat-like entity
6. — Octopus
7. Loveland —
9. Rhinoceros —

DOWN
1. Also known as Ryujin
2. Italian Bigfoot (2 w.)
4. — Claude
8. Lawton — Man

ACROSS
3. Payette Lake "Nessie"
5. Icelandic seashore creature (2 w.)
7. Warty pig of Pennsylvania

DOWN
1. Japanese Leviathan
2. — Man
3. — Stalker
4. Seen in the Wichita Mountains
6. — Fish

ACROSS

2. Gigantic island turtle
4. Croatian "forest girls" (2 w.)
6. Chilean troll without feet
8. Also known as "water owl"
9. Giant Australian tree frog

DOWN

1. Baboon monster from Mali
3. — Lake Monster
5. — Man
7. Ghost chimpanzee

ACROSS

1. South African giant snake with a horse's head.
3. Winged German Jackalope
4. It means "I see you now" in Spanish
5. — Beasts
8. Big — Monster
9. Prehistoric Utah canine (2 w.)

DOWN

2. Medieval marine monster
6. South African woolly marine elephant
7. Lake Utopia "Nessie" (2 w.)

ACROSS
4. African hominids
5. — Head
6. Dutch troll
7. Caucasian Amazonian tribe
8. Haunts the Tower of London (2 w.)
9. Evil South African monkey

DOWN
1. — Dogman
2. — Prisca
3. Aztec feathered snake

ACROSS

3. Icelandic poisonous pike fish
4. — Pigs
6. Haunted London's Newgate Prison (2 w.)
8. — Lake Monster
9. Prowls around the Capitol in Washington, DC

DOWN

1. It means "Bad Light" in Spanish
2. Giant Japanese serpent
5. In Chiloe Island it protects the entrance to a warlock's cave
7. — Horse of Bryn-y-maen, Wales

ACROSS
2. — Iceman
4. — Mud Man
6. Czech ghost
7. The Talking Mongoose
8. — Flying Squid

DOWN
1. Indian feline shape-shifter
3. — River Aliens
5. Lake Pepin's "Nessie"
6. Oviedo — Monster

ACROSS
1. Artificial human of Hebrew folklore
4. Native American lynx chimera
6. — Snowman
7. It lives in a maze
8. The basis for the western "genie"

DOWN
2. — Mermen
3. It has a hidden pot of gold at the end of the rainbow
5. Islamic demon
6. Winged unicorn

ACROSS

1. Brazilian shape-shifting dolphin
5. Balayang's brother
7. Japanese ghost whale
9. Also known as "ant-lion"
10. — Demon
11. Beast of —

DOWN

2. African trickster spider
3. Aboriginal bat deity
4. Babylonian creature with a scorpion tail
6. Welsh water horse
8. Sun-pushing beetle

ACROSS

3. Turned into bats by Hermes
5. Shape-shifting goblin
7. Shape-shifting trickster (2 w.)
8. Monster — of Big Blue
9. Mayan bat deity
10. Pocomoonshine Lake —

DOWN

1. Rainbow serpent of Australia
2. Black monster dog of English lore
4. Scottish bogeyman
6. — Island Swamp Monster

ACROSS

1. Half-man, half-horse
3. — Meter Monster
4. Part rooster, part snake
7. — Wild-woman of Iowa
8. Lybian race of men without heads

DOWN

1. It means "dog-headed" in Greek
2. Native American revenge spirit
4. It guards the entrance to Hades
5. Islamic Jackalope
6. — Monster

ACROSS

3. Brother of Cerberus
4. It had one hundred arms and fifty heads
7. Inuit monster wolf
9. It lived in the lake of Lerna
10. Spirit lookalike

DOWN

1. It lives in Lake Manitou
2. Killed by Hercules (2 w.)
5. A lion's body, a woman's head, and a love for riddles
6. — Monster
8. The Hesperian Dragon

ACROSS

3. Celtic child-eating hobgoblin
5. Mayan devil bird (2 w.)
7. A lion's body and a man's head
9. Slavic vampire werewolf

DOWN

1. Human head and a bird's body
2. Turned into a bear by Hera
4. Greek mother of monsters
6. Chilean ghost mollusk
8. Greek man-eating female monster

ACROSS

2. Children of Pricus (2 w.)
3. — Race Monster
5. Head of a woman, body of a vulture
6. Chinese winged lions
7. Japanese ghost cat

DOWN

1. — Eagle
2. — Puma
3. Evil Gorgon sister
4. Greek fire-breathing giant

ACROSS

2. — of Wisdom
6. Philippine vampire
8. Snake with a head at each end
9. Indian monster dog-wolf

DOWN

1. Turtle — Monster
3. Japanese monster shark
4. Wild bull with curved horns
5. Dominican wild-women of blue skin
7. Beast of —

ACROSS
3. Scottish monster rat
5. — Mud Monster
6. Swedish Jackalope
8. Shape-shifting Chinese dragon

DOWN
1. Blue-furred rhesus monkey (2 w.)
2. Japanese mind-reading ape
4. Carnivorous koala (2 w.)
6. — Monkey
7. Native American raccoon trickster

ACROSS

4. It means "sea-animal" in Sanskrit
7. — Monster
9. Evil Egyptian chimera
10. Aztec dragon
11. Tiny Hawaiian builders

DOWN

1. Sun-dwelling angels
2. European winged dragon
3. Philippine sea serpent
5. Job 40: 15
6. It actually exists (2 w.)
8. — Humanoids

SOLUTIONS

424

```
N     C       B
I  CHAMP   I
G     R     G
H     D  A  F
T     I  L  O
C  T  F  FLATWOODS
R  E  S  A  T  K
A  S     A  A  U
W  HITETHANG    N
L  E     H     K
E     CHUPACABRA  P
R        H        E
S     SASQUATCH
```

427

```
      P     MOON
      I     I
      A   W L LICK
      S   E T
   BLADENBORO
           D N
   CHESSIE  G
      P     O  K
      E        I
   NIGHTPEOPLE  S
      E
      BIGREDEYE
```

425

```
G           F
R     JACKALOPE
E        L  U
M        B  K
L     B  A  E
I  T  U  TOMMY
N  H  N  W  O
SPRING   I  N
   O  Y  M  T  S
   W  AMPUSCAT  T
   I  A  M  H  E
   N  N  M     R
   G     Y
```

428

```
            W     L
TOMBSTONE   E     O
H     O  H  R     V
E     M  I  LEAPER
G     O  R  W     L
RUNCH    DEMONDOG
N  K  E  Y  L     C
C  O  D  E  F     K
H  D  I  E  M     J
   I  GARGANTUAN  E
   K     N        N
                  N
                  Y
```

426

```
MOGOLLON     N
O  O     I   I
T  N     Z   M
H  A     A  JERSEY
M  K     R   R
A  A     D   I
N  DOGMAN    G
   E     A   A
   THUNDERBIRD
   O     G
   D
   OZARK
   G
```

429

```
           H
      PHANTOM
   U  K     G
   K  B     Z
GOWROW      I
   U  O     L     W
   D  H     L     H
   GOATMAN        I
   I  G     E     T
   E     SPACE    E
         S
         I
   BEAVERSHARK
```

430

431

432

433

434

435

463

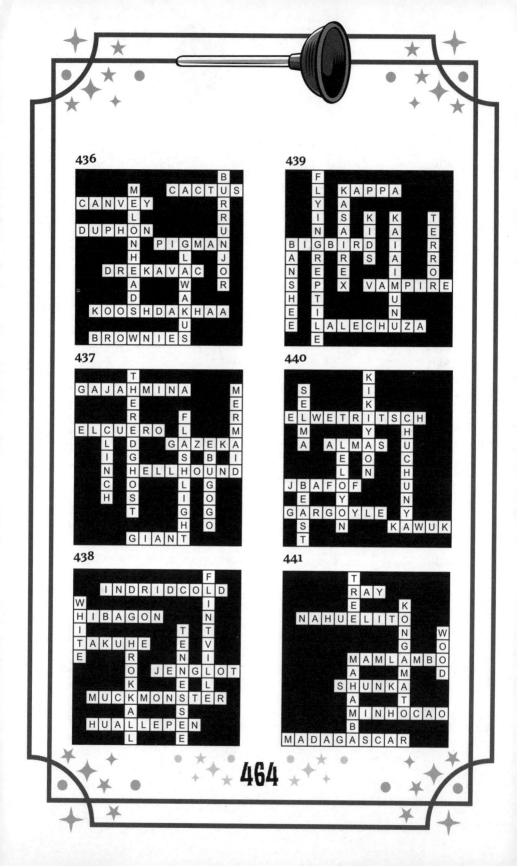

436

437

438

439

440

441

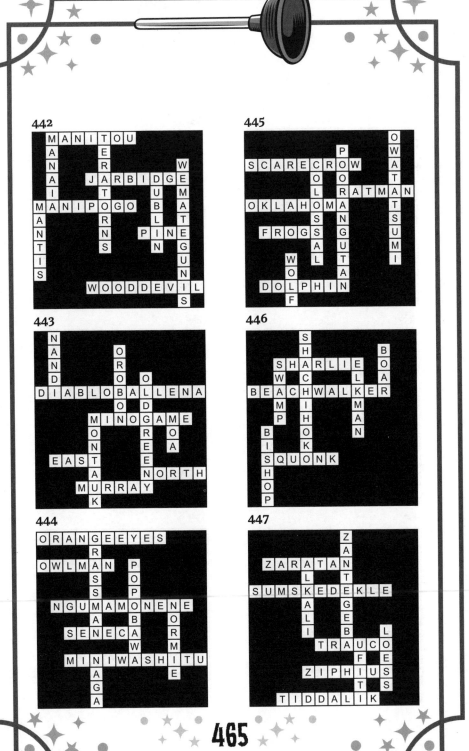

465

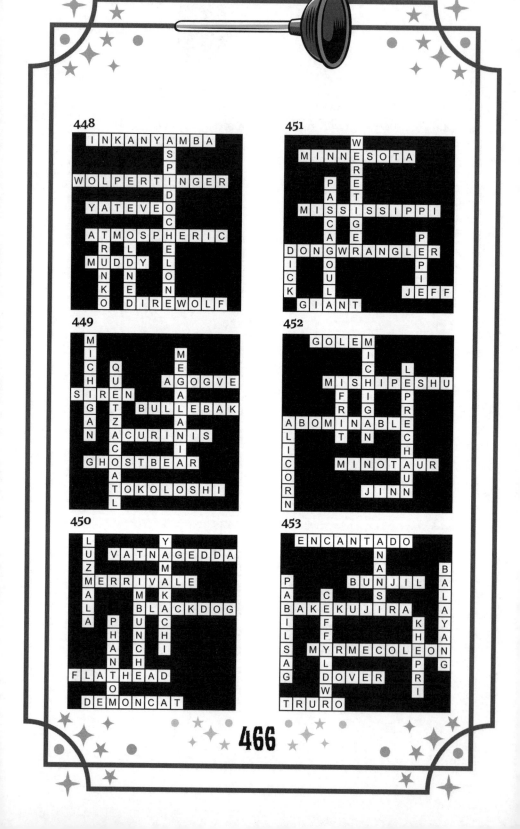

448

INKANYAMBA
WOLPERTINGER
YATEVEO
ATMOSPHERIC
MUDDY
DIREWOLF

449

AGOGVE
BULLEBAK
CURINIS
GHOSTBEAR
TOKOLOSHI

450

VATNAGEDDA
MERRIVALE
BLACKDOG
FLATHEAD
DEMONCAT

451

MINNESOTA
MISSISSIPPI
DONGWRANGLER
GIANT
JEFF

452

GOLEM
MISHIPESHU
ABOMINABLE
MINOTAUR
JINN

453

ENCANTADO
BUNJIL
BAKEKUJIRA
MYRMECOLEON
DOVER
TRURO

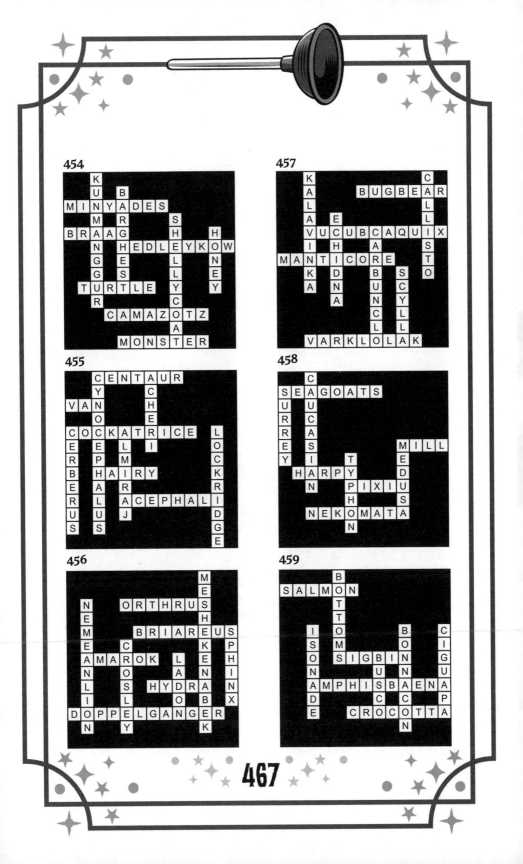

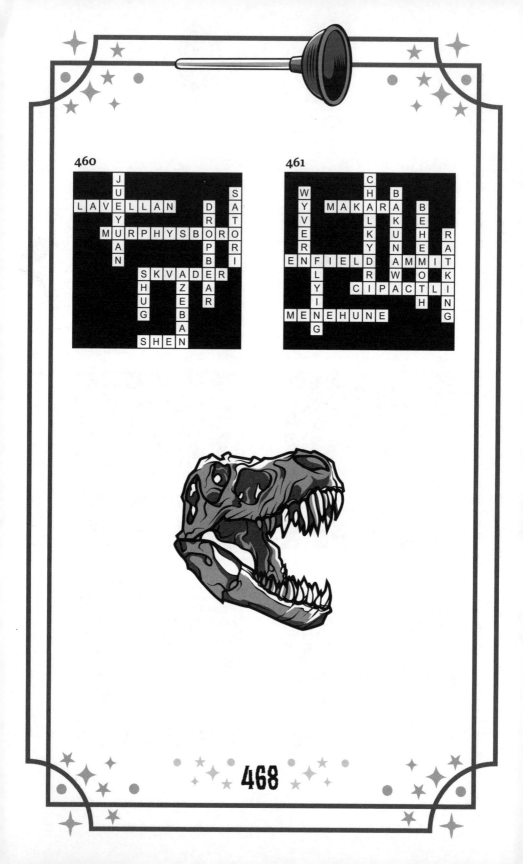

460

461

BONUS QUOTES

"I quote others only in order to better express myself."
—Michel de Montaigne

"If you can't beat them, arrange to have them beaten."
—George Carlin

"True success is figuring out your life and career so you never have to be around jerks."
—John Waters

"If the head is lost, all that perishes is the individual; if the balls are lost, all of human nature perishes."
—François Rabelais

"Screw normal. You know why? 'Cause if you're normal, the crowd will accept you. But if you're deranged, the crowd will make you their leader."
—Christopher Titus

"I am politically incorrect, that's true. Political correctness to me is just intellectual terrorism. I find that really scary, and I won't be intimidated into changing my mind. Everyone isn't going to love you all the time."
—Mel Gibson

ACKNOWLEDGMENTS

I would like to thank interviewees J. M. DeMatteis, Elizabeth Gracen, John H. Newton, Bruce A. Smith, Preston Dennett, Derek McGrath, and Stan Berkowitz who generously lent their time to this endeavor and gave thoughtful answers to all my questions.

I am also particularly grateful to all of my colleagues in the nonfiction racket. Their prose fills my nights, their inspiration keeps my creative flame alight, and their quotes make my trivia look good!

Last but not least, this book wouldn't have been possible without Jesse McHugh and Caroline Russomanno, who continue to believe.

BONUS QUOTES

"One loyal friend is worth
ten thousand relatives."
—Euripides

"I regret not death. I am going to meet my friends
in another world."
—Ludovico Ariosto

"Each of us bears the imprint of a friend met
along the way. In each the trace of each."
—Primo Levi

ABOUT THE AUTHOR

Maritza Mardones Castillo

DIEGO JOURDAN PEREIRA is an author of puzzle and activity books, including the *Giant Book of Games and Puzzles for Smart Kids*, *The Big Book of Brain-Boosting Puzzles*, *Bible Power Puzzles*, and the *Astonishing Bathroom Reader*. With a background in illustration, comic books, and graphic design, his clientele has ranged from Dover Publications to The Topps Company.

What is stopping you from reaching
your full potential?

FIND THE

ANSWER

THE BIG BOOK OF
BRAIN-BOOSTING
PUZZLES

has been expertly designed to keep your
mind young. All it takes is ONE PUZZLE A
DAY to boost your mental health.

How do you harness unlimited problem-solving skills?

UNLOCK THE TRUE POWER OF YOUR

THE BIG BOOK OF BRAIN-BOOSTING PIX-CROSS PUZZLES

features a revolutionary Japanese picture puzzle designed to improve the world's greatest computer—your own brain.

Order Yours Today!

THE BIG BOOK OF
BRAIN-BOOSTING
PIX-CROSS
PUZZLES

Use Numbers, Clues, and Logic to Reveal Hidden Pictures!

500 PICTURE PUZZLES

Diego Jourdan Pereira

LEARN WHAT

GOD'S WORD

CAN DO FOR YOU!

"...honor Christ the Lord as holy, always being prepared to make a defense to anyone who asks you for a reason for the hope that is in you..." 1 Peter 3:15 (ESV)

Order Yours Today!